3

DATE DUE

AG 06 '05			
FEB 1 4 2011			
JUL 1 5 2015			
FEB 1 8 2016			

ALABAMA WILDLIFE

~VOLUME 1~

A Checklist of Vertebrates and Selected Invertebrates: Aquatic Mollusks, Fishes, Amphibians, Reptiles, Birds, and Mammals

RALPH E. MIRARCHI

Published for, and in cooperation with,

The Division of Wildlife and Freshwater Fisheries
Alabama Department of Conservation and Natural Resources

and

The School of Forestry and Wildlife Sciences and
The Alabama Agricultural Experiment Station, Auburn University

by

The University of Alabama Press
Tuscaloosa and London

Alabama Agricultural
Experiment Station

AAES

∞
The paper on which this book is printed meets the minimum requirements of
American National Standard for Information Science–Permanence of Paper for
Printed Library Materials, ANSI Z39.48-1984.

Library of Congress Cataloging-in-Publication Data

Alabama wildlife / [edited by] Ralph E. Mirarchi ... [et al.].
    p. cm.
  Updates and expands: Vertebrate wildlife of Alabama. 1984 andVertebrate
animals of Alabama in need of special attention. 1986.
  "Published for, and in cooperation with, the Division of Wildlife and
Freshwater Fisheries, Department of Conservation and Natural Resources and
the School of Forestry and Wildlife Sciences and the Alabama Experiment
Station, Auburn University."
  Includes bibliographical references.
  Contents:
  — v.1. A checklist of vertebrates and selected invertebrates: Aquatic mollusks,
        fishes, amphibians, reptiles, birds, and mammals. ISBN 0-8173-5130-2
        (pbk. : alk paper)
  — v.2. Imperiled aquatic mollusks and fishes ISBN 0-8173-5131-0
  — v.3. Imperiled amphibians, reptiles, birds, and mammals.
        ISBN 0-8173-5132-9 (pbk. : alk paper)
  — v.4.Conservation and management recommendations for imperiled wildlife.
        ISBN 0-8173-5133-7 (pbk. : alk paper)
  1. Vertebrates—Alabama. 2. Endangered species—Alabama. I. Mirarchi,
R. E. (Ralph Edward), 1950– II. Alabama. Division of Wildlife and Freshwater
Fisheries. III. Auburn University. School of Forestry and Wildlife Sciences.
IV. Alabama Agricultural Experiment Station. V. Vertebrate wildlife of
Alabama. VI. Vertebrate animals of Alabama in need of special attention.

AL606.52.U6A58 2004
596'.09761—dc22

                                                            2003064557

The University of Alabama Press
Tuscaloosa, Alabama 35487-0380

TABLE OF CONTENTS

LIST OF FIGURES

COVER   Clockwise from top left: DeKays' brown snake, photo—John Jensen; tricolored heron, photo—Malcolm Pierson; yellow bass, photo—Patrick O'Neil; sooty elimia, photo—Arthur Bogan; pine woods treefrog, photo—Ericha Shelton; red fox, photo—U. S. Fish and Wildlife Service

MAPS

[v]

COUNTIES OF ALABAMA

MAJOR RIVERS, BASINS, AND DAMS OF ALABAMA

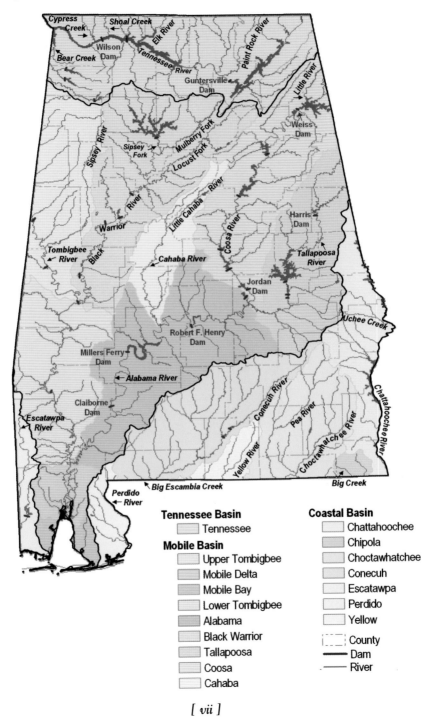

Tennessee Basin
- Tennessee

Mobile Basin
- Upper Tombigbee
- Mobile Delta
- Mobile Bay
- Lower Tombigbee
- Alabama
- Black Warrior
- Tallapoosa
- Coosa
- Cahaba

Coastal Basin
- Chattahoochee
- Chipola
- Choctawhatchee
- Conecuh
- Escatawpa
- Perdido
- Yellow
- County
- Dam
- River

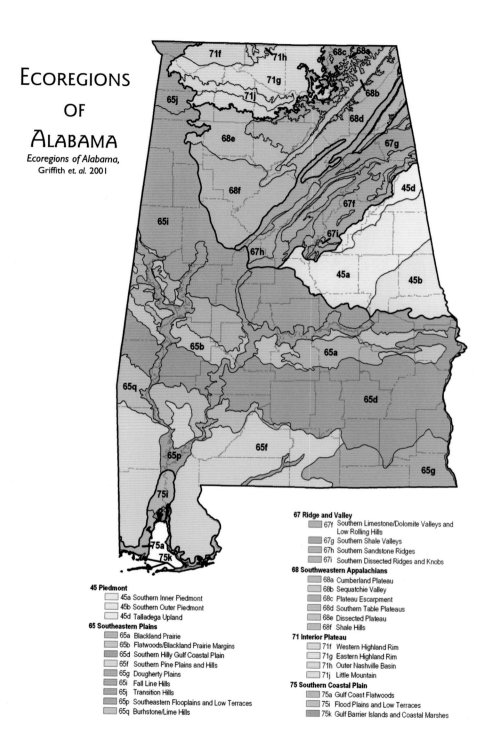

ECOREGIONS
OF
ALABAMA

Ecoregions of Alabama,
Griffith et. al. 2001

67 Ridge and Valley

- 67f Southern Limestone/Dolomite Valleys and Low Rolling Hills
- 67g Southern Shale Valleys
- 67h Southern Sandstone Ridges
- 67i Southern Dissected Ridges and Knobs

68 Southwestern Appalachians

- 68a Cumberland Plateau
- 68b Sequatchie Valley
- 68c Plateau Escarpment
- 68d Southern Table Plateaus
- 68e Dissected Plateau
- 68f Shale Hills

71 Interior Plateau

- 71f Western Highland Rim
- 71g Eastern Highland Rim
- 71h Outer Nashville Basin
- 71j Little Mountain

75 Southern Coastal Plain

- 75a Gulf Coast Flatwoods
- 75i Flood Plains and Low Terraces
- 75k Gulf Barrier Islands and Coastal Marshes

45 Piedmont

- 45a Southern Inner Piedmont
- 45b Southern Outer Piedmont
- 45d Talladega Upland

65 Southeastern Plains

- 65a Blackland Prairie
- 65b Flatwoods/Blackland Prairie Margins
- 65d Southern Hilly Gulf Coastal Plain
- 65f Southern Pine Plains and Hills
- 65g Dougherty Plains
- 65i Fall Line Hills
- 65j Transition Hills
- 65p Southeastern Floodplains and Low Terraces
- 65q Burhstone/Lime Hills

FOREWORD

Alabama is blessed with tremendous natural diversity that spans terrestrial habitats from the Gulf beaches to the lower Appalachian Mountains. The state also contains a wealth of water and wetland resources. Indeed, the Mobile-Tensaw Delta is recognized as one of the most significant and important delta complexes in the nation. This great physical diversity produces numerous habitat types and the abundance of wildlife species they support.

The volumes in this collection present detailed information about the known vertebrate and freshwater mussel and snail taxa in Alabama. Many are common on the landscape and well recognized by the public. Others are endemic, exist in very restrictive habitats, and are unknown to many. Regardless of their abundance, each species is part of the gift that has been bestowed upon us. Each has its place, role, and function. As the most intelligent beings on this planet, and those capable of impacting it the most, we have been given the responsibility to allow other organisms their space and to understand their roles and functions as best we can.

As we begin this century, these volumes are a good indicator of what is known about these species and what is yet to be learned. Some past actions were taken without an understanding of the consequences and some species have suffered. We are better today at predicting consequences, both beneficial and negative. As our knowledge increases so will our understanding of the outcome of our actions.

Human populations will continue to grow, effectively shrinking the natural world. Economic needs and demands will increase. The more we understand the natural world, the better we will be prepared to meet the needs of the various species. Economic development and growth can occur without creating drastic negative consequences for wildlife. It will be important to continually create opportunities for the public to enjoy the wildlife in our state and to become more aware of each species' habitat requirements.

We must recognize that the majority of wildlife habitat in Alabama is, and always will be, in the hands of private landowners. It will be their management decisions that determine the future for much of the wildlife in our state. Through developing a climate of cooperation and trust between private landowners and government agencies, wildlife will benefit.

The efforts of all the scientists and interested individuals who participated in the nongame wildlife conference and who contributed information for this publication are appreciated. The chief editor, Dr. Ralph Mirarchi, has provided great leadership and resolve to create these volumes. A special thank you for his efforts is deserved. In addition, all of the scientists who toiled in quest of gaining an answer to an often self-induced question about our natural world deserve recognition. It is the body of knowledge they created that is studied and built upon. I hope that these volumes provide understanding and direction to scientists as they seek answers to the many questions that still exist.

Gary H. Moody, Chief
Wildlife Section
Division of Wildlife and Freshwater Fisheries

DEDICATION

These volumes are dedicated to the memory of

Robert "Bob" C. McCollum, III
September 13, 1963 – January 22, 2002

Robert Clyde McCollum, III, son of Dr. Tom P. and Patsy L. Watson and the late Robert C. McCollum, Jr., was born in Albany, Georgia. Bob graduated from Hawkinsville High School, Hawkinsville, Georgia, in 1981. He attended both Middle Georgia College and the Georgia Institute of Technology prior to deciding on a career in wildlife management and enrolling at Auburn University in January 1987. He received a B.S. in Wildlife Science from the then-Department of Zoology and Wildlife Sciences, Auburn University, in June 1989 and an M.S. from the same program, under the auspices of the Alabama Cooperative Fish and Wildlife Research Unit, in August 1992. Bob worked as the Nongame Wildlife Coordinator for the Alabama Department of Conservation and Natural Resources, Division of Wildlife and Freshwater Fisheries from July 22, 1996, until his death.

Bob believed deeply in the conservation of nongame species and their associated habitats. He always endeavored to demonstrate the benefits of nonconsumptive activities associated with wildlife conservation to the public, whether through his daily routine, in developing birding trails, or by writing articles on wildlife. Bob loved all aspects of the outdoors. He enjoyed fly-fishing for trout and squirrel hunting as much as providing habitat in his yard for a variety of wildlife species. He was the moving force behind, and actively involved in, the initial planning for the Second Nongame Wildlife Conference at the time of his passing. He will be sorely missed, both as a wildlife professional and as a friend.

EDITOR'S NOTES

Authors making reference to this publication in its entirety should cite it as follows:

Mirarchi, R. E., ed. 2004. Alabama wildlife. Volume 1. A checklist of vertebrates and selected invertebrates: Aquatic mollusks, fishes, amphibians, reptiles, birds, and mammals. The University of Alabama Press, Tuscaloosa. 209 pp.

Authors making reference to individual sections of the publication should cite it as per the following example:

Haggerty, T. M., D. Cooley, G. Hill, G. D. Jackson, P. Kittle, R. E. Mirarchi, E. C. Soehren, and J. W. Tucker, Jr. 2004. Birds. Pp. 133-184 in R. E. Mirarchi, ed. Alabama wildlife. Volume 1. A checklist of vertebrates and selected invertebrates: Aquatic mollusks, fishes, amphibians, reptiles, birds, and mammals. The University of Alabama Press, Tuscaloosa.

ACKNOWLEDGMENTS

Those generous individuals who provided photographs for this volume are identified with each accompanying photograph. The Alabama Ornithological Society (AOS) and U.S. Fish and Wildlife Service (USFWS) also graciously allowed access to their photographic collections. However, numerous individuals, agencies, and organizations whose names do not appear elsewhere in this publication deserve recognition for contributions to the planning, execution, and funding of the most recent Nongame Conference and/or efforts that aided in the completion of this particular volume. They include: Gary H. Moody, Keith D. Guyse, Mark S. Sasser, and Ericha S. Shelton, Alabama Department of Conservation and Natural Resources (ADCNR), Division of Wildlife and Freshwater Fisheries; James B. Grand, Elise R. Irwin, Michael S. Mitchell, Amy L. Silvano, Cari-Ann Hayer, and Benton D. Taylor, Alabama Cooperative Fish and Wildlife Research Unit, Alabama Gap Analysis Team; Catherine L. Jackson, Teresa E. Rodriguez, Leigh Ann Stribling, Jamie Creamer, and Aimee Malone, Editorial Staff, Alabama Agricultural Experiment Station; Alabama Power Company (APC); Alabama Wildlife Federation; Auburn University (AU) Student Chapter of The Wildlife Society; AU Student Chapter of The American Fisheries Society; Black Warrior-Cahaba Rivers Land Trust; International Paper Company; MeadWestvaco Corporation; William R. and Fay Ireland Distinguished Professorship Endowment Fund; The Nature Conservancy of Alabama's Natural Heritage Program; ADCNR, State Lands' Natural Heritage Section: Sherry Bostick, U.S. Geological Survey; David Campbel and Jeff Sides, Univ. of Alabama-Tuscaloosa; Laura Mirarchi and Mike Gangloff, AU; Randy Haddock, Cahaba River Society; Bob Jones, Miss. Museum of Natural Science; Paul Parmalee, McClung Museum, Univ. of Tennessee; Malcolm Pierson, APC; Amy Sides, Alabama Rivers Alliance; Walt Burch, Greg Harber, Steve McConnell, Johndra Upton, all Nongame Wildlife Conference participants; and Richard Brinker, Dean, School of Forestry and Wildlife Sciences, for supporting the chief editor's request for professional improvement leave to complete this project.

PREFACE

State fish and wildlife agencies have been in existence for little more than a century. Their rudimentary beginnings most often began as expansions of sportsmen's clubs whose early interests centered on protecting game (those wild species sought for fur, flesh, sporting, and/or trophy value) often at the expense of other wild creatures, particularly those predatory in nature. Over succeeding decades, as the result of philosophical shifts in thinking about the interactions of humans and all wild things (e.g., see Leopold 1949) and the knowledge gleaned from research and experience, policies of these fledgling agencies and the attitudes of the public that support them have broadened such that nongame (all wild animals other than game) species also are now actively conserved under their umbrella of protection. Much of the impetus for statewide protection of nongame species along with game species came from the passage of the first federal endangered species legislation during the 1960s, and the birth of the general environmental movement during that same decade. Interest in all wildlife species has grown, and continues to grow as new terms such as *biodiversity* (the *variety* of *all* living organisms at *all* taxonomic levels) and their importance are described so cogently to the world by naturalists such as native Alabamian Edward O. Wilson (see Wilson 1992).

The state of Alabama is home to one of the richest wild faunas in the United States. New taxonomic forms (species or subspecies; hereafter *taxa*) of wildlife continue to be discovered and/or described within the state's boundaries. Alabama consistently is ranked among the top three to five states in terms of overall faunal biodiversity and ranks first among certain taxa (e.g., mussels), but it also holds the dubious honor of ranking second, only after Hawaii, in the number of taxa lost to extinction (The Nature Conservancy, 2002). Alabama was among the leaders in the area of game management during the early part of the twentieth century, but insulated by a wealth of natural resources and slow human population growth, and hindered by a weak education system and a struggling economy, it was not at the forefront of the early movement to protect nongame species. But it was not immune to it. In his fascinating historical text, James B. Trefethen rightly pointed out that the American conservation movement has occurred in fits and starts, sometimes thwarted by "political hacks," but inevitably pushed forward by the "giants among the pygmies" (Trefethen 1975:157). Such, too, was the case in Alabama relative to nongame wildlife resources. The original idea for the first symposium on endangered and threatened vertebrates (those animals with "backbones") in Alabama came from a meeting of Dan C. Holliman, Birmingham-Southern College (BSC); Tom Imhof and Helen Kittinger, the Alabama Ornithological Society; and James E. Keeler of the Alabama Department of Conservation and Natural Resources, Division of Game and Fish (ADCNR/DGF). The symposium subsequently convened at BSC in 1972, and the known vertebrate animal species of Alabama were categorized as *rare*, *endangered*, and *status undetermined*. Brief, descriptive annotations were provided for each, along with known distribution maps. The results were edited by J. E. Keeler, ADCNR/DGF, and published by that same agency (Keeler 1972).

Within a few short years, a group of visionary biologists (Herbert Boschung and Joab Thomas, University of Alabama-Tuscaloosa [UA-T]; Jack Brown, University of North Alabama [UNA]; George W. Folkerts, Auburn University [AU]; D. C. Holliman, BSC; and J. E. Keeler, ADCNR/DGF) saw the need to revise and expand that work and formed a steering committee to develop a second symposium that was held March 6-7, 1975, at UA-T. The scope of that symposium was expanded to include plants, mollusks, crayfishes, and shrimps, in addition to the vertebrates. In that publication (Boschung 1976), plant species were listed as *endangered*, *threatened*, or *of special concern*, and their habitats and distributions within the state were briefly noted. The status of each animal species was similarly described as were their physical characteristics, and their statewide distributions also were recorded. No specific conservation recommendations were made for these imperiled species, most likely because no ready and consistent source of funds for research and management to carry out such recommendations as yet existed at the state level.

It wasn't until the creation of an Alabama Nongame Wildlife Program in 1982 that the importance of those species was officially recognized by the state Legislature and responsibility for administration of the program was formally assigned to the ADCNR/DGF. Shortly thereafter, it was decided that a conference of specialists and laypersons should be convened to discuss common interests and concerns relative to Alabama's nongame wildlife resources and to build, with existing biological knowledge, a foundation upon which the program could be based. A steering committee (Gary H. Moody, Keith D. Guyse, Jack Hagopian, Frank P. Handley, J. E. Keeler [retired], ADCNR/DGF; Guy A. Baldassarre, Julian L. Dusi, G. W. Folkerts, Kirby L. Hays, Ralph E. Mirarchi, Robert H. Mount, AU; D. C. Holliman, BSC; John S. Ramsey, Alabama

Cooperative Fisheries Research Unit; David T. Rogers, UA-T; and C. William Summerour, Jacksonville State University) developed plans for the conference. The goals were: (1) to develop complete annotated lists of all vertebrate species and/or subspecies in Alabama; (2) to assign priority categories to those needing special attention; and (3) to develop a prioritized list of practicable measures that should be taken to enhance the welfare of nongame wildlife within the respective groups.

The first "official" (albeit the third meeting of biologists concerned with imperiled taxa) Nongame Wildlife Conference was held at AU on July 15 and 16, 1983, being jointly sponsored by the ADCNR/DGF and the Alabama Agricultural Experiment Station. This conference was essentially a "workshop" during which four committees of specialists—one each for fishes, amphibians and reptiles, birds, and mammals—discussed and arrived at consensus opinion relative to the status of the various components of the state's vertebrate fauna. The committees also developed lists of general and specific practicable measures that should be taken to enhance the welfare of nongame wildlife. Committee meetings were open to the public, and the public's input was solicited.

The first two objectives were achieved with the publication of the conference results, which were edited and compiled by R. H. Mount and distributed as two separate publications—an annotated checklist of all vertebrate species entitled *Vertebrate Wildlife of Alabama* (Mount 1984). The second publication was a more technical and detailed work entitled *Vertebrate Animals of Alabama in Need of Special Attention* (Mount 1986) and consisted of individual accounts for each species whose status, according to the conferees, was such that placement in one of four priority categories (*poorly known, special concern, threatened,* and *endangered*) was warranted. These works were much more complete and detailed at the vertebrate level than the previous publications and included color photographs of selected species on the checklist, and color photographs and detailed state distribution maps of each taxon in need of special attention. The intention was that funds from the Nongame Program would be matched with federal endangered species monies to fund research and management activities in support of conservation efforts for these taxa in need of special attention. However, plants and invertebrate species were not included in the conference discussions or publications, presumably because of the lack of funds that would be available to conduct such research.

Eventually the ADCNR/DGF developed a position for a Nongame Wildlife Coordinator. The position first was filled by Joseph Meyers (1984-

1990) and subsequently by James Woehr (1992-1994), and Robert "Bob" McCollum (1996). Even so, the third objective of the conference proved more difficult to achieve, primarily due to a lack of state and federal funds specifically dedicated to the conservation of nongame wildlife and the lack of a prioritization of research needs.

Approximately 15 years passed after the First Nongame Wildlife Conference and the resulting publications became available. In 2001, the U.S. Congress passed legislation (Wildlife Conservation Restoration Program) that provided a one-time appropriation to the various states "to address the unmet needs for a diverse array of wildlife and associated habitats" for wildlife conservation, conservation education, and wildlife-associated recreation. To be eligible for these, and potentially future, funds each state must develop a Wildlife Conservation Strategy. As such, Bob McCollum began discussions with various biologists in the state to develop plans for a Second Nongame Wildlife Conference that would play an important role in the formulation of that strategy for Alabama.

The Conference was initially planned to re-evaluate and update the efforts of the first Conference. Publications were to be revised and updated and project recommendations were to be solicited. Additionally, some taxonomic groups (mussels and aquatic snails) of invertebrate species also were to be included. Planning for the conference began under the direction of Bob McCollum, and a chief editor (R. E. Mirarchi, AU) was selected to coordinate the revision and updating of the previous publications. Conference plans were slowed during the winter of 2002 with the sudden and tragic passing of Bob McCollum. However, other personnel of the now-ADCNR/Division of Wildlife and Freshwater Fisheries (DWFF)—in particular Ericha S. Shelton, G. H. Moody, and K. D. Guyse—worked closely with the chief editor to get the planned meeting back on schedule. Committee chairs/co-editors from a cross section of biological/ecological backgrounds, regions of the state, and professional affiliations were selected for each wildlife group to be represented (Jeffrey T. Garner, ADCNR/DWFF, mollusks; Maurice F. Mettee, Alabama Geological Survey, fishes; Mark A. Bailey, Conservation Southeast, Inc., amphibians and reptiles; Thomas M. Haggerty, UNA, birds; and Troy L. Best, AU, mammals), and they, in turn, selected expert committee members to finalize the process. During the spring and early summer the chief editor, committee chairs/co-editors, and ADCNR/DWFF personnel, including the new Nongame Wildlife Coordinator, Mark Sasser, finished plans for the meeting, and developed important criteria for assessing the status, distribution, and conservation needs of all vertebrate, and the selected invertebrate (mussels and aquatic snails), wildlife taxa of the state.

Prior to the Conference, committee chairs were required to submit a "draft" annotated checklist of taxa for each wildlife group (mussels and aquatic snails, fishes, amphibians and reptiles, birds, and mammals) under consideration. Additionally, priority status designations were developed by the chief editor and chairs/co-editors of each committee to assess status for each species/taxon. These priority designations were defined as:

Extinct - taxa that historically occurred in Alabama, but are no longer alive anywhere within their former distribution.

Extirpated - taxa that historically occurred in Alabama, but are now absent; may be rediscovered in the state, or be reintroduced from populations existing outside the state.

Extirpated/Conservation Action Underway - taxa that historically occurred in Alabama, were absent for a period of time, and currently are being reintroduced, or have a plan for being reintroduced, into the state from populations outside the state.

Priority 1/Highest Conservation Concern - taxa critically imperiled and at risk of extinction/extirpation because of extreme rarity, restricted distribution, decreasing population trend/population viability problems, and specialized habitat needs/habitat vulnerability due to natural/human-caused factors. Immediate research and/or conservation action required.

Priority 2/High Conservation Concern - taxa imperiled because of three of four of the following: rarity; very limited, disjunct, or peripheral distribution; decreasing population trend/population viability problems; specialized habitat needs/habitat vulnerability due to natural/human-caused factors. Timely research and/or conservation action needed.

Priority 3/Moderate Conservation Concern - taxa with conservation problems because of insufficient data or because of two of four of the following: small populations; limited, disjunct, or peripheral distribution; decreasing population trend/population viability problems; specialized habitat needs/habitat vulnerability due to natural/human-caused factors. Research and/or conservation action recommended.

Priority 4/Low Conservation Concern - taxa that are secure, yet conservation concerns exist because of one of four of the following: relative abundance; limited, disjunct, or peripheral distribution; decreasing population trend/population viability problems; specialized habitat needs/increasing habitat vulnerability due to natural/human-caused factors. Research on specific problem suggested.

Priority 5/Lowest Conservation Concern - taxa that are demonstrably secure, with size of population stable/increasing, geographical distribution stable/expanding, population trend/ population viability stable/increasing, relatively limited habitat vulnerability due to natural/ human caused factors, **or** an unusual visitor to the state. No specific monitoring or conservation action needed.

The Second Nongame Wildlife Conference was held at the Auburn University Hotel and Dixon Conference Center on July 23-24, 2002. Some 140 participants were involved in the meeting, which consisted of discussion groups led by the committees of experts on the various animal groups. During the meeting, members of the audience were encouraged to interact with the committee of experts in discussing the status, distribution, habitats of, and priority conservation designation for each taxon. Input from these interactions was used to modify the draft checklists presented at the meeting and resulted in a final annotated checklist (herewith) of all taxa in each group. Those species from each group designated as **Extirpated, Extirpated/Conservation Action Underway, Priority 1,** or **Priority 2** were assigned to various experts for preparation of more in-depth individual species accounts that are contained in Volumes 2 (Imperiled Aquatic Mollusks and Fishes) and 3 (Imperiled Amphibians, Reptiles, Birds, and Mammals) of this series. General conservation recommendations for preservation and management of specific ecosystems, communities, and habitats within Alabama, along with prioritized and detailed conservation recommendations for research and management actions for individual taxa, are contained in Volume 4. Details associated with the compilation of Volumes 2-4 are outlined in the preface of each of those texts.

This volume includes a brief, introductory overview of each animal group's history, dynamics, and prognosis, and anything else thought unique and relevant by the group's co-editor. Also included is the source of the taxonomic classification used in the annotated list. All taxonomic classifications follow the most recently accepted guidelines for the respective scientific societies, unless otherwise noted. Individual annotations begin with taxonomic designation from Class through Family. Each species annotation then includes, in order, the common name, scientific name, relative abundance, descriptive terms relative to distribution in the state (basic ecoregions or other accepted criteria for each group as outlined in the groups introductory comments), reproductive status (breeds in state or not), seasonal use of state (for migratory species), brief but descriptive phrase describing typical habitat where found, other information deemed interesting, priority status designation, and any appropriate designation as a federally imperiled taxon. Outlined below are definitions of terms commonly used to describe distributions and activities of various taxa throughout the annotations:

Abundant - generally distributed in suitable habitats and in substantial numbers.

Accidental - sighting/occurrence verified but not part of the established biota; far outside normal geographical distribution, and not expected to be seen again.

Breeds/Breeder - successful reproduction (nests, eggs, and/or young) verified on regular basis.

Breeds Occasionally/Occasional Breeder - successful reproduction verified only on occasional basis.

Bred Historically/Historical Breeder - successful reproduction once verified, but no longer occurs.

Breeding Probable - successful reproduction probable, but no verification exists.

Common - easily found/seen in suitable habitats.

Endangered - in danger of extinction or extirpation in all or a majority of geographical distribution in the foreseeable future; may be federally designated as such.

Exotic - non-native that has become established naturally, or as a result of human activity, as a self-sustaining wild population within state.

Fairly Common - often found/seen in suitable habitats.

Fall - August through November.

Hypothetical - sightings having acceptable documentation, but not supported with physical evidence or corroborated by several experienced observers.

Local Breeder - breeding restricted to a very small area, usually within a single county.

Locally Common - easily found/seen in suitable habitats, but absent or less common in intervening areas; characteristic of certain species having narrow habitat requirements.

Nonbreeder - species that migrates through, or winters, but does not successfully reproduce in the state.

Occasional - an infrequent visitor from outside normal geographical distribution that may be seen irregularly, or for birds, a species that is seldom found and unexpected; not seen annually.

Peripheral - present, but in low numbers because of being at extremes of overall geographical distribution.

Poorly Known - forms for which data on status, distribution, and/or life histories are insufficient to permit categorization.

Possible Breeder - reproduction suspected (e.g., species in habitat during breeding season, territorial behavior, courtship behavior, pair detected), but without verification.

Potentially Occurs - forms that occur so close to state boundaries that their presence is suspected, but not confirmed.

Problematic - regularly occurring, but widely and unreliably distributed, with sites/habitats for potential conservation difficult to determine.

Rare - seldom found/seen in suitable habitats and unexpected, but within normal geographical distribution; can be seen annually.

Special Concern - forms that should be closely monitored because of threats to habitat, limited distribution, and/or life history may cause them to become threatened or endangered within foreseeable future.

Spring - March through May.

Summer - June through July.

Threatened - forms likely to become endangered in all or a majority of their geographical distribution within foreseeable future; may be federally designated as such.

Uncommon - seldom found/seen in suitable habitats, but expected.

Winter - December through February.

Finally, the maps on pages *vi* through *viii* are provided to assist the reader in locating many of the geographic, ecological, and specific site loca-

tions mentioned in the text. Only major rivers, and those creeks and dams frequently mentioned in the text, were labeled. All dams on major rivers were
included (Mettee *et al.* 1993), although not all were labeled. These decisions
were made by the editor in an attempt to avoid unnecessary cluttering of the
map.

I anticipate that this volume will be used extensively in the field by
educators, researchers, students, recreationists, governmental and private conservation entities, planners, and the lay public who may become involved in
decision-making processes that affect Alabama's wildlife resources. As such, it
was particularly designed and sized for ease of use in the outdoors. I encourage
you to take along a copy each time you venture forth to enjoy Alabama's
diverse and beautiful wildlife resources and to "check off" those animals you
encounter on each trip.

Ralph E. Mirarchi, Editor

FRESHWATER MUSSELS
AND
SNAILS

Banded Mysterysnail
Viviparus georgianaus

INTRODUCTION

The precipitous decline of North American freshwater mollusks has resulted in increased awareness of this fauna over the past two decades. With the most diverse assemblage of unionids and one of the most diverse assemblages of aquatic snails in the world, Alabama often has been the focal point of this interest. This state is, or was historically, home to 174 species of freshwater snails representing 10 families, and 173 species and subspecies of freshwater mussels representing two families. Embedded in this great diversity is a high degree of endemism. One hundred two snail and 11 mussel taxa never have been collected outside the boundaries of Alabama. When taxa endemic to drainages that Alabama shares with adjacent states are included, these numbers increase to 115 snails and 58 mussels (Lydeard and Mayden 1995, numbers adjusted to currently accepted taxonomy). As would be expected with such a level of endemism, there are many species with very restricted distributions and specialized habitat requirements, making them highly vulnerable to extinction. Unfortunately, many of those taxa have been unable to cope with modern perturbations to their habitat and are no longer with us. Herein, we list, as possibly extinct, 42 taxa of aquatic snails and 27 taxa of freshwater mussels historically found in Alabama. These numbers represent 98 percent and 79 percent of the Northern American snails and mussels, respectively, considered to be extinct by The American Fisheries Society. The fingernail, pill, or pea clams (Family Sphaeriidae) also are mollusks native to Alabama. Although widespread and sometimes very common, these small, cryptic species have received little scientific attention. There are 39 species, representing four genera, recognized in North America. Representatives of all four genera occur in Alabama, but no systematic survey of them has ever been performed in the state. Therefore, they were not included in the checklist, but conservation priorities in the near future should include an organized survey of this group in the state.

Although several factors probably have contributed to the decline of Alabama's mollusks, destruction of shoal habitat by impoundments and channelization of our rivers has been the major culprit. As such, it is critically important that this group of animals be given the long overdue attention they deserve. The Priority Status Designation assigned by this committee to each extant and some extirpated species was based on the most current information available from recent fieldwork, the mollusk literature, and, after roundtable discussion, among committee members and others attending the mollusk working group at the 2002 Alabama Nongame Wildlife Conference.

Additionally, relatively new threats from exotic introductions such as zebra mussels and Asian clams may further complicate conservation of our native species. Zebra mussels are sessile, clinging to solid substrata with byssal threads, and have reached densities of more than 100,000 per square meter (9,290 per square foot) in more northerly regions. Such densities make resources needed by native species unavailable, smother native species with their excessive numbers, and often hinder them from opening and closing their shells. With the exception of areas with intensive barge traffic, densities in most Alabama reaches of the Tennessee River are less than one per square meter (less than one per square foot), but anecdotal evidence suggests a steady increase, so the potential for future detriment to native species is great. Asian clams presumably compete with native species for resources, but their effects appear to have stabilized since they found their way into Alabama around the middle of the twentieth century. Although densities of more than 100 per square meter are not uncommon in some habitats, native species usually outnumber Asian clams in the free-flowing habitats favored by the rarer native species.

Most recent and current mollusk work has dealt with freshwater mussels. The large number of snail species assigned a priority status designation of Moderate Conservation Concern is based primarily on a lack of current information on their status, and is reflective of the dearth of knowledge about them. Recent additions of some snail species to the federal endangered species list have brought them some attention, but much basic survey and taxonomic work remains to be done. A few extirpated species of mussels and snails also were assigned the Extirpated/Conservation Action Underway designation based on the likelihood of their being reintroduced to portions of their historic distribution within Alabama. Several such projects are under way, or are being considered, and only those species involved were assigned this rank.

Geographical distributions provided in the annotations refer to the state of Alabama (e.g., the Spectaclecase, *Cumberlandia monodonta*, is widespread in the Mississippi River system, but restricted to the Tennessee River in Alabama), unless otherwise specified. Cumberlandian Region refers to the area encompassing the Tennessee and Cumberland River drainages. References to the Apalachicola Basin include the Chattahoochee and Chipola Rivers and tributaries. Gulf Coast systems refer to the smaller drainages of south-central and southeastern Alabama that flow directly into the Gulf of Mexico, including the Choctawhatchee, Pea, Yellow, and Conecuh Rivers and tributaries. The "eastern reaches" of the Mobile Basin include the Coosa, Tallapoosa, and Cahaba Rivers and tributaries, whereas the "western reaches" of said basin include the Tombigbee and Black Warrior Rivers and tributaries.

The reader will note some unique situations involving the mollusks listed here. The common names of freshwater mussels and snails often are unusual, and usually are visually or morphologically descriptive. Many of the names of mussels date back to the period in which they were harvested for the pearl button industry during the late 1800s and first half of the 1900s. These names generally are colorful, with a few too colorful for modern publication, and reflect what they resembled to the mussel fishermen. During the 1980s, in an attempt to standardize usage of common names of freshwater mollusks, scientists working with the group assigned names to most species. Names used by commercial mussel fishermen were retained when applicable, and less colorful, but still descriptive, names were given to those ignored by them, and to the freshwater snails. Common and scientific names followed Turgeon et al. (1998) except, on occasion, when recent taxonomic changes were included or when extinct species not previously given common names were assigned such.

Jeffrey T. Garner

COMMITTEE

Mr. Jeffrey T. Garner, Alabama Department of Conservation and Natural Resources, Division of Wildlife and Freshwater Fisheries, Florence, AL, Chairperson/Compiler

Mrs. Holly N. Blalock-Herod, U.S. Fish and Wildlife Service, Panama City, FL

Dr. Arthur E. Bogan, North Carolina Museum of Natural Sciences, Raleigh, NC

Mr. Robert S. Butler, U.S. Fish and Wildlife Service, Asheville, NC

Dr. Wendell R. Haag, Center for Bottomland Hardwood Research, U.S. Forest Service, Oxford, MS

Mr. Paul D. Hartfield, U.S. Fish and Wildlife Service, Jackson, MS

Mr. Jeffrey J. Herod, U.S. Fish and Wildlife Service, Jackson Guard at Eglin Air Force Base, Niceville, FL

Dr. Paul D. Johnson, Tennessee Aquarium Research Institute, Cohutta, GA

Mr. Stuart W. McGregor, Geological Survey of Alabama, Tuscaloosa, AL

Dr. James D. Williams, Florida Caribbean Science Center, U.S. Geological Survey, Gainesville, FL

BIVALVES
CLASS BIVALVIA

FRESHWATER MUSSELS
ORDER UNIONOIDA

FAMILY MARGARITIFERIDAE

Spectaclecase *Cumberlandia monodonta*. Rare. Restricted to the Tennessee River. Extant only in the riverine reaches downstream of Wilson and Guntersville Dams. **HIGHEST CONSERVATION CONCERN.**

Alabama Pearlshell *Margaritifera marrianae*. Rare. Endemic to small area of south-central Alabama. Most populations found in Escambia River system in Butler, Conecuh, and Crenshaw Counties. In the Alabama River system, known from Limestone Creek, Monroe County. Found in small tributaries. **Candidate for federal protection. HIGHEST CONSERVATION CONCERN.**

FAMILY UNIONIDAE

Mucket *Actinonaias ligamentina*. Rare. Restricted to Tennessee River drainage. Apparently rare even prior to impoundment. Possibly extant in Second and Shoal Creeks, Lauderdale County. Restricted to shoal habitats. **HIGHEST CONSERVATION CONCERN.**

Pheasantshell *Actinonaias pectorosa*. **Extirpated.** Endemic to Cumberlandian Region. Historically occurred in Tennessee River downstream to Muscle Shoals. Not reported since the river was impounded. Limited to shoal habitats.

Elktoe *Alasmidonta marginata*. **Extirpated.** Restricted to Tennessee River system. Historically found in main stem and large tributaries across northern Alabama. No records since the early twentieth century. Found in shoal habitats.

Coosa Elktoe *Alasmidonta mccordi*. **Extinct.** Known only from one specimen collected from the Coosa River in St. Clair County prior to its impoundment.

Southern Elktoe *Alasmidonta triangulata*. Rare. Endemic to Apalachicola Basin. Extant in Uchee Creek system in Lee and Russell Counties. Usually found in sandy mud substrata. **HIGHEST CONSERVATION CONCERN.**

Slippershell Mussel *Alasmidonta viridis*. Rare. Restricted to Tennessee River drainage. Extant in a few tributaries. Usually found in small creeks. **HIGHEST CONSERVATION CONCERN**.

Coosa Fiveridge *Amblema elliotti*. Special concern. Endemic to the eastern reaches of Mobile Basin upstream of the Fall Line. Primarily in riverine habitats. MODERATE CONSERVATION CONCERN. **(Fig. 1, p. 25)**

Threeridge *Amblema plicata*. Common. Found in Tennessee River drainage, western and lower reaches of Mobile Basin, and some Gulf Coast rivers. Common in many areas of Tennessee drainage, but declining in parts of Mobile Basin and Gulf Coast. May be found in riverine or impounded areas. Important commercial species. Low Conservation Concern. **(Fig. 2, p. 25)**

Apalachicola Floater *Anodonta heardi*. Poorly known. Apparently endemic to Apalachicola Basin. In Alabama, known from a single recent record from Uchee Creek, Russell County. Also records from other portions of the Apalachicola Basin in Georgia and Florida. Found predominantly in sluggish water. MODERATE CONSERVATION CONCERN.

Flat Floater *Anodonta suborbiculata*. Fairly common. Widespread in Tennessee River system, with localized populations in Mobile Basin impoundments. May be a recent invader of Mobile Basin. An odd form similar to *A. suborbiculata* found in Gulf Coast areas may represent an undescribed species. Usually found in soft sediments in sluggish water. Low Conservation Concern.

Rayed Creekshell *Anodontoides radiatus*. Uncommon. Widespread south of Tennessee River drainage, but declining. Often found in soft sediments in sluggish water. **HIGH CONSERVATION CONCERN**.

Rock Pocketbook *Arcidens confragosus*. Fairly common. Common in parts of Tennessee River system, but declining in parts of Mobile Basin. May occur in riverine or impounded habitats. MODERATE CONSERVATION CONCERN.

Purple Wartyback *Cyclonaias tuberculata*. Common. Restricted to Tennessee River system. Usually found in riverine habitat and occasionally in impounded areas where siltation is limited. Lowest Conservation Concern.

Fanshell *Cyprogenia stegaria*. Rare. Restricted to Tennessee River system. Extant only in Wilson Dam tailwaters. Restricted to lotic habitats. **Listed as *endangered* by the U.S. Fish and Wildlife Service. HIGHEST CONSERVATION CONCERN**.

Dromedary Pearlymussel *Dromus dromas*. **Extirpated**. Endemic to Cumberlandian Region. Not reported from Alabama since the Tennessee River was impounded. Restricted to lotic habitats. Reintroduction program planned for Wilson Dam tailwaters. **Listed as *endangered* by the U.S. Fish and Wildlife Service. CONSERVATION ACTION UNDERWAY.**

Butterfly *Ellipsaria lineolata*. Fairly common. Distributed widely in Tennessee River system and Mobile Basin. Found almost exclusively in riverine habitats. Low Conservation Concern. **(Fig. 3, p. 25)**

Alabama Spike *Elliptio arca*. Restricted to Mobile Basin. Apparently imperiled throughout, except in Sipsey River. May be found in riffles or pools. **HIGHEST CONSERVATION CONCERN.**

Delicate Spike *Elliptio arctata*. Uncommon. Widespread but uncommon in Mobile Basin. Some confusion as to the taxonomic status of a similar form in the Gulf Coast systems. Usually encountered in areas with at least some current. Often found under large rocks. **HIGHEST CONSERVATION CONCERN.**

Chipola Slabshell *Elliptio chipolaensis*. **Extirpated**. In Alabama, known only from a single record from Howard's Mill Creek, Houston County, in the Chattahoochee River system. Also records from other portions of the Apalachicola Basin in Georgia and Florida. Occurs in muddy sand in moderate current. **Listed as *threatened* by the U.S. Fish and Wildlife Service.**

Eastern Elliptio *Elliptio complanata*. Common. Found only in headwaters of Chipola River and tributaries of Chattahoochee River. Occurs in a variety of habitats. Lowest Conservation Concern.

Elephantear *Elliptio crassidens*. Abundant in many areas, but possibly declining in Mobile Basin and Gulf Coast drainages. Found throughout Alabama, except in Choctawhatchee River system. The dominant species in many areas, primarily in riverine habitats. Lowest Conservation Concern. **(Fig. 4, p. 25)**

Spike *Elliptio dilatata*. Rare. Limited to Tennessee River system. Extant in riverine areas downstream of Wilson and Guntersville Dams. Restricted to lotic habitats. **HIGHEST CONSERVATION CONCERN.**

Brother Spike *Elliptio fraterna*. **Extirpated**. In Alabama, known from a single Chattahoochee River record from Russell County. Also records from other portions of the Apalachicola Basin in Georgia and Florida.

Variable Spike *Elliptio icterina*. Common. Restricted to Gulf Coast systems. Taxonomic status uncertain. Possible species complex, but may be a distinct species. Part of a widely distributed complex of lanceolate *Elliptio* that occurs from southern Alabama through-out much of the Atlantic coast. May occur in current or sluggish areas. Lowest Conservation Concern.

Fluted Elephantear *Elliptio mcmichaeli*. Locally common, but declining. Apparently endemic to, and now restricted to, the lower reaches of the Choctawhatchee River system. Further taxonomic work may reveal similar forms in adjacent drainages belong to this species. Usually found in habitats with at least some current. **HIGHEST CONSERVATION CONCERN.**

Winged Spike *Elliptio nigella*. **Extinct**. Endemic to Apalachicola Basin. Known from a few Alabama records. Last reportedly collected in 1958.

Inflated Spike *Elliptio purpurella*. Rare. Endemic to Apalachicola Basin. Historically found in Chattahoochee and Chipola River systems. Possibly extant in Big Creek, Houston County. Usually found in sand or limestone substrata. **HIGHEST CONSERVATION CONCERN.**

Purple Bankclimber *Elliptoideus sloatianus*. Rare. Restricted to Chattahoochee River system. Thought extirpated from system until a live specimen recently was collected in upper Goat Rock impoundment. Usually found in moderate current. **Listed as threatened by the U.S. Fish and Wildlife Service. HIGHEST CONSERVATION CONCERN.**

Sugarspoon *Epioblasma arcaeformis*. **Extinct**. Endemic to Cumberlandian Region. Occurred in Tennessee River downstream to Muscle Shoals. Has not been reported since the river was impounded.

Angled Rifleshell *Epioblasma biemarginata*. **Extinct**. Endemic to Cumberlandian Region. Occurred in Tennessee River and major tributaries downstream to Muscle Shoals.

Cumberlandian Combshell *Epioblasma brevidens*. Rare. Endemic to Cumberlandian Region. Extant only in a short reach of Bear Creek, Colbert County. Limited to shoal habitats. Reintroduction program planned for Tennessee River in Wilson Dam tailwaters. **Listed as endangered by the U.S. Fish and Wildlife Service. HIGHEST CONSERVATION CONCERN.**

Oyster Mussel *Epioblasma capsaeformis*. **Extirpated**. Endemic to Cumberlandian Region. Historically occurred downstream to Muscle Shoals and in Paint Rock and Elk Rivers. Restricted to shoal habitats. Reintroduction program planned for Wilson Dam tailwaters. **Listed as endangered by the U.S. Fish and Wildlife Service. CONSERVATION ACTION UNDERWAY.**

Leafshell *Epioblasma flexuosa*. **Extinct**. Once found throughout Tennessee River. Has not been reported since the river was impounded.

Yellow Blossom *Epioblasma florentina florentina*. **Possibly extinct**. Endemic to Cumberlandian Region. Historically in Tennessee River downstream to Muscle Shoals and some major tributaries. Has not been reported since early twentieth century. **Listed as *endangered* by the U.S. Fish and Wildlife Service.**

Acornshell *Epioblasma haysiana*. **Extinct**. Endemic to Cumberlandian Region. Occurred in Tennessee River downstream to Muscle Shoals and in lower Elk River. Has not been reported since the river was impounded.

Narrow Catspaw *Epioblasma lenior*. **Extinct**. Endemic to Cumberlandian Region. Known from Paint Rock River system. Has not been reported since early twentieth century.

Forkshell *Epioblasma lewisii*. **Extinct**. Endemic to Cumberlandian Region. Occurred in Tennessee River downstream to Muscle Shoals. Has not been reported since the river was impounded.

Upland Combshell *Epioblasma metastriata*. **Extirpated**. Endemic to Mobile Basin. Historically occurred throughout the system. Not reported recently and last collected from Conasauga River. Restricted to shoal habitats. **Listed as *endangered* by the U.S. Fish and Wildlife Service.**

Catspaw *Epioblasma obliquata obliquata*. **Extirpated**. Historically found throughout Tennessee River. Has not been reported since the river was impounded. Restricted to shoal habitats. **Listed as *endangered* by the U.S. Fish and Wildlife Service.**

Southern Acornshell *Epioblasma othcaloogensis*. **Extirpated**. Endemic to Coosa and Cahaba River systems upstream of Fall Line. Not reported in recent years. Restricted to shoal habitats. **Listed as *endangered* by the U.S. Fish and Wildlife Service.**

Southern Combshell *Epioblasma penita*. Rare. Endemic to Mobile Basin. Historically distributed throughout the system. Known to be extant only in Buttahatchee River. Possibly distributed upstream into Alabama. Found in shoal habitats. **Listed as *endangered* by the U.S. Fish and Wildlife Service. HIGHEST CONSERVATION CONCERN**.

Rounded Combshell *Epioblasma personata*. **Extinct**. Historically distributed throughout Tennessee River. Has not been reported since the river was impounded.

Tennessee Riffleshell *Epioblasma propinqua*. **Extinct**. Historically occurred throughout Tennessee River. Has not been reported since the river was impounded.

Cumberland Leafshell *Epioblasma stewardsonii*. **Extinct**. Endemic to Tennessee River system. Has not been reported since the river was impounded.

Tubercled Blossom *Epioblasma torulosa torulosa*. **Possibly extinct**. Historically found across northern Alabama in Tennessee River. Has not been reported since the river was impounded. **Listed as *endangered* by the U.S. Fish and Wildlife Service.**

Snuffbox *Epioblasma triquetra*. Rare. Historically occurred across northern Alabama in Tennessee River and some major tributaries. Known to be extant only in Paint Rock River. Restricted to shoal habitats. **HIGHEST CONSERVATION CONCERN.**

Turgid Blossom *Epioblasma turgidula*. **Possibly extinct**. Historically distributed across northern Alabama in Tennessee River proper and some major tributaries. Has not been reported since early twentieth century. Was restricted to shoal habitats. **Listed as *endangered* by the U.S. Fish and Wildlife Service.**

Tennessee Pigtoe *Fusconaia barnesiana*. Local and uncommon. Endemic to Cumberlandian Region. Distributed across northern Alabama. Extant in a few tributaries, but extirpated from Tennessee River proper. Limited to shoal habitats. **HIGH CONSERVATION CONCERN.**

Gulf Pigtoe *Fusconaia cerina*. Common. Endemic to Mobile Basin and widespread within the system. Ecomorphs from small streams to large rivers divergent in shell morphology. Usually found in habitats with at least moderate current. Lowest Conservation Concern. **(Fig. 5, p. 25)**

Shiny Pigtoe *Fusconaia cor*. Rare. Endemic to Cumberlandian Region. Once distributed across northern Alabama, but now extant only in Paint Rock River. Restricted to shoal habitats. **Listed as *endangered* by the U.S. Fish and Wildlife Service. HIGHEST CONSERVATION CONCERN.**

Finerayed Pigtoe *Fusconaia cuneolus*. Rare. Endemic to Cumberlandian Region. Once distributed across northern Alabama, but now extant only in Paint Rock River. Found in shoal habitats. **Listed as *endangered* by the U.S. Fish and Wildlife Service. HIGHEST CONSERVATION CONCERN.**

Ebonyshell *Fusconaia ebena*. Abundant. Widespread in Mobile Basin and Tennessee River system, primarily in large rivers. Often the dominant species in riverine areas. Important commercial species. Lowest Conservation Concern. **(Fig. 6, p. 25)**

Narrow Pigtoe *Fusconaia escambia*. Rare. Endemic to Gulf Coast drainages, but found primarily in Escambia River system. One historic record from lower Yellow River. Generally found in areas with at least some current. **HIGHEST CONSERVATION CONCERN.**

Round Ebonyshell *Fusconaia rotulata*. Rare. Endemic to Escambia River system. Usually found in habitats with at least moderate current. **HIGHEST CONSERVATION CONCERN.**

Longsolid *Fusconaia subrotunda*. Rare. Restricted to Tennessee River system. Extant only in tailwaters of Wilson and Guntersville Dams. Found only in riverine habitats. **HIGHEST CONSERVATION CONCERN.**

Purple Pigtoe *Fusconaia succissa*. Fairly common. Endemic to Gulf Coast drainages. Found in Choctawhatchee, Escambia, and Yellow Rivers. Usually in habitats with at least some current. Low Conservation Concern.

Round Pearlshell *Glebula rotundata*. Poorly known. Found across extreme southern Alabama. Usually in sluggish water. MODERATE CONSERVATION CONCERN.

Cracking Pearlymussel *Hemistena lata*. Rare. Restricted to Tennessee River system. Only extant in Elk River above impounded reach. Limited to riverine habitats. **Listed as *endangered* by the U.S. Fish and Wildlife Service. HIGHEST CONSERVATION CONCERN.**

Pink Mucket *Lampsilis abrupta*. Rare. Restricted to Tennessee River system. Extant only in tailwaters of Tennessee River dams and in a short reach of Bear Creek in Colbert County. Found in riverine habitats. **Listed as *endangered* by the U.S. Fish and Wildlife Service. HIGHEST CONSERVATION CONCERN.**

Finelined Pocketbook *Lampsilis altilis*. Rare. Endemic to the eastern reaches of Mobile Basin. Extant in some tributaries of most major rivers within its distribution. Further taxonomic work may reveal this to be a species complex. Usually found in habitats with at least some current. **Listed as *endangered* by the U.S. Fish and Wildlife Service. HIGH CONSERVATION CONCERN.**

Southern Sandshell *Lampsilis australis*. Rare. Endemic to Gulf Coast drainages. Found in Choctawhatchee, Escambia, and Yellow River systems usually in soft sediments with at least some current. **HIGHEST CONSERVATION CONCERN.**

Lined Pocketbook *Lampsilis binominata*. ***Extinct***. Endemic to Apalachicola Basin. Historically occurred in Chattahoochee River, but has not been reported from Alabama since the early 1940s. Was reported from Apalachicola Basin as late as the 1960s.

Wavyrayed Lampmussel *Lampsilis fasciola*. Special concern. Restricted to Tennessee River drainage. Extant only in Bear Creek, Colbert County, and Paint Rock River system. Limited to shoal habitats. MODERATE CONSERVATION CONCERN. (**Fig. 7, p. 25**)

Haddleton Lampmussel *Lampsilis haddletoni*. **Extinct**. Known from only two specimens from West Fork Choctawhatchee River. Not collected for almost 50 years.

Southern Pocketbook *Lampsilis ornata*. Fairly common. Widespread in Mobile Basin. Also found sparingly in the Conecuh River drainage. Occurs in a variety of habitats. Low Conservation Concern.

Pocketbook *Lampsilis ovata*. Fairly common. Found only in Tennessee River drainage. Extant in tailwaters of Tennessee River dams and some large tributaries. Found in shoals and pools in tributaries, but only in riverine habitats in large rivers. Low Conservation Concern. **(Fig. 8, p. 26)**

Orangenacre Mucket *Lampsilis perovalis*. Rare. Endemic to western Mobile Basin. Found in the Tombigbee River system and some of its tributaries. Usually in habitats with at least moderate current. **Listed as threatened by the U.S. Fish and Wildlife Service. HIGH CONSERVATION CONCERN.**

Southern Fatmucket *Lampsilis straminea claibornensis*. Fairly common. Found throughout Alabama south of Tennessee River drainage, except in the Black Belt where replaced by *L. s. straminea*. Appears to be smooth-shelled ecomorph of *L. s. straminea*. Usually found in slow to moderate current, but generally absent from impoundments. Low Conservation Concern.

Rough Fatmucket *Lampsilis straminea straminea*. Poorly known. Endemic to the Black Belt region of Alabama and Mississippi. Replaced by smooth-shelled *L. s. claibornensis* outside of Black Belt. Found most often in sluggish to moderate current. MODERATE CONSERVATION CONCERN. **(Fig. 9, p. 26)**

Shinyrayed Pocketbook *Lampsilis subangulata*. Rare. Restricted to Chattahoochee and Chipola River systems. Only known extant populations are in Uchee Creek, Russell County, and Big Creek, Houston County. **Listed as endangered by the U.S. Fish and Wildlife Service. HIGHEST CONSERVATION CONCERN.**

Yellow Sandshell *Lampsilis teres*. Common. Distributed throughout Alabama. Often found in both free-flowing and impounded rivers. May be found in gravel, sand, or mud. Lowest Conservation Concern. **(Fig. 10, p. 26)**

Alabama Lampmussel *Lampsilis virescens*. Rare. Endemic to Tennessee River system. Historically occurred downstream to Muscle Shoals. Eliminated throughout its distribution except in Paint Rock River system. Occurs in moderate current. **Listed as endangered by the U.S. Fish and Wildlife Service. HIGHEST CONSERVATION CONCERN.**

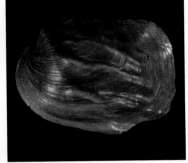

Fig. 2. Threeridge, *Amblema plicata,* **p. 18.** *Photo–Art Bogan*

Fig. 1. Coosa Fiveridge, *Amblema elliotti,* **p. 18.** *Photo–Mike Gangloff*

Fig. 3. Butterfly, *Ellipsaria lineolata,* **p. 19.** *Photo–Mike Gangloff*

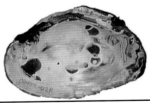

Fig. 4. Elephantear, *Elliptio crassidens,* **p. 19.** *Photo–Mike Gangloff*

Fig. 5. Gulf Pigtoe, *Fusconaia cerina,* **p. 22.** *Photo–Art Bogan*

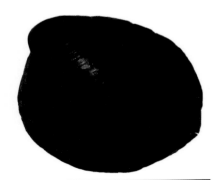

Fig. 6. Ebonyshell, *Fusconaia ebena,* **p. 22.** *Photo–Mike Gangloff*

Fig. 7. Wavyrayed Lampmussel, *Lampsilis fasciola,* **p. 23.** *Photo–Art Bogan*

Fig. 8. Pocketbook, *Lampsilis ovata,* **p. 24.** *Photo–Art Bogan*

Fig. 9. Rough Fatmucket, *Lampsilis straminea straminea,* **p. 24.** *Photo–Mike Gangloff*

Fig. 10. Yellow Sandshell, *Lampsilis teres,* **p. 24.**
Photo–Wendell Haag

Fig. 11. Fragile Papershell, *Leptodea fragilis,* **p. 29.** *Photo–Mike Gangloff*

Fig. 12. Washboard, *Megalonaias nervosa,* **p. 30.** *Photo–Mike Gangloff*

Fig. 13. Threehorn Wartyback, *Obliquaria reflexa,* **p. 30.** *Photo–Mike Gangloff*

Fig. 14. Southern Hickorynut, *Obovaria jacksoniana,* **p. 30.** *Photo–Pat O'Neil*

Fig. 15. Bankclimber, *Plectomerus dombeyanus,* **p. 31.** *Photo–Art Bogan*

Fig. 16. Bleufer, *Potamilus purpuratus,* **p. 34.** *Photo–Mike Gangloff*

Fig. 17. Giant Floater, *Pyganodon grandis,* **p. 35.** *Photo–Mike Gangloff*

Fig. 18. Southern Mapleleaf, *Quadrula apiculata,* **p. 35.** *Photo–Mike Gangloff*

Fig. 19. Alabama Orb, *Quadrula asperata,* **p. 35.** *Photo–Mike Gangloff*

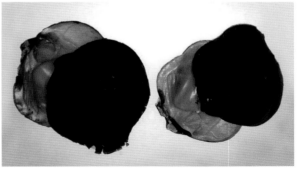

Fig. 20. Monkeyface, *Quadrula metanerva,* **p. 35.** *Photo–Art Bogan*

Fig. 21. Pimpleback, *Quadrula pustulosa pustulosa*, **p. 35.**
Photo–Wendell Haag

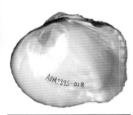

Fig. 22. Ridged Mapleleaf, *Quadrula rumphiana*, **p. 36.**
Photo–Mike Gangloff

Fig. 23. Pistolgrip,
Tritogonia verrucosa, **p. 37.**
Photo–Mike Gangloff

Fig. 24. Fawnsfoot,
Truncilla donaciformis,
p. 37. *Photo–Mike Gangloff*

Fig. 25. Pondhorn,
Uniomerus tetralasmus,
p. 37. *Photo–Mike Gangloff*

Fig. 26. Paper Pondshell,
Utterbackia imbecillis,
p. 37. *Photo–Mike Gangloff*

Fig. 27. Little Spectaclecase, *Villosa lienosa*, **p. 38.** *Photo–Mike Gangloff*

Fig. 28. Alabama Rainbow,
Villosa nebulosa, **p. 38.**
Photo–Mike Gangloff

Fig. 29. Southern Rainbow, *Villosa vibex*,
p. 38. *Photo–Mike Gangloff*

White Heelsplitter *Lasmigona complanata complanata*. Special concern. Restricted to Tennessee River system. Found in impounded reaches in Wheeler Reservoir and free-flowing reaches of some large tributaries. MODERATE CONSERVATION CONCERN.

Alabama Heelsplitter *Lasmigona complanata alabamensis*. Special concern. Endemic to Mobile Basin. Found primarily in free-flowing reaches, but may occur in pools. MODERATE CONSERVATION CONCERN.

Flutedshell *Lasmigona costata*. Uncommon. Limited to Tennessee River system. Extant in Paint Rock and Elk Rivers and a short reach of Bear Creek in Colbert County. Usually found in shoal habitats. **HIGH CONSERVATION CONCERN**.

Tennessee Heelsplitter *Lasmigona holstonia*. Uncommon. Found in Tennessee River tributaries and a few headwater tributaries of Coosa River. Usually occurs in small streams. **HIGH CONSERVATION CONCERN**.

Green Floater *Lasmigona subviridis*. **Extirpated**. In Alabama, known from a single Chattahoochee River record from Russell County collected in nineteenth century. Other records available from Apalachicola Basin in Georgia and Florida.

Birdwing Pearlymussel *Lemiox rimosus*. **Extirpated**. Endemic to Tennessee River system. Historically occurred downstream to Muscle Shoals. Not reported since the river was impounded. Reintroduction program for Wilson Dam tailwaters planned. **Listed as endangered by the U.S. Fish and Wildlife Service. CONSERVATION ACTION UNDERWAY**.

Fragile Papershell *Leptodea fragilis*. Fairly common. Widespread in Tennessee River system and Mobile Basin. Occurs in both riverine and impounded habitats. Lowest Conservation Concern. **(Fig. 11, p. 26)**

Scaleshell *Leptodea leptodon*. **Extirpated**. Historically occurred in Tennessee River upstream to Muscle Shoals. Not reported since the river was impounded. **Listed as endangered by the U.S. Fish and Wildlife Service.**

Slabside Pearlymussel *Lexingtonia dolabelloides*. Rare. Endemic to Tennessee River system. Only extant populations are in Paint Rock River system and a short reach of Bear Creek, Colbert County. Found in shoal habitats. **HIGHEST CONSERVATION CONCERN**.

Black Sandshell *Ligumia recta*. Uncommon in Tennessee River system, rare in Mobile Basin. Found in riverine habitats. **HIGH CONSERVATION CONCERN**.

Pondmussel *Ligumia subrostrata*. Poorly known. Widespread, but localized. Known from at least one small impoundment in Mobile County. Found in sluggish water. MODER-ATE CONSERVATION CONCERN.

Alabama Moccasinshell *Medionidus acutissimus*. Uncommon. Occurs in the Mobile Basin and Gulf Coast drainages. Widespread but localized in Mobile Basin. Apparently extirpated from Gulf Coast systems. Usually occurs in riffles and shoals. **Listed as threatened by the U.S. Fish and Wildlife Service. HIGH CONSERVATION CONCERN.**

Cumberland Moccasinshell *Medionidus conradicus*. Rare. Endemic to Cumberlandian Region. Extant in Paint Rock River system and Spring Creek system in Colbert County. Occurs in moderate to swift current. **HIGHEST CONSERVATION CONCERN.**

Coosa Moccasinshell *Medionidus parvulus*. **Extirpated.** Endemic to Mobile Basin. Historically widespread in the system, now in a few localized populations in Coosa River headwater tributaries in Georgia. Found in riffles and shoals. **Listed as *endangered* by the U.S. Fish and Wildlife Service.**

Gulf Moccasinshell *Medionidus penicillatus*. Rare. Endemic to Apalachicola Basin and Econfina Creek, Florida. Occurred in Chattahoochee and Chipola River systems. Known to be extant only in Big Creek, Houston County. **Listed as *endangered* by the U.S. Fish and Wildlife Service. HIGHEST CONSERVATION CONCERN.**

Washboard *Megalonaias nervosa*. Fairly common. Distributed throughout Alabama, with exception of Choctawhatchee and Yellow River systems. Found in both riverine and impounded areas. Important commercial species. Lowest Conservation Concern. **(Fig. 12, p. 26)**

Threehorn Wartyback *Obliquaria reflexa*. Common. Occurs throughout Tennessee River system and Mobile Basin. Found in both riverine and impounded habitats. Lowest Conservation Concern. **(Fig. 13, p. 26)**

Southern Hickorynut *Obovaria jacksoniana*. Special concern. Restricted to the western reaches of the Mobile Basin. Extant in some tributaries. Usually occurs in shoal habitats. MODERATE CONSERVATION CONCERN. **(Fig. 14, p. 26)**

Hickorynut *Obovaria olivaria*. **Extirpated.** Historically occurred in Tennessee River upstream to Muscle Shoals. Last reported in the late 1970s.

Ring Pink *Obovaria retusa*. Rare. Restricted to Tennessee River system. Possibly extant in tailwaters of Wilson Dam. Usually found in lotic habitats. **Listed as *endangered* by the U.S. Fish and Wildlife Service. HIGHEST CONSERVATION CONCERN.**

Round Hickorynut *Obovaria subrotunda*. Rare. Restricted to Tennessee River system. Extant only in Paint Rock River system. Usually found in areas of moderate current. **HIGHEST CONSERVATION CONCERN.**

Alabama Hickorynut *Obovaria unicolor*. Restricted to the western reaches of Mobile Basin. Common only in Sipsey River, rare elsewhere. Extant in some Tombigbee River tributaries. Usually found in areas with at least some current. **HIGH CONSERVATION CONCERN.**

Littlewing Pearlymussel *Pegias fabula*. **Extirpated.** Endemic to Cumberlandian Region. Historically occurred in some northern Alabama tributaries. Not reported from Alabama since early twentieth century. **Listed as *endangered* by the U.S. Fish and Wildlife Service.**

Bankclimber *Plectomerus dombeyanus*. Common. Found primarily in Alabama and Tombigbee Rivers and also in extreme lower reaches of Coosa and Cahaba Rivers. Occurs in both sluggish and flowing water, often on steep slopes. Lowest Conservation Concern. **(Fig. 15, p. 27)**

White Wartyback *Plethobasus cicatricosus*. Rare. Restricted to Tennessee River. Apparently eliminated throughout its distribution except in Wilson Dam tailwaters. Restricted to riverine habitats. **Listed as *endangered* by the U.S. Fish and Wildlife Service. HIGHEST CONSERVATION CONCERN.**

Orangefoot Pimpleback *Plethobasus cooperianus*. Rare. Restricted to Tennessee River. May be extant in tailwaters of Wilson and/or Guntersville Dams. Restricted to riverine habitats. **Listed as *endangered* by the U.S. Fish and Wildlife Service. HIGHEST CONSERVATION CONCERN.**

Sheepnose *Plethobasus cyphyus*. Rare. Found only in Tennessee River. Extant in riverine reaches downstream of Wilson and Guntersville Dams. Restricted to riverine habitats. **HIGHEST CONSERVATION CONCERN.**

Highnut *Pleurobema altum*. **Extinct.** Endemic to Mobile Basin. Has not been reported since early twentieth century.

Hazel Pigtoe *Pleurobema avellanum*. **Extinct.** Endemic to Mobile Basin. Has not been reported since mid-twentieth century.

Painted Clubshell *Pleurobema chattanoogaense*. Rare. Endemic to upper Coosa River system. Listed as probably extinct in some recent publications. Extant in Weiss Bypass on Coosa River. Restricted to shoal habitats. **HIGHEST CONSERVATION CONCERN.**

Clubshell *Pleurobema clava*. **Extirpated**. Historically found across northern Alabama in Tennessee River. Has not been reported from the state since the river was impounded. Restricted to lotic habitats. **Listed as *endangered* by the U.S. Fish and Wildlife Service.**

Ohio Pigtoe *Pleurobema cordatum*. Special concern. Found throughout Tennessee River in northern Alabama. Historically the most abundant species. Today found only in small numbers in tailwaters of Guntersville and Wilson Dams. Restricted to riverine habitats. Formerly an important commercial species. MODERATE CONSERVATION CONCERN.

Black Clubshell *Pleurobema curtum*. **Extirpated**. Endemic to Tombigbee River system. Possibly extant only in East Fork Tombigbee River in Mississippi. Found in riffles and runs. **Listed as *endangered* by the U.S. Fish and Wildlife Service.**

Southern Clubshell *Pleurobema decisum*. Uncommon. Found throughout Mobile Basin, except the Mobile Delta. Still widespread but localized. Restricted to shoal habitats. **Listed as *endangered* by the U.S. Fish and Wildlife Service. HIGH CONSERVATION CONCERN.**

Yellow Pigtoe *Pleurobema flavidulum*. **Extinct**. Endemic to Mobile Basin. Has not been reported since early twentieth century.

Dark Pigtoe *Pleurobema furvum*. Rare. Endemic to Black Warrior River system upstream of the Fall Line. Extant only in Sipsey Fork and North River. Found in riffles and shoals. **Listed as *endangered* by the U.S. Fish and Wildlife Service. HIGHEST CONSERVATION CONCERN.**

Southern Pigtoe *Pleurobema georgianum*. Rare. Endemic to Coosa River system.Extant in a few tributaries. Restricted to shoal habitats. **Listed as *endangered* by the U.S. Fish and Wildlife Service. HIGHEST CONSERVATION CONCERN.**

Brown Pigtoe *Pleurobema hagleri*. **Extinct**. Endemic to the Black Warrior River system upstream of the Fall Line. Has not been reported since early twentieth century.

Georgia Pigtoe *Pleurobema hanleyianum*. **Extinct**. Endemic to Mobile Basin. Has not been reported since mid-twentieth century.

Alabama Pigtoe *Pleurobema johannis*. **Extinct**. Endemic to Mobile Basin. Has not been reported since early twentieth century.

Flat Pigtoe *Pleurobema marshalli*. **Extirpated**. Endemic to Tombigbee River system. Has not been reported since completion of Tennessee-Tombigee Waterway. Restricted to shoals and runs. **Listed as *endangered* by the U.S. Fish and Wildlife Service.**

Coosa Pigtoe *Pleurobema murrayense*. **Extinct**. Endemic to Mobile Basin. Has not been reported since mid-twentieth century.

Longnut *Pleurobema nucleopsis*. **Extinct**. Endemic to Mobile Basin. Has not been reported since early twentieth century.

Tennessee Clubshell *Pleurobema oviforme*. Rare. Endemic to Cumberlandian Region. Extant in Alabama only in Paint Rock River system. Found in lotic habitats. **HIGHEST CONSERVATION CONCERN**.

Ovate Clubshell *Pleurobema perovatum*. Rare. Endemic to Mobile Basin. Widely distributed in the system, but in low numbers and localized. Occurs in shoals and runs. **Listed as endangered by the U.S. Fish and Wildlife Service. HIGHEST CONSERVATION CONCERN**.

Rough Pigtoe *Pleurobema plenum*. Rare. Historically distributed throughout Tennessee River. Extant only in tailwaters of Wilson Dam and possibly Guntersville Dam. Found in lotic habitats. **Listed as endangered by the U.S. Fish and Wildlife Service. HIGHEST CONSERVATION CONCERN**.

Oval Pigtoe *Pleurobema pyriforme*. Rare. Found only in a few Gulf Coast river systems. Extant only in Big Creek, Houston County. Usually found in areas with at least some current. **Listed as endangered by the U.S. Fish and Wildlife Service. HIGHEST CONSERVATION CONCERN**.

Warrior Pigtoe *Pleurobema rubellum*. **Extinct**. Endemic to Mobile Basin. Has not been reported since early twentieth century.

Pyramid Pigtoe *Pleurobema rubrum*. Rare. Historically distributed throughout Tennessee River. Extant only in tailwaters of Wilson and Guntersville Dams. Found in lotic habitats. **HIGHEST CONSERVATION CONCERN**.

Round Pigtoe *Pleurobema sintoxia*. Rare. Historically distributed throughout Tennessee River. Extant only in tailwaters of Wilson and Guntersville Dams. Found in lotic habitats. **HIGHEST CONSERVATION CONCERN**.

Fuzzy Pigtoe *Pleurobema strodeanum*. Special concern. Endemic to Gulf Coast drainages. Found in Choctawhatchee, Escambia, and Yellow River systems. Occurs both in current and sluggish areas. **HIGH CONSERVATION CONCERN**.

Heavy Pigtoe *Pleurobema taitianum*. Rare. Endemic to Mobile Basin. Historically occurred in main stem habitats of Tombigbee, Alabama, Coosa, and Cahaba Rivers. Extant in very localized populations in Alabama and Tombigbee Rivers. Found in flowing water. **Listed as *endangered* by the U.S. Fish and Wildlife Service. HIGHEST CONSERVATION CONCERN.**

True Pigtoe *Pleurobema verum*. **Extinct**. Endemic to Mobile Basin. Has not been reported since early twentieth century.

Pink Heelsplitter *Potamilus alatus*. Common. Restricted to Tennessee River system in both riverine and impounded habitats. Lowest Conservation Concern.

Inflated Heelsplitter *Potamilus inflatus*. Uncommon. Restricted to Mobile Basin. Localized populations extant in Black Warrior, Tombigbee, and Alabama Rivers. Found in soft substrata in slow to moderate current. **Listed as *threatened* by the U.S. Fish and Wildlife Service. HIGH CONSERVATION CONCERN.**

Pink Papershell *Potamilus ohiensis*. Fairly common. Restricted to Tennessee River system. Found primarily in soft substrata of impounded areas. Low Conservation Concern.

Bleufer *Potamilus purpuratus*. Fairly common. Restricted to Mobile Basin where widespread. Occurs both in pools and shoals. Often found under large rocks on shoals. Lowest Conservation Concern. **(Fig. 16, p. 27)**

Kidneyshell *Ptychobranchus fasciolaris*. Rare. Restricted to Tennessee River system. Extant in tailwaters of Wilson and Guntersville Dams, Paint Rock River system, and a short reach of Bear Creek in Colbert County. Always found in flowing water. **HIGHEST CONSERVATION CONCERN.**

Triangular Kidneyshell *Ptychobranchus greenii*. Rare. Endemic to Mobile Basin upstream of the Fall Line. Extant in a few tributaries of most major rivers in that system. Possible species complex. Occurs in shoal habitats. **Listed as *endangered* by the U.S. Fish and Wildlife Service. HIGHEST CONSERVATION CONCERN.**

Southern Kidneyshell *Ptychobranchus jonesi*. Rare. Endemic to Gulf Coast drainages. Historically found in Choctawhatchee, Escambia, and Yellow River systems. Only known extant population is in West Fork Choctawhatchee River. Usually found in areas with at least some current. **HIGHEST CONSERVATION CONCERN.**

Fluted Kidneyshell *Ptychobranchus subtentum*. **Extirpated**. Endemic to Cumberlandian Region. Historically occurred downstream to Muscle Shoals. Has not been reported from Alabama since river was impounded. Restricted to shoal habitats. **Recent candidate for federal protection.**

Eastern Floater *Pyganodon cataracta*. Poorly known. Restricted to Chattahoochee and possibly Chipola River systems. Not reported from the state since the 1970s. Usually

found in soft sediments in sluggish water. Habitat often overlooked in surveys. MOD-
ERATE CONSERVATION CONCERN.

Giant Floater *Pyganodon grandis*. Common. Found throughout Alabama. Occurs in almost
any habitat, including farm ponds. Lowest Conservation Concern. **(Fig. 17, p. 27)**

Southern Mapleleaf *Quadrula apiculata*. Common. Formerly restricted to the Mobile
Basin. Introduced into lower Tennessee River. Highly variable in shell morphology and
may represent a species complex. Found in riverine and impounded habitats. Important
commercial species. Lowest Conservation Concern. **(Fig. 18, p. 27)**

Alabama Orb *Quadrula asperata*. Common. Endemic to Mobile Basin. Widespread and
often common. Usually found in habitats with at least some current. Unsculptured form
in Tallapoosa River system may be a valid species (*Q. archeri*). Lowest Conservation
Concern. **(Fig. 19, p. 27)**

Rabbitsfoot *Quadrula cylindrica cylindrica*. Rare. Restricted to Tennessee River system.
Extant in Paint Rock River system and a short reach of Bear Creek, Colbert County.
Usually found along margins of shoals, but may be found in pools. **HIGHEST CON-
SERVATION CONCERN.**

Cumberland Monkeyface *Quadrula intermedia*. ***Extirpated***. Endemic to Tennessee River
system. Historically occurred downstream to Muscle Shoals. Has not been reported from
Alabama since the river was impounded. Restricted to lotic habitats. Potential for reintroduction into Wilson Dam tailwaters. **Listed as *endangered* by the U.S. Fish and
Wildlife Service. CONSERVATION ACTION UNDERWAY.**

Monkeyface *Quadrula metanevra*. Uncommon. Found in Tennessee River system and
Mobile Basin. Almost always occurs in riverine habitats. MODERATE CONSERVA-
TION CONCERN. **(Fig. 20, p. 27)**

Pimpleback *Quadrula pustulosa pustulosa*. Common. Restricted to Tennessee River system. Found in Tennessee River proper and large tributaries. Occurs in riverine and
impounded habitats. Lowest Conservation Concern. **(Fig. 21, p. 28)**

Mapleleaf *Quadrula quadrula*. Common. Apparently restricted to Tennessee River system. Specimens with similar shell morphology in Mobile Basin are probably aberrant *Q.
apiculata*. Found both in current and sluggish water. Does well in impoundments.
Important commercial species. Lowest Conservation Concern.

Purple Pimpleback *Quadrula refulgens*. Poorly known. Possibly of marginal occurrence in
Alabama. One record from Escatawpa River in extreme southwestern Alabama may represent a transplanted shell. MODERATE CONSERVATION CONCERN.

Ridged Mapleleaf *Quadrula rumphiana*. Fairly common. Endemic to Mobile Basin. Widespread in the system, it is highly variable in shell morphology and may represent a species complex. Found most commonly in areas with at least some current. Low Conservation Concern. **(Fig. 22, p. 28)**

Stirrupshell *Quadrula stapes*. **Possibly extinct**. Endemic to Mobile Basin. Found only in Tombigbee River system historically. Prehistoric shells occasionally found on Alabama River. Not reported since construction of Tennessee-Tombigee Waterway. **Listed as endangered by the U.S. Fish and Wildlife Service.**

Tapered Pigtoe *Quincuncina burkei*. Uncommon. Endemic to Choctawhatchee River system. Found most commonly in areas with at least some current. **HIGH CONSERVATION CONCERN.**

Sculptured Pigtoe *Quincuncina infucata*. Rare. Restricted to some tributaries of Chattahoochee and Chipola Rivers. Extant in Alabama only in Big Creek, Houston County, and a few tributaries of Chattahoochee River. Found in both pools and shoals. **HIGHEST CONSERVATION CONCERN.**

Alabama Creekmussel *Strophitus connasaugaensis*. Uncommon. Endemic to Mobile Basin. Found in Coosa and Cahaba River systems. May occur in areas with little to moderate current. **HIGH CONSERVATION CONCERN.**

Southern Creekmussel *Strophitus subvexus*. Special concern. Found throughout Alabama south of Tennessee River system. Often found in sluggish water. MODERATE CONSERVATION CONCERN.

Creeper *Strophitus undulatus*. Rare. Limited to Tennessee River drainage. Extant only in a short reach of Bear Creek, Colbert County. Occurs in a variety of habitats. **HIGHEST CONSERVATION CONCERN.**

Southern Purple Lilliput *Toxolasma corvunculus*. Rare. Endemic to Mobile Basin. Formerly widespread in the system, now in small, highly localized populations. Not reported for several years. **HIGHEST CONSERVATION CONCERN.**

Pale Lilliput *Toxolasma cylindrellus*. Rare. Endemic to middle reaches of Tennessee River system. Extirpated throughout its distribution except in Paint Rock River system. Usually found in moderate current. **Listed as endangered by the U.S. Fish and Wildlife Service. HIGHEST CONSERVATION CONCERN.**

Purple Lilliput *Toxolasma lividus*. Fairly common. Restricted to Tennessee River drainage. Found in both riverine and impounded areas. Low Conservation Concern.

Lilliput *Toxolasma parvus*. Poorly known. Recognized from Tennessee River system, Mobile Basin, and Gulf Coast drainages. Taxonomic work may reveal a species complex and restrict this distribution. Occurs primarily in soft sediments in sluggish water. MODERATE CONSERVATION CONCERN.

Iridescent Lilliput *Toxolasma paulus*. Poorly known. Restricted to Apalachicola Basin and Gulf Coast drainages. Populations west of Apalachicola River system may represent one or more undescribed species. Occurs both in current and sluggish water. MODERATE CONSERVATION CONCERN.

Pistolgrip *Tritogonia verrucosa*. Fairly common. Widely distributed in Tennessee River drainage and Mobile Basin. Usually found in riverine habitats, but occasionally in reservoirs. Low Conservation Concern. **(Fig. 23, p. 28)**

Fawnsfoot *Truncilla donaciformis*. Common in much of Tennessee River drainage, uncommon in Mobile Basin. Most often found in riverine areas, but occasionally in impounded areas with sandy substrata. MODERATE CONSERVATION CONCERN. **(Fig. 24, p. 28)**

Deertoe *Truncilla truncata*. Rare. Found in Tennessee River system. Extant in Wilson Dam tailwaters and several large tributaries. **HIGHEST CONSERVATION CONCERN**.

Florida Pondhorn *Uniomerus carolinianus*. Poorly known. Restricted to Chattahoochee and Chipola River systems. Apparently extant only in Uchee Creek, Russell County. May be found in areas with little or no current. MODERATE CONSERVATION CONCERN.

Pondhorn *Uniomerus tetralasmus*. Fairly common. Found across the Gulf Coast west of the Apalachicola Basin, and much of the Mobile Basin. Often found in areas with little or no current, and may occur in intermittent ponds and streams. Low Conservation Concern. **(Fig. 25, p. 28)**

Paper Pondshell *Utterbackia imbecillis*. Common. Found statewide. Utilizes almost any habitat, including farm ponds. Lowest Conservation Concern. **(Fig. 26, p. 28)**

Florida Floater *Utterbackia peggyae*. Poorly known. Restricted to Apalachicola Basin. In, Alabama, known from a single record from Big Creek Lake, Houston County. Other records from Apalachicola Basin in Georgia and Florida. Habitat often overlooked during surveys. MODERATE CONSERVATION CONCERN.

Choctaw Bean *Villosa choctawensis*. Rare. Endemic to Gulf Coast drainages. Found in Choctawhatchee, Escambia, and Yellow River systems. Usually found in areas with at least some current. **HIGH CONSERVATION CONCERN**.

Rainbow *Villosa iris.* Special concern. Restricted to Tennessee River system. Extant in several tributaries. Usually in shoal habitats. MODERATE CONSERVATION CONCERN.

Little Spectaclecase *Villosa lienosa.* Common. Occurs throughout Alabama south of the Tennessee River drainage. Found in a variety of habitats. Lowest Conservation Concern. **(Fig. 27, p. 28)**

Alabama Rainbow *Villosa nebulosa.* Special concern. Found in Mobile Basin upstream of the Fall Line. Occurs in small streams. MODERATE CONSERVATION CONCERN. **(Fig. 28, p. 28)**

Painted Creekshell *Villosa taeniata.* Special concern. Endemic to Cumberlandian Region. Usually in small to medium creeks in shoal habitats. MODERATE CONSERVATION CONCERN.

Cumberland Bean *Villosa trabalis.* **Extirpated.** Endemic to Cumberlandian Region. Historically occurred downstream to Muscle Shoals. Has not been reported since the river was impounded. Restricted to lotic habitats. **Listed as *endangered* by the U.S. Fish and Wildlife Service.**

Mountain Creekshell *Villosa vanuxemensis.* Fairly common. Endemic to Tennessee and Cumberland River systems. Extant in several tributaries. Relict population in tailwaters of Wilson Dam. May occur in shoal or pool habitats. Low Conservation Concern.

Coosa Creekshell *Villosa umbrans.* Rare. Endemic to Mobile Basin. Highly localized in tributaries upstream of the Fall Line. Found primarily in small streams. **HIGH CONSERVATION CONCERN.**

Southern Rainbow *Villosa vibex.* Common. Found in a variety of habitats throughout Alabama south of the Tennessee River drainage. Lowest Conservation Concern. **(Fig. 29, p. 28)**

Downy Rainbow *Villosa villosa.* Rare. Found in extreme southeastern Alabama in small tributaries in the Chattahoochee and Choctawhatchee River systems and possibly in the headwaters of the Chipola River. May be in riffle or pool habitats. **HIGH CONSERVATION CONCERN.**

ORDER VENEROIDA

FAMILY DREISSENIDAE

Zebra Mussel *Dreissena polymorpha*. **Exotic**. In Alabama, not reported outside of main channel of Tennessee River. Densities increasing slowly but steadily since early 1990s.

FAMILY CORBICULIDAE

Asian Clam *Corbicula fluminea*. **Exotic**. Introduced in the mid-1900s and now found throughout Alabama. Densities vary, but may reach several hundred per square meter and may be cyclic with extensive mortality events reported regularly.

GASTROPODS
CLASS GASTROPODA

FRESHWATER SNAILS
ORDER ARCHITAENIOGLOSSA

LIVE-BEARING SNAILS - FAMILY VIVIPARIDAE

Slender Campeloma *Campeloma decampi*. Rare. Endemic to small region of Tennessee River drainage in north-central Alabama. Extant in Limestone, Piney, and Round Island Creeks, Limestone County. Occurs both in gravel and soft sediments in slow to moderate current. **Listed as *endangered* by the U.S. Fish and Wildlife Service. HIGHEST CONSERVATION CONCERN.**

Pointed Campeloma *Campeloma decisum*. Fairly common. Widespread in Tennessee River system. Found primarily in soft sediments in slow to moderate current. Low Conservation Concern. **(Fig. 30, p. 41)**

Ovate Campeloma *Campeloma geniculum*. Poorly known. Endemic to Gulf Coast drainages. Found primarily in soft sediments in slow to moderate current. MODERATE CONSERVATION CONCERN.

Cylinder Campeloma *Campeloma regulare*. Common. Endemic to Mobile Basin. Found primarily in soft sediments in slow to moderate current. Low Conservation Concern.

Cylindrical Lioplax *Lioplax cyclostomaformis*. Rare. Endemic to Mobile Basin. Historically found throughout Alabama. Known to be extant in a short reach of Cahaba River. Generally found in soft sediments under boulders in shoal habitats. **Listed as *endangered* by the U.S. Fish and Wildlife Service. HIGHEST CONSERVATION CONCERN.**

Furrowed Lioplax *Lioplax sulculosa*. Poorly known. Restricted to Tennessee River. Found primarily in soft sediments in slow to moderate current. MODERATE CONSERVATION CONCERN.

Tulotoma *Tulotoma magnifica*. Rare, locally common. Endemic to Mobile Basin. Historically occurred from Coosa River in St. Clair County to Alabama River in Monroe County. Known to be extant in Jordan Dam tailwaters, Coosa River, and six Coosa River tributaries. Generally occurs under cobble and boulders in shoal habitats. **Listed as *endangered* by the U.S. Fish and Wildlife Service. HIGHEST CONSERVATION CONCERN**.

Banded Mysterysnail *Viviparus georgianus*. Common. Presumably found in streams throughout Alabama. Apparently more common in Tennessee River system. Found primarily in soft sediments and detritus in slow current. Lowest Conservation Concern. **(Fig. 31, p. 41)**

Olive Mysterysnail *Viviparus subpurpureus*. Common. Apparently restricted to main stem Tennessee River. Found in gravel or soft sediments in slow to swift current. Often found under cobble and boulders. Low Conservation Concern. **(Fig. 32, p. 41)**

APPLE SNAILS - FAMILY AMPULLARIIDAE

Florida Applesnail *Pomacea paludosa*. Poorly known. Restricted to Gulf Coast drainages. Usually found in areas with little to moderate current. MODERATE CONSERVATION CONCERN.

ORDER NEOTAENIOGLOSSA

HORN, RIVER, AND ROCK SNAILS - FAMILY PLEUROCERIDAE

Anthony Riversnail *Athearnia anthonyi*. Rare. Endemic to Tennessee River system. Historically found in Tennessee River from Muscle Shoals to Knoxville and in lower reaches of large tributaries. Now restricted to a short reach of Tennessee River in Jackson County and in lower Limestone Creek, Limestone County. Found in lotic habitats. **Listed as *endangered* by the U.S. Fish and Wildlife Service. HIGHEST CONSERVATION CONCERN**.

Acute Elimia *Elimia acuta*. Special concern. Endemic to Tennessee River tributaries in north-central Alabama. Usually found in lotic habitats. MODERATE CONSERVATION CONCERN. **(Fig. 33, p. 41)**

Mud Elimia *Elimia alabamensis*. Poorly known. Endemic to the middle reaches of Coosa River and adjacent tributaries. Usually found in lotic habitats. MODERATE CONSERVATION CONCERN.

Fig. 30. Pointed Campeloma, *Campeloma* *decisum,* **p. 39.** *Photo–Jeff Garner*

Fig. 31. Banded Mysterysnail, *Viviparus georgianus,* **p. 40.** *Photo–Jeff Garner*

Fig. 32. Olive Mysterysnail, *Viviparus* *subpurpureus,* **p. 40.** *Photo–Jeff Garner*

Fig. 33. Acute elimia, *Elimia acuta,* **p. 40.** *Photo–Art Bogan*

Fig. 34. Walnut Elimia, *Elimia* *bellula,* **p. 45.** *Photo–Malcolm Pierson*

Fig. 35. Rippled Elimia, *Elimia caelatura,* **p. 45.** *Photo–Malcolm Pierson*

Fig. 37. Sharp-crest Elimia, *Elimia carinifera,* **p. 45.** *Photo–Art Bogan*

Fig. 38. Fluted Elimia, *Elimia carinocostata,* **p. 45.** *Photo–Art Bogan*

Fig. 36. Cahaba Elimia, *Elimia cahawbensis,* **p. 45.** *Photo–Art Bogan*

Fig. 39. Riffle Elimia, *Elimia clara,* **p. 46.** *Photo–Malcolm Pierson*

Fig. 40. Cylinder Elimia, *Elimia cylindracea,* **p. 46.** *Photo–Art Bogan*

Fig. 41. Coldwater Elimia, *Elimia gerhardti,* **p. 47** *Photo–Art Bogan*

Fig. 42. Silt Elimia, *Elimia haysiana,* **p. 47.**
Photo–Malcolm Pierson

Fig. 44. Sooty Elimia, *Elimia paupercula,* **p. 48.** *Photo–Art Bogan*

Fig. 43. Slowwater Elimia, *Elimia interveniens,* **p. 47.** *Photo–Art Bogan*

Fig. 45. Onyx Rocksnail, *Leptoxis praerosa,* **p. 51.** *Photo–Art Bogan*

Fig. 46. Rugged Hornsnail,
Pleurocera alveare, **p. 52.**
Photo–Art Bogan

Fig. 47. Silty Hornsnail,
Pleurocera canaliculatum,
p. 52. *Photo–Jeff Garner*

Fig. 49. Two-ridge Rams-horn,
Helisoma anceps, **p. 57.** *Photo–Art Bogan*

Fig. 48. Brook Hornsnail, *Pleurocera vestita,*
p. 53. *Photo–Malcolm Pierson*

Ample Elimia *Elimia ampla*. Uncommon. Endemic to Cahaba River system. Usually found in lotic habitats. **HIGH CONSERVATION CONCERN**.

Lilyshoals Elimia *Elimia annettae*. Uncommon. Endemic to Cahaba River, Bibb County. Usually found in lotic habitats. **HIGH CONSERVATION CONCERN**.

Princess Elimia *Elimia bellacrenata*. Rare. Endemic to tributaries of the Cahaba River. Typically found in springs and small streams. **HIGHEST CONSERVATION CONCERN**.

Walnut Elimia *Elimia bellula*. Poorly known. Endemic to the middle reaches of Coosa River and Yellowleaf and Choccolocco Creeks. Usually found in lotic habitats. MODERATE CONSERVATION CONCERN. **(Fig. 34, p. 41)**

Rusty Elimia *Elimia bentonensis*. Poorly known. Endemic to Coosa River tributaries in Calhoun, St. Clair, and Talladega Counties. Usually found in lotic habitats. MODERATE CONSERVATION CONCERN.

Short-spire Elimia *Elimia brevis*. **Extinct**. Endemic to middle and lower reaches of Coosa River. Not reported since the river was impounded. Was restricted to shoal habitats.

Rippled Elimia *Elimia caelatura*. Special concern. Endemic to Coosa River system from headwaters downstream to Talladega County. Several isolated populations are extant and highly variable, suggesting a possible species complex. Usually found in lotic habitats. MODERATE CONSERVATION CONCERN. **(Fig. 35, p. 41)**

Cahaba Elimia *Elimia cahawbensis*. Common. Endemic to Mobile Basin. Widespread in Black Warrior and Coosa River tributaries and in Cahaba River system. Usually found in lotic habitats. Low Conservation Concern. **(Fig. 36, p. 42)**

Spindle Elimia *Elimia capillaris*. **Extinct**. Endemic to Coosa River. Historically found from the headwaters downstream to Coosa County. Not reported since the river was impounded. Was restricted to shoal habitats.

Sharp-crest Elimia *Elimia carinifera*. Common. Endemic to Mobile Basin. Widespread in streams above the Fall Line. Found primarily in streams, but occasionally in rivers. Usually in lotic habitats. Lowest Conservation Concern. **(Fig. 37, p. 42)**

Fluted Elimia *Elimia carinocostata*. Common. Endemic to Mobile Basin. Found in tributaries of Black Warrior and Coosa Rivers and in upper Cahaba River system. Usually found in lotic habitats. Low Conservation Concern. **(Fig. 38, p. 42)**

Prune Elimia *Elimia chiltonensis*. Poorly known. Endemic to Coosa River tributaries. Usually found in lotic habitats. MODERATE CONSERVATION CONCERN.

Riffle Elimia *Elimia clara*. Common. Endemic to Cahaba River system. Usually found in lotic habitats. Low Conservation Concern. **(Fig. 39, p. 42)**

Closed Elimia *Elimia clausa*. **Extinct**. Endemic to Coosa River in St. Clair County. Not reported since the river was impounded. Was restricted to shoal habitat.

Slackwater Elimia *Elimia clenchi*. Special concern. Endemic to Gulf Coast area. Found in tributaries of Choctawhatchee, Chipola, and Conecuh Rivers. Usually found in habitats with at least some current. MODERATE CONSERVATION CONCERN.

Cockle Elimia *Elimia cochliaris*. Rare. Endemic to tributaries of Little Cahaba River. Occurs in springs and spring branches. **HIGHEST CONSERVATION CONCERN**.

Hispid Elimia *Elimia comma*. Special concern. Endemic to Black Warrior River drainage in Blount and Jefferson Counties. Found in springs and small streams. MODERATE CONSERVATION CONCERN.

Lacy Elimia *Elimia crenatella*. Rare. Endemic to Coosa River system. Historically found in Coosa River and tributaries from St. Clair to Talladega Counties. Known to be extant in Cheaha, Emauhee, and Weewoka Creeks, Talladega County. Usually found in lotic habitats. **Listed as *threatened* by the U.S. Fish and Wildlife Service. HIGHEST CONSERVATION CONCERN**.

Graphite Elimia *Elimia curvicostata*. Special concern. Restricted to Choctawhatchee River system. MODERATE CONSERVATION CONCERN.

Cylinder Elimia *Elimia cylindracea*. Special concern. Endemic to western reaches of Mobile Basin. Widespread in Tombigbee River system. Usually found in areas with at least some current. Often locally common on rock ledges. MODERATE CONSERVATION CONCERN. **(Fig. 40, p. 42)**

Stately Elimia *Elimia dickinsoni*. Poorly known. Restricted to Choctawhatchee and Chipola River systems. Usually found in water with at least some current. MODERATE CONSERVATION CONCERN.

Banded Elimia *Elimia fascians*. Poorly known. Endemic to Coosa River tributaries from Calhoun to Coosa Counties. Usually found in lotic habitats. MODERATE CONSERVATION CONCERN.

Yellow Elimia *Elimia flava*. Common. Endemic to Tallapoosa River system. Usually found in lotic habitats. Low Conservation Concern.

Fusiform Elimia *Elimia fusiformis*. **Extinct**. Endemic to Coosa River from Shelby to Elmore Counties. Not reported since the river was impounded. Was restricted to shoal habitats.

Coldwater Elimia *Elimia gerhardti*. Common. Endemic to Coosa River system. Widespread in tributaries. Usually found in lotic habitats. Lowest Conservation Concern. **(Fig. 41, p. 42)**.

Shouldered Elimia *Elimia gibbera*. **Extinct**. Endemic to Coosa River in St. Clair County. Not reported since the river was impounded. Was restricted to shoal habitats.

High-spired Elimia *Elimia hartmaniana*. **Extinct**. Endemic to Coosa River from St. Clair to Elmore Counties. Not reported since the river was impounded. Was restricted to shoal habitats.

Silt Elimia *Elimia haysiana*. Common. Endemic to lower Coosa River. Usually found in lotic habitats. Low Conservation Concern. **(Fig. 42, p. 43)**

Gladiator Elimia *Elimia hydei*. Special concern. Endemic to Black Warrior River system. Usually found in areas with at least some current. MODERATE CONSERVATION CONCERN.

Constricted Elimia *Elimia impressa*. **Extinct**. Endemic to Coosa River from St. Clair to Coosa Counties. Not reported since the river was impounded. Was restricted to shoal habitat.

Slowwater Elimia *Elimia interveniens*. Special concern. Endemic to Tennessee River drainage. Found in lower reaches of tributaries in northern Alabama, primarily in lotic habitats. Possibly synonymous with *E. paupercula*. MODERATE CONSERVATION CONCERN. **(Fig. 43, p. 43)**

Hearty Elimia *Elimia jonesi*. **Extinct**. Endemic to Coosa River from St. Clair to Chilton Counties. Not reported since the river was impounded. Was restricted to shoal habitats.

Teardrop Elimia *Elimia lachryma*. **Extinct**. Endemic to Coosa River from Etowah to Talladega Counties. Not reported since the river was impounded. Was restricted to shoal habitats.

Ribbed Elimia *Elimia laeta*. **Extinct**. Endemic to Coosa River from Cherokee to Elmore Counties. Not reported since the river was impounded. Was restricted to shoal habitats.

Panel Elimia *Elimia laqueata*. Special concern. Endemic to Tennessee River system. Apparently restricted to Elk River system and adjacent Tennessee River. Found primarily in lotic habitats. MODERATE CONSERVATION CONCERN.

Wrinkled Elimia *Elimia macglameriana*. **Extinct**. Endemic to Coosa River from its head-waters to St. Clair County. Not reported since the river was impounded. Was restricted to shoal habitat.

Black Mudalia *Elimia melanoides*. Locally common. Endemic to Black Warrior River sys-tem. Known to be extant only in upper reaches of Locust Fork. Restricted to lotic habi-tats. **HIGH CONSERVATION CONCERN.**

Oak Elimia *Elimia mutabilis*. Poorly known. Endemic to Mobile Basin. Restricted to a few springs and streams tributary to Alabama River. MODERATE CONSERVATION CONCERN.

Round-rib Elimia *Elimia nassula*. Rare. Endemic to Tennessee River system in northern Alabama. Extant in five springs in Colbert, Lawrence, Madison, and Morgan Counties. Found only in spring and spring-run habitats. **HIGHEST CONSERVATION CON-CERN.**

Caper Elimia *Elimia olivula*. Special concern. Endemic to Mobile Basin. Found in Alabama and Cahaba Rivers downstream of the Fall Line. Primarily found in areas with at least some current. MODERATE CONSERVATION CONCERN.

Sooty Elimia *Elimia paupercula*. Special concern. Endemic to Tennessee River tributar-ies. Found across northern Alabama. Usually in springs and headwaters. May represent headwater complex of several species. MODERATE CONSERVATION CONCERN. **(Fig. 44, p. 43)**

Engraved Elimia *Elimia perstriata*. Rare. Endemic to a small area of the Tennessee River drainage in north-central Alabama. Extant only in a few streams in Madison and Lawrence Counties. Found in lotic habitats of small to medium streams. **HIGHEST CONSERVATION CONCERN.**

Rough-lined Elimia *Elimia pilsbryi*. **Extinct**. Endemic to Coosa River, Talladega to Chilton Counties. Not reported since the river was impounded. Was restricted to shoal habitats.

Pupa Elimia *Elimia pupaeformis*. **Extinct**. Endemic to Coosa River from St. Clair to Elmore Counties. Not reported since the river was impounded. Was restricted to shoal habitats.

Bot Elimia *Elimia pupoidea*. **Extinct**. Endemic to Mobile Basin. Known from Cahaba and Black Warrior River systems and Alabama River near the mouth of the Cahaba River. Not reported recently. Found primarily in lotic habitats.

Spring Elimia *Elimia pybasi*. Poorly known. Endemic to the Tennessee River drainage of northern Alabama. Found in springs and small streams. MODERATE CONSERVA-TION CONCERN.

Pygmy Elimia *Elimia pygmaea*. **Extinct**. Endemic to Coosa River, Talladega County. Not reported since the river was impounded. Was restricted to shoal habitats.

Compact Elimia *Elimia showalteri*. Poorly known. Endemic to Cahaba River. Found primarily in lotic habitats. MODERATE CONSERVATION CONCERN.

Dented Elimia *Elimia taitiana*. Poorly known. Endemic to south-central Alabama. Occurs in Mobile Basin streams in Sumter, Marengo, Monroe, and Wilcox Counties. A disjunct population exists in Sepulga River, Escambia River system. Usually found in water with at least some current. MODERATE CONSERVATION CONCERN.

Cobble Elimia *Elimia vanuxemiana*. **Extinct**. Endemic to middle and lower reaches of Coosa River and a few tributaries. Not reported since the river was impounded. Was restricted to shoal habitats.

Puzzle Elimia *Elimia varians*. Uncommon. Endemic to Cahaba River system. Found primarily in lotic habitats. **HIGH CONSERVATION CONCERN.**

Squat Elimia *Elimia variata*. Uncommon. Endemic to Cahaba River system. Found primarily in lotic habitats. **HIGH CONSERVATION CONCERN.**

Slough Elimia *Elimia viennaensis*. Poorly known. Endemic to Apalachicola Basin. Restricted to Uchee Creek, Russell County. Usually found in lotic habitats. MODERATE CONSERVATION CONCERN.

Excised Slitshell *Gyrotoma excisa*. **Extinct**. Endemic to Coosa River. Historically found in shoals from St. Clair to Elmore Counties. Not reported since the river was impounded. Was restricted to shoal habitats.

Striate Slitshell *Gyrotoma lewisii*. **Extinct**. Endemic to Coosa River. Historically found in shoals of Talladega and Shelby Counties. Not reported since the river was impounded. Was restricted to shoal habitats.

Pagoda Slitshell *Gyrotoma pagoda*. **Extinct**. Endemic to Coosa River. Historically found in shoals from Chilton to Elmore Counties. Not reported since the river was impounded. Was restricted to shoal habitats.

Ribbed Slitshell *Gyrotoma pumila*. **Extinct**. Endemic to Coosa River. Historically found in shoals from Shelby to Elmore Counties. Not reported since the river was impounded. Was restricted to shoal habitats.

Pyramid Slitshell *Gyrotoma pyramidata*. **Extinct**. Endemic to Coosa River. Historically found in shoals of St. Clair and Shelby Counties. Not reported since the river was impounded. Was restricted to shoal habitats.

Round Slitshell *Gyrotoma walkeri*. **Extinct**. Endemic to Coosa River. Historically found in shoals from Shelby to Coosa Counties. Not reported since the river was impounded. Was restricted to shoal habitats.

Spiny Riversnail *Io fluvialis*. **Extirpated**. Endemic to Tennessee River system. Historically occurred downstream to Muscle Shoals. Not reported since the river was impounded. Found only in lotic habitats. Recently reintroduced into riverine reaches of upper Guntersville Reservoir in Tennessee. **CONSERVATION ACTION UNDERWAY**.

Round Rocksnail *Leptoxis ampla*. Uncommon. Endemic to Mobile Basin. Historically found in Coosa and Cahaba Rivers and tributaries. Known to be extant in some reaches of Cahaba River and three tributaries. Found in lotic habitats. **Listed as threatened by the U.S. Fish and Wildlife Service. HIGH CONSERVATION CONCERN**.

Agate Rocksnail *Leptoxis clipeata*. **Extinct**. Endemic to the middle reaches of Coosa River. Not reported since the river was impounded. Was restricted to shoal habitats.

Oblong Rocksnail *Leptoxis compacta*. **Extinct**. Endemic to Mobile Basin. Known from Cahaba River and at least one Coosa River tributary. Not reported recently. Was restricted to shoal habitats.

Interrupted Rocksnail *Leptoxis downiei*. **Extinct**. Endemic to Coosa River. Not reported since the river was impounded. Was restricted to shoal habitats.

Interrupted Rocksnail *Leptoxis foremani*. **Extirpated**. Endemic to middle and upper Coosa River system, including headwater tributaries. Apparently extant only in Oostanaula River, Georgia. Was restricted to shoal habitats. Has potential for reintroduction. **CONSERVATION ACTION UNDERWAY**.

Maiden Rocksnail *Leptoxis formosa*. **Extinct**. Endemic to upper and middle reaches of Coosa River; also occurred in some tributaries. Not reported since the river was impounded. Was restricted to shoal habitats.

Rotund Rocksnail *Leptoxis ligata*. **Extinct**. Endemic to middle and lower reaches of Coosa River. Not reported since the river was impounded. Was restricted to shoal habitats.

Lirate Rocksnail *Leptoxis lirata*. **Extinct**. Endemic to middle reaches of Coosa River. Not reported since the river was impounded. Was restricted to shoal habitats.

Knob Mudalia *Leptoxis minor*. **Extinct**. Endemic to Tennessee River at Muscle Shoals. Not reported since the river was impounded. Occurred in shoal habitats.

Bigmouth Rocksnail *Leptoxis occultata*. **Extinct**. Endemic to middle reaches of Coosa River. Not reported since the river was impounded. Was restricted to shoal habitats.

Spotted Rocksnail *Leptoxis picta*. Uncommon. Endemic to Alabama River. Extant in riverine reaches downstream of Claiborne, Millers Ferry, and Jones Bluff Dams. Restricted to lotic habitats. **HIGH CONSERVATION CONCERN**.

Plicate Rocksnail *Leptoxis plicata*. Rare. Endemic to Black Warrior River system and adjacent Tombigbee River. Known to be extant in middle reaches of Locust Fork, Jefferson County. Restricted to lotic habitats. **Listed as *endangered* by the U.S. Fish and Wildlife Service. HIGHEST CONSERVATION CONCERN**.

Onyx Rocksnail *Leptoxis praerosa*. Common. Widespread in Tennessee River drainage of northern Alabama. Restricted to lotic habitats. Low Conservation Concern. **(Fig. 45, p. 43)**

Coosa Rocksnail *Leptoxis showalteri*. **Extinct**. Endemic to middle reaches of Coosa River. Not reported since the river was impounded. Was restricted to shoal habitats.

Painted Rocksnail *Leptoxis taeniata*. Uncommon. Endemic to Mobile Basin. Known from Coosa, Cahaba, and Alabama Rivers and tributaries. Extant in lower reaches of Choccolocco, Buxahatchee, and Ohatchee Creeks of the Coosa River system. Found primarily in lotic habitats. **Listed as *threatened* by the U.S. Fish and Wildlife Service. HIGH CONSERVATION CONCERN**.

Squat Rocksnail *Leptoxis torrefacta*. **Extinct**. Endemic to Coosa River. Not reported since the river was impounded. Was restricted to shoal habitats.

Smooth Mudalia *Leptoxis virgata*. **Extirpated**. Endemic to Tennessee River. Historically occurred downstream to northeastern Alabama. Not reported since the river was impounded. Restricted to shoal habitats.

Striped Rocksnail *Leptoxis vittata*. **Extinct**. Endemic to middle and lower reaches of Coosa River. Not reported since the river was impounded. Was restricted to shoal habitats.

Armored Rocksnail *Lithasia armigera*. Special concern. Restricted to Tennessee River in the vicinity of Muscle Shoals. Extant in Wilson Dam tailwaters. **HIGH CONSERVATION CONCERN**.

Knobby Rocksnail *Lithasia curta*. **Extirpated**. Endemic to lower Tennessee River, from near mouth upstream to Muscle Shoals. Limited to lotic habitats.

Warty Rocksnail *Lithasia lima*. Special concern. Some taxonomic questions regarding this form. Endemic to Tennessee River system. Extant in Bear Creek in Colbert and Franklin Counties, and Sugar Creek and Elk River in Limestone County. Found only in lotic habitats. **HIGH CONSERVATION CONCERN**.

Muddy Rocksnail *Lithasia salebrosa*. Special concern. Endemic to Tennessee River system. Restricted to Wilson Dam tailwaters. Found only in lotic habitats. **HIGH CONSERVATION CONCERN**.

Varicose Rocksnail *Lithasia verrucosa*. Common. Found in Tennessee River across northern Alabama. Extant in tailwaters of Wilson, Wheeler, Guntersville, and Nickajack Dams. Restricted to lotic habitats. Low Conservation Concern.

Rugged Hornsnail *Pleurocera alveare*. Uncommon. Restricted to Tennessee River in the tailwaters of Wilson, Wheeler, and possibly Guntersville Dams. Found primarily in lotic habitats. **HIGH CONSERVATION CONCERN. (Fig. 46, p. 44)**

Ringed Hornsnail *Pleurocera annulifera*. Common. Endemic to, and widespread in, Black Warrior River system. Found in both lotic and lentic habitats. Low Conservation Concern.

Spiral Hornsnail *Pleurocera brumbyi*. Special concern. Endemic to tributaries of Tennessee River in northern Alabama. Found in both lentic and lotic habitats. MODERATE CONSERVATION CONCERN.

Silty Hornsnail *Pleurocera canaliculatum*. Abundant. Restricted to Tennessee River system. Found throughout. High variability with regard to shell morphology may indicate a species complex. Found in a variety of habitats. Lowest Conservation Concern. **(Fig. 47, p. 44)**

Corpulent Hornsnail *Pleurocera corpulenta*. Rare. Endemic to Tennessee River. Historically found across northern Alabama. Known to be extant only in upper Guntersville Reservoir, Jackson County. Found only in lotic habitats. **HIGHEST CONSERVATION CONCERN**.

Shortspire Hornsnail *Pleurocera curta*. Poorly known. Endemic to Tennessee River system. Historically reported from across northern Alabama. Not reported in several years. MODERATE CONSERVATION CONCERN.

Rough Hornsnail *Pleurocera foremani*. Rare. Endemic to Mobile Basin. Known from Cahaba and Coosa Rivers. Extant in lower Yellowleaf Creek and Coosa River at Wetumpka. Usually found in areas with at least some current. **HIGHEST CONSERVATION CONCERN**.

Noble Hornsnail *Pleurocera nobilis*. Poorly known. Endemic to Tennessee River system.

Known from Jackson County possibly downstream to Madison County. Found in a variety of habitats. Appears to intergrade with *P. canaliculatum*. MODERATE CONSERVATION CONCERN.

Broken Hornsnail *Pleurocera postelli*. Poorly known. Endemic to Tennessee River system in northwestern Alabama. Found in small streams. Taxonomic status uncertain. MODERATE CONSERVATION CONCERN.

Smooth Hornsnail *Pleurocera prasinata*. Common. Endemic to Mobile Basin. Found in Alabama River, and in lower Coosa and Cahaba Rivers. Found in a variety of habitats. Low Conservation Concern.

Skirted Hornsnail *Pleurocera pyrenella*. Special concern. Endemic to a small area of Tennessee River drainage in north-central Alabama. Found in both lentic and lotic habitats. **HIGH CONSERVATION CONCERN.**

Upland Hornsnail *Pleurocera showalteri*. Special concern. Endemic to upper Coosa River. Usually found in areas with at least some current. MODERATE CONSERVATION CONCERN.

Sulcate Hornsnail *Pleurocera trochiformis*. Poorly known. Endemic to Tennessee River system and reported from across northern Alabama. Found in a variety of habitats.Taxonomic status uncertain. MODERATE CONSERVATION CONCERN.

Brook Hornsnail *Pleurocera vestita*. Special concern. Endemic to Mobile Basin. Known from tributaries of Coosa and Alabama Rivers. Usually found in lotic habitats. MODERATE CONSERVATION CONCERN. **(Fig. 48, p. 44)**

Telescope Hornsnail *Pleurocera walkeri*. Special concern. Endemic to Tennessee River system. Extant in several tributaries of Tennessee River in northwestern Alabama. Usually found in lotic habitats. MODERATE CONSERVATION CONCERN.

PEBBLESNAILS - FAMILY HYDROBIIDAE

Mud Amnicola *Amnicola limosa*. Common and widespread. Found in tailwaters of Tennessee River dams and possibly in the Mobile Basin. Lowest Conservation Concern.

Manitou Cavesnail *Antrorbis breweri*. Poorly known. Known only from its type locality, Manitou Cave, Fort Payne, DeKalb County. MODERATE CONSERVATION CONCERN.

Globe Siltsnail *Birgella subglobosa*. Poorly known. Widespread, but distribution within state unknown. Found in muddy sand. MODERATE CONSERVATION CONCERN.

Cahaba Pebblesnail *Clappia cahabensis*. **Extinct**. Endemic to a short reach of Cahaba River. Was restricted to shoal habitats.

Umbilicate Pebblesnail *Clappia umbilicata*. **Extinct**. Endemic to Coosa River. Not reported since the river was impounded. Was restricted to shoal habitats.

Flat Pebblesnail *Lepyrium showalteri*. Rare. Historically widespread in Coosa, Cahaba, and Little Cahaba Rivers. Known to be extant at one site each in Cahaba and Little Cahaba Rivers. Restricted to shoal habitats. **Listed as *endangered* by the U.S. Fish and Wildlife Service. HIGHEST CONSERVATION CONCERN.**

Ghost Marstonia *Marstonia arga*. Common. Widespread in Tennessee River and tributaries across northern Alabama. Found primarily in streams in submerged clumps of bryophytes and tree roots, usually adjacent to current. Found in submerged macrophytes in reservoirs. Lowest Conservation Concern.

Coosa Pyrg *Marstonia hershleri*. Poorly known. Known only from Coosa River. MODERATE CONSERVATION CONCERN.

Olive Marstonia *Marstonia olivacea*. **Extinct**. Known only from Big Spring Creek, Madison County.

Armored Marstonia *Marstonia pachyta*. Rare, but locally common. Endemic to Limestone Creek system, Limestone County. Found primarily in submerged clumps of tree roots and bryophytes. **Listed as *endangered* by the U.S. Fish and Wildlife Service. HIGHEST CONSERVATION CONCERN.**

Alligator Siltsnail *Notogillia wetherbyi*. Poorly known. Distribution within the state unknown. MODERATE CONSERVATION CONCERN.

Moss Pyrg *Pyrgulopsis scalariformis*. Rare, but locally common. Once widespread, but apparently reduced to a single extant population in Flint River, Madison County. Found primarily in submerged clumps of tree roots and bryophytes. Usually adjacent to current. **HIGHEST CONSERVATION CONCERN.**

Teardrop Snail *Rhapinema dacryon*. Poorly known. Endemic to the Chipola River system. MODERATE CONSERVATION CONCERN.

Golden Pebblesnail *Somatogyrus aureus*. Poorly known. Endemic to Tennessee River. Not reported since the river was impounded. MODERATE CONSERVATION CONCERN.

Angular Pebblesnail *Somatogyrus biangulatus*. Poorly known. Endemic to Tennessee River. Known only from Muscle Shoals. Not reported since the river was impounded. MODERATE CONSERVATION CONCERN.

Knotty Pebblesnail *Somatogyrus constrictus*. Poorly known. Endemic to Coosa River. Not reported since the river was impounded. MODERATE CONSERVATION CONCERN.

Coosa Pebblesnail *Somatogyrus coosaensis*. Poorly known. Endemic to Coosa River. MODERATE CONSERVATION CONCERN.

Stocky Pebblesnail *Somatogyrus crassus*. Poorly known. Endemic to Coosa River. Not reported since the river was impounded. MODERATE CONSERVATION CONCERN.

Tennessee Pebblesnail *Somatogyrus currierianus*. Poorly known. Endemic to Tennessee River drainage. Known only from Madison County. MODERATE CONSERVATION CONCERN.

Hidden Pebblesnail *Somatogyrus decipens*. Poorly known. Endemic to Coosa River. Not reported since the river was impounded. MODERATE CONSERVATION CONCERN.

Ovate Pebblesnail *Somatogyrus excavatus*. Poorly known. Endemic to Tennessee River drainage. Known only from Shoal Creek, Lauderdale County. MODERATE CONSERVATION CONCERN.

Cherokee Pebblesnail *Somatogyrus georgianus*. Poorly known, but widespread. Known from Alabama, Cahaba, and Tennessee Rivers. Not reported recently. MODERATE CONSERVATION CONCERN.

Fluted Pebblesnail *Somatogyrus hendersoni*. Poorly known. Endemic to Coosa River. Not reported since the river was impounded. MODERATE CONSERVATION CONCERN.

Granite Pebblesnail *Somatogyrus hinkleyi*. Poorly known. Endemic to Coosa and Tallapoosa Rivers. Not reported since those rivers were impounded. MODERATE CONSERVATION CONCERN.

Atlas Pebblesnail *Somatogyrus humerosus*. Poorly known. Endemic to Tennessee River. Known only from Muscle Shoals. MODERATE CONSERVATION CONCERN.

Dwarf Pebblesnail *Somatogyrus nanus*. Poorly known. Endemic to Coosa River. Not reported since the river was impounded. MODERATE CONSERVATION CONCERN.

Moon Pebblesnail *Somatogyrus obtusus*. Poorly known. Endemic to Coosa River. Not reported since the river was impounded. MODERATE CONSERVATION CONCERN.

Tallapoosa Pebblesnail *Somatogyrus pilsbryanus*. Poorly known. Endemic to Tallapoosa River. Not reported since the river was impounded. MODERATE CONSERVATION CONCERN.

Compact Pebblesnail *Somatogyrus pumilus*. Poorly known. Reported from Black Warrior River and at least one Coosa River tributary. MODERATE CONSERVATION CONCERN.

Pygmy Pebblesnail *Somatogyrus pygmaeus*. Poorly known. Endemic to Coosa River. Not reported since the river was impounded. MODERATE CONSERVATION CONCERN.

Quadrate Pebblesnail *Somatogyrus quadratus*. Poorly known. Endemic to Tennessee River system. Known only from Muscle Shoals and adjacent Shoal Creek, Lauderdale County. Not reported since the river was impounded. MODERATE CONSERVATION CONCERN.

Mud Pebblesnail *Somatogyrus sargenti*. Poorly known. Endemic to Tennessee River tributaries. MODERATE CONSERVATION CONCERN.

Rolling Pebblesnail *Somatogyrus strengi*. Poorly known. Endemic to, and formerly widespread in, Tennessee River system. Not reported since the river was impounded. MODERATE CONSERVATION CONCERN.

Choctaw Pebblesnail *Somatogyrus substriatus*. Poorly known. Reported from widespread localities throughout Alabama. MODERATE CONSERVATION CONCERN.

Opaque Pebblesnail *Somatogyrus tennesseensis*. Poorly known. Endemic to Tennessee River system. Reported only from Shoal Creek, Lauderdale County. MODERATE CONSERVATION CONCERN.

Gulf Coast Pebblesnail *Somatogyrus walkerianus*. Poorly known. Endemic to Conecuh River, Escambia County. MODERATE CONSERVATION CONCERN.

Sculpin Snail *Stiobia nana*. Poorly known. Endemic to Coldwater Spring Run, Calhoun County. MODERATE CONSERVATION CONCERN.

SEEP SNAILS - FAMILY POMATIOPSIDAE
Southern Seep Snail *Pomatiopsis hinkleyi*. **Extinct**. Historically in a spring at Muscle Shoals. Not collected since impoundment of the Tennessee River. Possibly a form of *P. lapidaria*.

Slender Walker *Pomatiopsis lapidaria*. Common. Widespread in springs of Tennessee River system. Often found on wet rocks adjacent to springs. Lowest Conservation Concern.

ORDER HETEROSTROPHA
VALVATAS - FAMILY VALVATIDAE
Two-ridge Valvata *Valvata bicarinata*. Poorly known. Restricted to Tennessee River system. MODERATE CONSERVATION CONCERN.

ORDER BASOMMATOPHORA

PONDSNAILS - FAMILY LYMNAEIDAE

Golden Fossaria *Fossaria obrussa*. Common. Apparently found throughout Alabama. Found in streams, rivers, and ponds, often marginally. Lowest Conservation Concern.

Mimic Lymnaea *Pseudosuccinea columella*. Common. Apparently found throughout Alabama. Found in streams and rivers, often marginally. Lowest Conservation Concern.

POUCH SNAILS - FAMILY PHYSIDAE

Tadpole Physa *Physella gyrina*. Common. Apparently found throughout Alabama. Occurs in streams, rivers, and ponds. Lowest Conservation Concern.

Bayou Physa *Physella hendersoni*. Common. Apparently found throughout Alabama. Occurs in streams, rivers, and ponds. Lowest Conservation Concern.

Pewter Physa *Physella heterostropha*. Common. Apparently found throughout Alabama. Occurs in streams, rivers, and ponds. Lowest Conservation Concern.

RAMS-HORN SNAILS - FAMILY PLANORBIDAE

Shoal Sprite *Amphigyra alabamensis*. **Extinct**. Endemic to Coosa River. Not reported since the river was impounded. Was restricted to shoal habitats.

Ash Gyro *Gyraulus parvus*. Common. Presumably occurs throughout Alabama. Found in streams and rivers, often on woody debris and submerged clumps of bryophytes and tree roots. Lowest Conservation Concern.

Two-ridge Rams-horn *Helisoma anceps*. Common. Presumably found throughout Alabama. Usually occurs in sluggish water. Lowest Conservation Concern. **(Fig. 49, p. 44)**

Disc Sprite *Micromenetus brogniartianus*. Poorly known. Reported only from Jackson County. MODERATE CONSERVATION CONCERN.

Bugle Sprite *Micromenetus dilatatus*. Common. Presumably occurs throughout Alabama. Found in streams and rivers, often on woody debris and submerged clumps of bryophytes and tree roots. Lowest Conservation Concern.

Carinate Flat-top Snail *Neoplanorbis carinatus*. **Extinct**. Endemic to Coosa River. Not reported since the river was impounded. Was restricted to shoal habitats.

Angled Flat-top Snail *Neoplanorbis smithi*. **Extinct**. Endemic to Coosa River. Not reported since the river was impounded. Was restricted to shoal habitats.

Little Flat-top Snail *Neoplanorbis tantillus*. **Extinct**. Endemic to Coosa River. Not reported since the river was impounded. Was restricted to shoal habitats.

Umbilicate Flat-top Snail *Neoplanorbis umbilicatus*. **Extinct**. Endemic to Coosa River. Not reported since the river was impounded. Was restricted to shoal habitats.

Thicklip Rams-horn *Planorbula armigera*. Poorly known. Presumably found throughout Alabama. Usually found in sluggish water. MODERATE CONSERVATION CONCERN.

Marsh Rams-horn *Planorbella trivolvis*. Common. Apparently restricted to Tennessee River system. Usually found in sluggish water. Lowest Conservation Concern.

FRESHWATER LIMPETS - FAMILY ANCYLIDAE

Fragile Ancylid *Ferrissia fragilis*. Common. Presumably found throughout Alabama. Occurs in a variety of habitats. Lowest Conservation Concern.

Hood Ancylid *Ferrissia mcneili*. Poorly known. Known only from Mobile County. MODERATE CONSERVATION CONCERN.

Creeping Ancylid *Ferrissia rivularis*. Poorly known. Presumably found throughout Alabama. Occurs in a variety of habitats. MODERATE CONSERVATION CONCERN.

Cymbal Ancylid *Laevapex diaphanous*. Poorly known. Restricted to Tennessee River. MODERATE CONSERVATION CONCERN.

Dusky Ancylid *Laevapex fuscus*. Common. Presumably found throughout Alabama. Occurs in a variety of habitats. Lowest Conservation Concern.

Domed Ancylid *Rhodacmea elatior*. Poorly known. Reported from Tennessee and Cahaba River systems. MODERATE CONSERVATION CONCERN.

Wicker Ancylid *Rhodacmea filosa*. Poorly known. Reported from Black Warrior and Coosa River systems and possibly the Tennessee River system. MODERATE CONSERVATION CONCERN.

Knobby Ancylid *Rhodacmea hinkleyi*. Poorly known. Reported from Coosa and Tennessee Rivers. MODERATE CONSERVATION CONCERN.

FISHES

Ashy Darter
Etheostoma cinereum

INTRODUCTION

The number of fish species occurring in Alabama's fresh waters is difficult to estimate because many estuarine and marine fishes enter fresh waters during their daily movements and seasonal migrations. Boschung (1992) reported in excess of 900 species of fishes occurring in Alabama and adjacent states that share fresh waters, including marine waters from the Mississippi River Delta to Cape San Blas and seaward to the 200-meter (656-foot) isobath. The diversity of fishes occurring in Alabama's 124,000 kilometers (77,000 miles) of fresh water river and stream channels has been reported to be more than 300 species (Smith-Vaniz 1968; Boschung 1992; and Mettee et al. 1996). Listed below are 317 species the committee considered that live exclusively in fresh water, invade fresh waters on a routine basis, or that live in coastal environments of varying salinity. Of this total, 24 species move freely between fresh, brackish, and (or) saline waters and 10 species are exotics introduced to state waters. Fourteen species are listed as either threatened or endangered by the U.S. Fish and Wildlife Service, nine species are extirpated from state waters, and two species are extinct, the Harelip Sucker *Moxostoma lacerum* and the Whiteline Topminnow *Fundulus albolineatus*. Also included in the list are 14 taxa recognized as unique yet not formally described in the scientific literature.

The scientific classification follows the American Fisheries Society, Committee on Names of Fishes recommendations (published in 2003), with the exception that common names are capitalized following the editorial preferences of the Alabama Nongame Wildlife Conference Steering Committee. Comments relative to abundance, seasonality, and distribution of fishes were derived from observations and reports of the committee members and information in Mettee et al. (1996). Comments relative to abundance and distribution are self explanatory. The term *basin* is used to denote a major group of drainages interconnected by a master river or estuary (i.e., Mobile Basin); the term *drainage* is used to distinguish a group of interconnected stream systems the main channel of which enters an ocean, estuary, or the main stem of a basin (i.e., Alabama River drainage); and the term *system* is used to describe a smaller division of a drainage (i.e., Cahaba River system).

Conservation designations were derived by nomination of a species for consideration followed by a majority vote or general consensus of the Committee. Highest Conservation Concern status was assigned to 22 species; High Conservation Concern was assigned to 25 species; Moderate Conservation Concern was assigned to 33 species; Low Conservation Concern was assigned to 35 species; and Lowest Conservation Concern was assigned to 181 species. Many of the highest and high conservation concern species are found in springs and spring-fed tributaries above the Fall Line or in main river channels that have been substantially modified.

Alabama's fish diversity thrives through a unique association of a diverse geologic template, an abundant water resource, and a mild subtropical climate. However, several activities have substantially altered the character of fish communities in some areas and threaten fish diversity in others. One is modification of main stream and river channels. Except for a few hundred miles of free-flowing river channels, most of Alabama's major river trunks were dammed by the early 1970s for flood control, navigation, power production, and recreation. Consequently, many large-river species once common in state waters now exist only as marginal populations, and several are listed as protected species. Another activity threatening fish populations is degradation of habitat. Habitat changes are caused by a variety of reasons, but water quality deterioration associated with polluted runoff, such as sediment and nutrients, appears to be a particularly pervasive and chronic problem. These pollutants degrade physical habitat, which in turn causes substantial changes in fish communities, and affect the survival of uniquely adapted species. Assessing the aquatic effects of polluted runoff can be difficult using conventional pollution monitoring techniques, but because fishes respond to water quality and habitat impairment through changes in the structure of their communities, they are ideal monitoring tools as we struggle to examine, define, and manage the impacts of pollutants acting at the watershed scale.

"Fish watching" has never been a popular pastime of the population at large, but recreational fishing and commercial fish harvest are visible and valuable economic activities in the state. Several species of black basses and sunfishes, locally known as "bream" and "crappie," and the channel catfish contribute millions of dollars to Alabama's economy annually and provide some of the best recreational opportunities in the United States. In 2001, approximately 851,000 resident and nonresident anglers spent $719.2 million on fishing-related activities.

As providers of sustenance, recreation, and as harbingers of environmental change, fishes have served this state well. Their current state of conservation indicates that we have failed in some measure to fully appreciate the degree to which water and the resources of aquatic environments are altered by our actions. Water is a resource whose supply will become limiting in the future, even for states such as Alabama with seemingly unlimited quantities. Alabama's aquatic habitats undoubtedly will change as the state's human population grows and uses her vast water resources in different ways. It is hoped this list of fishes and their associated conservation designations will assist in responsible development and management of those resources.

Patrick E. O'Neil

COMMITTEE

Dr. Maurice F. (Scott) Mettee, Geological Survey of Alabama, Tuscaloosa, AL, Co-chairperson/Compiler

Dr. Patrick E. O'Neil, Geological Survey of Alabama Tuscaloosa, AL, Co-chairperson/Compiler

Dr. Henry L. Bart, Royal D. Suttkus Museum of Natural History, Tulane University, Belle Chase, LA

Dr. Paul D. Blanchard, Department of Biology, Samford University, Birmingham, AL

Dr. Herbert T. Boschung, Department of Biological Sciences, University of Alabama, Tuscaloosa, AL

Mr. Daniel J. Drennen, U.S. Fish and Wildlife Service, Jackson, MS

Dr. Robert W. Hastings, Alabama Natural Heritage Program, The Nature Conservancy, Huntingdon College, Montgomery, AL

Dr. Elise Irwin, U.S. Geological Survey, Alabama Cooperative Fish and Wildlife Research Unit, Department of Fisheries and Allied Aquacultures, Auburn University, AL

Dr. Carol E. Johnston, Department of Fisheries and Allied Aquacultures, Auburn University, AL

Dr. Bernard R. Kuhajda, Department of Biological Sciences, University of Alabama, Tuscaloosa, AL

Mr. Greg Lein, Alabama Department of Conservation and Natural Resources, State Lands Division, Montgomery, AL

Mr. Frank Paruka, U.S. Fish and Wildlife Service, Panama City, FL

Mr. J. Malcolm Pierson, Alabama Power Company, Birmingham, AL

Mr. Thomas E. Shepard, Geological Survey of Alabama, Tuscaloosa, AL

Ms. Peggy Shute, Tennessee Valley Authority National Heritage Project, Norris, TN

Dr. John R. Shute, Conservation Fisheries, Inc., Knoxville, TN

Dr. Robert A. Stiles, Department of Biology, Samford University, Birmingham, AL

Dr. Melvin L. Warren, Center for Bottomland Hardwoods Research, Southern Research Station, U.S. Forest Service, Oxford, MS

LAMPREYS
CLASS CEPHALASPIDOMORPHI

LAMPREYS
ORDER PETROMYZONTIFORMES

LAMPREYS - FAMILY PETROMYZONTIDAE

Ohio Lamprey *Ichthyomyzon bdellium*. Uncommon and localized parasitic species in Tennessee River drainage whose distribution is problematic. Lowest Conservation Concern.

Chestnut Lamprey *Ichthyomyzon castaneus*. A widespread and sometimes fairly common parasitic species found most frequently in larger streams and rivers of the Mobile River Basin and Tennessee River drainage. Lowest Conservation Concern.

Southern Brook Lamprey *Ichthyomyzon gagei*. A widespread but uncommon nonparasitic species of small streams and headwaters in the Mobile River Basin and coastal drainages; less frequent in the Tennessee River drainage. Lowest Conservation Concern.

Mountain Brook Lamprey *Ichthyomyzon greeleyi*. A localized and rare nonparasitic species known only in Alabama from Shoal Creek, a Tennessee River tributary in Lauderdale County. Widespread north of Alabama. MODERATE CONSERVATION CONCERN.

Least Brook Lamprey *Lampetra aepyptera*. A widespread, nonparasitic species common throughout small streams and headwater branches in the Mobile River Basin, Tennessee River, and Conecuh River drainages. Lowest Conservation Concern. (**Fig. 50, p. 75**)

American Brook Lamprey *Lampetra appendix*. Distribution of this uncommon to rare nonparasitic species poorly known. Found only in the Bear Creek and Piney Creek systems in the Tennessee River drainage. MODERATE CONSERVATION CONCERN.

CARTILAGINOUS FISHES
CLASS CHONDRICHTHYES

SHARKS
ORDER CARCHARHINIFORMES

REQUIEM SHARKS - FAMILY CARCHARHINIDAE

Bull Shark *Carcharhinus leucas*. Occasionally encountered in the lower reaches of the Mobile-Tensaw River Delta and Mobile River. Lowest Conservation Concern.

RAY-FINNED FISHES
CLASS ACTINOPTERYGII

STURGEONS AND PADDLEFISHES
ORDER ACIPENSERIFORMES

STURGEONS - FAMILY ACIPENSERIDAE

Lake Sturgeon *Acipenser fulvescens*. **Extirpated**. Records known only from the Tennessee and Coosa Rivers, but none in more than 50 years likely means species is extirpated.

Gulf Sturgeon *Acipenser oxyrinchus desotoi*. Made seasonal migration runs to above the Fall Line in many rivers of Alabama prior to their impoundment. Spawning populations known in the Choctawhatchee and Yellow Rivers and occasional individuals caught or sighted in the Mobile-Tensaw River Delta and lower Tombigbee and Alabama Rivers. **Listed as *threatened* by the U.S. Fish and Wildlife Service. HIGH CONSERVATION CONCERN.**

Shovelnose Sturgeon *Scaphirhynchus platorynchus*. **Extirpated**. The few historical records of this species in Alabama are from the Tennessee River prior to impoundment. The lack of collections in more than 50 years likely means this species is extirpated.

Alabama Sturgeon *Scaphirhynchus suttkusi*. Endemic to the lower Alabama, Tombigbee, and Cahaba Rivers, and is one of the rarest vertebrates in the state. **Listed as *endangered* by the U.S. Fish and Wildlife Service. HIGHEST CONSERVATION CONCERN.**

PADDLEFISHES - FAMILY POLYODONTIDAE

Paddlefish *Polyodon spathula*. Once common throughout main river channels of the Mobile Basin and Tennessee River drainage, but past over-harvest resulted in a fishing moratorium for the "spoonbill cat" in 1988. Populations have recovered somewhat, and are now more common in the lower Alabama and Tombigbee Rivers. Low Conservation Concern.

GARS
ORDER LEPISOSTEIFORMES

GARS - FAMILY LEPISOSTEIDAE

Alligator Gar *Atractosteus spatula*. Generally uncommon throughout the Alabama, Tombigbee, and Conecuh Rivers but this may be due, in part, to the difficulty of locating and collecting this long-lived predator. This magnificent fish can grow to three meters (9.8 feet) long and is bow hunted for sport in the Mobile-Tensaw River Delta. MODERATE CONSERVATION CONCERN.

Spotted Gar *Lepisosteus oculatus*. Widespread and common in larger rivers and backwaters throughout the state. Lowest Conservation Concern.

Longnose Gar *Lepisosteus osseus*. Widespread and common in larger rivers and streams in Alabama and one of its largest freshwater fishes. Reaches lengths approaching two meters (6.5 feet). Lowest Conservation Concern.

Shortnose Gar *Lepisosteus platostomus*. **Extirpated**. Status in Alabama somewhat problematic. No specimens have been found in recent years despite extensive collecting throughout the Tennessee River Basin.

BOWFINS
ORDER AMIIFORMES

BOWFIN - FAMILY AMIIDAE

Bowfin *Amia calva*. "Grinnel" are primitive, long-lived fishes widespread throughout the state but uncommon in the Tennessee River drainage. Prefer sloughs, backwaters, oxbows, and main river channels. Lowest Conservation Concern. **(Fig. 51, p. 75)**

MOONEYES
ORDER HIODONTIFORMES

MOONEYES - FAMILY HIODONTIDAE

Goldeye *Hiodon alosoides*. **Extirpated**. Last collected in 1938, this riverine species is now considered extirpated.

Mooneye *Hiodon tergisus*. An uncommon but widespread predator in larger rivers and streams in the Mobile River Basin below the Fall Line, and in the Tennessee River drainage. Low Conservation Concern.

EELS
ORDER ANGUILLIFORMES

FRESHWATER EELS - FAMILY ANGUILLIDAE

American Eel *Anguilla rostrata*. A catadromous piscivore, widespread and fairly common below the Fall Line in the Mobile River Basin and all coastal rivers, but uncommon in the Tennessee drainage. Large individuals infrequently captured in smaller streams. Low Conservation Concern.

ANCHOVIES AND HERRINGS
ORDER CLUPEIFORMES

ANCHOVIES - FAMILY ENGRAULIDAE

Bay Anchovy *Anchoa mitchilli*. An abundant forage fish in estuarine waters. Seasonally inhabits the lower Alabama and Tombigbee Rivers. A population has been found in the lower Black Warrior River 434 kilometers (270 miles) upstream of Mobile Bay. Lowest Conservation Concern.

HERRINGS - FAMILY CLUPEIDAE

Alabama Shad *Alosa alabamae*. Anadromous and found seasonally during spring spawning migrations in the Choctawhatchee and Conecuh Rivers. Occurs sporadically in the Alabama and Black Warrior Rivers. **The U.S. Department of Commerce, National Marine Fisheries Service is considering this species for *protected* status. HIGH CONSERVATION CONCERN.**

Skipjack Herring *Alosa chrysochloris*. Widely distributed throughout the Mobile River Basin below the Fall Line, in coastal rivers, and in the Tennessee River drainage. Occurs most commonly in large rivers and reservoirs during spring spawning period. MODERATE CONSERVATION CONCERN.

Gizzard Shad *Dorosoma cepedianum*. Widespread and common in all Alabama waters, especially larger rivers and reservoirs. Lowest Conservation Concern.

Threadfin Shad *Dorosoma petenense*. A widespread and abundant fish in rivers, impoundments, and lakes throughout Alabama. The common bait shad for most anglers. Lowest Conservation Concern. (**Fig. 52, p. 75**)

CARPS, MINNOWS, AND SUCKERS
ORDER CYPRINIFORMES

CARPS AND MINNOWS - FAMILY CYPRINIDAE

Largescale Stoneroller *Campostoma oligolepis*. Widespread and locally abundant in headwaters, streams, and small rivers in the Mobile River Basin and Tennessee River drainage; more common above the Fall Line. Lowest Conservation Concern.

Bluefin Stoneroller *Campostoma pauciradii*. Endemic to Chattahoochee River tributaries but spotty in distribution, and occurring in low numbers above the Fall Line in the Halawakee, Wacoochee, and Uchee Creek systems. MODERATE CONSERVATION CONCERN.

Goldfish *Carassius auratus*. **Exotic**. A non-native introduced species found sporadically throughout the state.

Rosyside Dace *Clinostomus funduloides*. A colorful stream-dwelling species found in cooler streams of the Tennessee River drainage, mainly in the Highland Rim. Lowest Conservation Concern. (**Fig. 53, p. 75**)

Grass Carp *Ctenopharyngodon idella*. **Exotic**. A species native to Southeast Asia, but introduced into ponds throughout Alabama for aquatic weed control. Escapees found regularly in rivers and impoundments throughout the state.

Blue Shiner *Cyprinella caerulea*. Endemic to the Mobile Basin, uncommonly found in a few flowing streams of the Coosa River system. Evidence suggests it has been extirpated in the Cahaba River. **Listed as *threatened* by the U.S. Fish and Wildlife Service. HIGH CONSERVATION CONCERN.**

Alabama Shiner *Cyprinella callistia*. Endemic to the Mobile River Basin. Ubiquitous and locally abundant in streams and flowing rivers above the Fall Line and sporadically in the Coastal Plain. Lowest Conservation Concern.

Bluestripe Shiner *Cyprinella callitaenia*. An iridescent shiner infrequently found in streams, impounded stream mouths, and the main channel of the Chattahoochee

River. Populations may have declined in recent years. MODERATE CONSERVA-
TION CONCERN.

Whitetail Shiner *Cyprinella galactura*. Widespread in Tennessee River streams where it
can be locally abundant. Lowest Conservation Concern.

Tallapoosa Shiner *Cyprinella gibbsi*. Occurs widely in smaller streams of the Tallapoosa
River system above the Fall Line. Low Conservation Concern. **(Fig. 54, p. 75)**

Red Shiner *Cyprinella lutrensis*. **Exotic**. This aggressive shiner became established in
the Coosa and Chattahoochee Rivers sometime in the 1960s.

Spotfin Shiner *Cyprinella spiloptera*. Widespread, common, and sometimes locally
abundant throughout streams in the Tennessee River drainage. Lowest Conservation
Concern.

Tricolor Shiner *Cyprinella trichroistia*. A colorful shiner common in the Coosa and
Cahaba River systems. Most frequently found in small streams above the Fall Line, in
a few tributaries to the Alabama River, and a few tributaries to the upper Black
Warrior River. Lowest Conservation Concern.

Blacktail Shiner *Cyprinella venusta*. This very hardy shiner is widespread and common
throughout the lower three-fourths of Alabama and has recently invaded the Tennessee
River drainage via the Tennessee-Tombigbee Waterway. Lowest Conservation Concern.

Steelcolor Shiner *Cyprinella whipplei*. More common in larger waters of the Tennessee
drainage, with a well-established population in Mulberry Fork of Black Warrior River.
Lowest Conservation Concern.

Common Carp *Cyprinus carpio*. **Exotic**. Introduced to American waters in the 1870s
from Europe and now found in all major rivers of the state.

Spotfin Chub *Erimonax monachus*. **Extirpated**. A Tennessee River drainage endemic
last collected in Alabama in 1937. **Listed as *threatened* by the U.S. Fish and Wildlife
Service.**

Streamline Chub *Erimystax dissimilis*. An uncommon, shoal-inhabiting species, found
only in the Shoal Creek, Elk River, and Paint Rock River systems of the Tennessee
Valley. **HIGH CONSERVATION CONCERN.**

Blotched Chub *Erimystax insignis*. More widespread throughout the Tennessee River
Valley and generally more abundant than the streamline chub. MODERATE CON-
SERVATION CONCERN.

Flame Chub *Hemitremia flammea*. A dazzling chub restricted to limestone spring-runs and small headwater tributaries throughout the Tennessee River Valley. Most commonly encountered in the Highland Rim, and in a few Coosa River springs. Low Conservation Concern.

Cypress Minnow *Hybognathus hayi*. Pools and backwater sloughs of main river channels in the Mobile River Basin and the larger coastal rivers are preferred by this uncommon minnow. Possibly extirpated from the Tennessee River drainage. Low Conservation Concern.

Mississippi Silvery Minnow *Hybognathus nuchalis*. A common and sometimes locally abundant inhabitant of the lower Alabama and Tombigbee River systems. Apparently extirpated in the Tennessee River drainage in Alabama. Low Conservation Concern.

Bigeye Chub *Hybopsis amblops*. Clear, flowing, silt-free streams in the Tennessee River Valley are preferred by this widespread and fairly common chub. Lowest Conservation Concern.

Lined Chub *Hybopsis lineapunctata*. Upland streams of modest flow in the Tallapoosa River and upper Coosa River systems are frequented by this bottom-dwelling chub. Lowest Conservation Concern.

Clear Chub *Hybopsis winchelli*. A straw-colored chub frequently found in a variety of Coastal Plain aquatic habitats in the Mobile River Basin with a few populations above the Fall Line, and in the Escatawpa River. Lowest Conservation Concern.

Coastal Chub *Hybopsis* sp. cf. *winchelli*. This undescribed cousin of the Clear Chub is common in coastal drainages from the Perdido River east to the Chattahoochee River. Lowest Conservation Concern.

Silver Carp *Hypophthalmichthys molitrix*. **Exotic**. This cultured native of eastern Asia is rarely encountered in state waters.

Bighead Carp *Hypophthalmichthys nobilis*. **Exotic**. Another cultured native of eastern Asia, occasionally found in Alabama rivers.

Striped Shiner *Luxilus chrysocephalus*. A widespread and sometimes abundant species found in small to moderate-sized streams throughout the Mobile River Basin and Tennessee River drainage. Lowest Conservation Concern.

Warpaint Shiner *Luxilus coccogenis*. This uniquely colored species prefers cooler stream waters of Shoal and Cypress Creeks in Lauderdale County, and in headwater streams of Lookout Creek in DeKalb County. Low Conservation Concern. **(Fig. 55, p. 75)**

Bandfin Shiner *Luxilus zonistius*. A widespread and locally abundant species found in small to moderate tributaries of the Chattahoochee and Tallapoosa Rivers in eastern Alabama. Lowest Conservation Concern.

Warrior Shiner *Lythrurus alegnotus*. This upland cousin of the pretty shiner is endemic to the upper Black Warrior River system above the Fall Line. Lowest Conservation Concern.

Blacktip Shiner *Lythrurus atrapiculus*. This delicate shiner is a common forage species in streams throughout the Coastal Plain of southeastern Alabama, from the Conecuh River east to the Chattahoochee River. Lowest Conservation Concern.

Pretty Shiner *Lythrurus bellus*. Ubiquitous and common throughout the Mobile River Basin below the Fall Line and penetrating upland in the Cahaba and Tallapoosa Rivers. Lowest Conservation Concern.

Scarlet Shiner *Lythrurus fasciolaris*. A strikingly colored fish common in flowing waters throughout the Tennessee River drainage. Has invaded the upper Locust Fork system. Lowest Conservation Concern.

Ribbon Shiner *Lythrurus fumeus*. This lackluster shiner is found in streams of lowland or disturbed character in Franklin, Colbert, and Lauderdale Counties in the Tennessee River drainage. MODERATE CONSERVATION CONCERN.

Mountain Shiner *Lythrurus lirus*. This bronze-colored shiner is uncommon in clear, small to moderate streams of good quality in the Coosa River system, and the Tennessee River drainage where it occurs commonly in the Paint Rock River system. Low Conservation Concern.

Cherryfin Shiner *Lythrurus roseipinnis*. A small, dusky fish found in small tributaries of the extreme lower Alabama and Tombigbee Rivers, the Mobile-Tensaw River Delta, and the Escatawpa River. Lowest Conservation Concern.

Shoal Chub *Macrhybopsis aestivalis hyostoma*. This rare chub is known only from the Elk River main channel near the Tennessee state line. **HIGH CONSERVATION CONCERN**.

Undescribed Chubs *Macrhybopsis* sp. cf. *aestivalis*. Two forms occur in the Mobile River Basin and only are found in larger free-flowing streams and rivers. Low Conservation Concern.

Florida Chub *Macrhybopsis* sp. cf. *aestivalis*. The coastal form prefers large sand and gravel shoals typical of the Conecuh, Choctawhatchee, and Yellow Rivers. Low Conservation Concern.

Silver Chub *Macrhybopsis storeriana*. This large minnow is common in larger streams, rivers, and impoundments of the Mobile River Basin below the Fall Line and in the Tennessee River drainage. Lowest Conservation Concern.

Bluehead Chub *Nocomis leptocephalus*. This nest builder is widespread and common in smaller streams throughout the Coastal Plain of the Mobile River Basin, yet surprisingly absent in Black Belt streams. Also widespread in the Tallapoosa system above the Fall Line and occurs in Bear Creek in the Tennessee River system and upper Sipsey Fork. Lowest Conservation Concern.

River Chub *Nocomis micropogon*. Found sporadically in Tennessee Valley creeks and streams particularly during the spring breeding season. Low Conservation Concern.

Golden Shiner *Notemigonus crysoleucas*. A popular bait bucket minnow found throughout the state in all drainages, preferring sluggish pools and streams. Lowest Conservation Concern.

Palezone Shiner *Notropis albizonatus*. This rare shiner is known only from clear tributaries with excellent water quality in the upper Paint Rock River system. **Listed as endangered by the U.S. Fish and Wildlife Service. HIGHEST CONSERVATION CONCERN.**

Orangefin Shiner *Notropis ammophilus*. Easily recognized by its bright orange fins, this sand-loving shiner is widespread and abundant in most streams and rivers in the Mobile River Basin Coastal Plain. Lowest Conservation Concern. **(Fig. 56, p. 75)**

Popeye Shiner *Notropis ariommus*. **Extirpated**. Last collected in Alabama during the 1880s from Cypress Creek near Florence. Recently collected in the Elk River system north of the Alabama-Tennessee state line.

Burrhead Shiner *Notropis asperifrons*. A Mobile River Basin endemic that prefers small, upland streams above the Fall Line. A relict population occurs in the lower Alabama River tributaries in the Lime Hills region. Lowest Conservation Concern.

Emerald Shiner *Notropis atherinoides*. Sand bars and shoals along main river channels in the Mobile River Basin and Tennessee River drainage are preferred habitat for this widespread and common species. Lowest Conservation Concern.

Rough Shiner *Notropis baileyi*. Abundant in the Mobile River Basin below the Fall Line, penetrates upland habitats in the upper Sipsey Fork, Tallapoosa River, and Bear Creek of the Tennessee drainage. Absent in sluggish, turbid Black Belt streams. Lowest Conservation Concern.

Bigeye Shiner *Notropis boops*. Occurs uncommonly in clear streams of the Tennessee River drainage and may be locally abundant in preferred habitat. Lowest Conservation Concern.

Silverjaw Minnow *Notropis buccatus*. This widespread and common minnow of Alabama's Coastal Plain is characterized by its unique head morphology. Lowest Conservation Concern.

Ghost Shiner *Notropis buchanani*. Status in Alabama poorly known. Likely common prior to impoundment of the Tennessee River, but now limited to impounded backwaters and flowing sections of the Elk River. **HIGH CONSERVATION CONCERN.**

Cahaba Shiner *Notropis cahabae*. Thought to be endemic to the Cahaba River main channel where it occurred only sporadically and in low numbers; however, discovery of a larger population in the Locust Fork system in 1998 doubled its known distribution. **Listed as *endangered* by the U.S. Fish and Wildlife Service. HIGHEST CONSERVATION CONCERN.**

Silverside Shiner *Notropis candidus*. Main river channels below the Fall Line are home to this abundant endemic species of the Mobile River Basin. Lowest Conservation Concern.

Ironcolor Shiner *Notropis chalybaeus*. Status in Alabama poorly known. Typically few in number when found and sporadically distributed in coastal streams across southern Alabama. **HIGHEST CONSERVATION CONCERN.**

Rainbow Shiner *Notropis chrosomus*. Exquisitely colored during breeding season. Prefers small, clear streams and spring runs in the Cahaba and Coosa River systems, with isolated populations in the lower Alabama and Black Warrior River systems, and a few records from Tennessee River tributaries. Lowest Conservation Concern. **(Fig. 57, p. 75)**

Dusky Shiner *Notropis cummingsae*. Status in Alabama poorly known. Low-gradient blackwater-like streams in the Uchee Creek system of the Chattahoochee River drainage and one stream in the Chipola River system are preferred by this delicate shiner. **HIGH CONSERVATION CONCERN.**

Fluvial Shiner *Notropis edwardraneyi*. Like the silverside shiner, this abundant shiner is confined to main river channels in the Mobile River Basin below the Fall Line. Lowest Conservation Concern.

Redeye Chub *Notropis harperi*. A spring-dwelling species with a spotty distribution from the Conecuh River east to the Chattahoochee River. Often abundant when found. Lowest Conservation Concern.

Highscale Shiner *Notropis hypsilepis*. Limited distribution in Alabama and found commonly in only a few Piedmont tributaries to the Chattahoochee River. MODERATE CONSERVATION CONCERN.

Tennessee Shiner *Notropis leuciodus*. One of Alabama's more colorful shiners during the breeding season. Locally common in clear, cool streams of Shoal Creek and Paint Rock River systems. Low Conservation Concern.

Longnose Shiner *Notropis longirostris*. Large schools can be found over shifting sand shoals in Alabama's coastal streams from the Escatawpa River east to the Chattahoochee River. Lowest Conservation Concern.

Taillight Shiner *Notropis maculatus*. The exquisite taillight shiner is occasionally found in swampy, mud-bottomed backwaters of Coastal Plain rivers and large tributaries. Its perceived rarity can be attributed to sampling difficulty in its preferred habitat. Low Conservation Concern.

Highland Shiner *Notropis micropteryx*. Found occasionally in Tennessee River streams. Acquires a light raspberry flush during the breeding season. MODERATE CONSERVATION CONCERN.

Coastal Shiner *Notropis petersoni*. Only found in small tributaries to the Mobile-Tensaw Delta, Mobile Bay, and in small streams bordering the Alabama-Florida state line. Lowest Conservation Concern.

Silver Shiner *Notropis photogenis*. Once thought rare in Alabama. Has been found at several new locations in the Tennessee River Valley, preferring the clear, flowing waters in Shoal Creek and the Elk River. MODERATE CONSERVATION CONCERN.

Silverstripe Shiner *Notropis stilbius*. Common and abundant in the Mobile River Basin most frequently above the Fall Line. Lowest Conservation Concern.

Telescope Shiner *Notropis telescopus*. Fairly common and somewhat widespread throughout the Tennessee Valley with good populations found in the clear waters of Shoal Creek, Paint Rock River, and Bear Creek. Lowest Conservation Concern.

Weed Shiner *Notropis texanus*. Perhaps one of the most widespread and common fishes in Alabama's Coastal Plain, it has recently invaded the Tennessee River through the Tennessee-Tombigee Waterway. Lowest Conservation Concern.

Skygazer Shiner *Notropis uranoscopus*. This unique Mobile Basin endemic is restricted in distribution, but sometimes abundant in the flowing main channels and larger tributaries of the Cahaba and lower Tallapoosa Rivers below the Fall Line. Once occurred in the lower Alabama River, but now appears to be extirpated there. MODERATE CONSERVATION CONCERN.

Mimic Shiner *Notropis volucellus*. This taxonomically complex species group is widespread but usually uncommon when found in streams throughout the Tennessee River drainage and Mobile River Basin. Lowest Conservation Concern.

Channel Shiner *Notropis wickliffi*. Scattered across the Tennessee River Valley preferring impounded backwaters, stream mouths, and pooled areas in larger streams. Lowest Conservation Concern.

Coosa Shiner *Notropis xaenocephalus*. Prefers clear upland streams of the Coosa and Tallapoosa River systems. Lowest Conservation Concern.

Sawfin Shiner *Notropis* sp. cf. *spectrunculus*. This attractive shiner is common in cool, clear streams with clean substrate in the Paint Rock River and Shoal Creek systems of the Tennessee River. Also found in the flowing section of the Elk River. Low Conservation Concern.

Pugnose Minnow *Opsopoeodus emiliae*. Prefers weedy, sluggish waters of lowland character throughout the Coastal Plain. Lowest Conservation Concern.

Riffle Minnow *Phenacobius catostomus*. Larger, flowing streams with cobble and gravel in the Cahaba, Coosa, and Tallapoosa River systems are preferred by this terete benthic minnow. Limited populations are found in the lower Alabama and upper Black Warrior systems. Lowest Conservation Concern.

Suckermouth Minnow *Phenacobius mirabilis*. Common to the upper Mississippi River Basin, but rare in Alabama where it occurs peripherally in the Bear Creek system of the Tennessee River drainage. **HIGHEST CONSERVATION CONCERN.**

Stargazing Minnow *Phenacobius uranops*. Uniquely adapted for a riffle existence, this benthic minnow is uncommon in the Tennessee River Valley. Found only in Shoal Creek, Cypress Creek, and the Elk River. **HIGH CONSERVATION CONCERN.**

Southern Redbelly Dace *Phoxinus erythrogaster*. One of Alabama's most colorful minnows preferring small, clear streams and headwaters in the Highland Rim of the Tennessee River drainage. Lowest Conservation Concern. **(Fig. 58, p. 75)**

Bluntnose Minnow *Pimephales notatus*. Common in the Tennessee River drainage and the Mobile River Basin below the Fall Line, but strangely absent in streams of the Fall Line Hills region. Lowest Conservation Concern. **(Fig. 59, p. 76)**

Fig. 50. Least Brook Lamprey, *Lampetra aepyptera,* **p. 63.**
Photo–Patrick O'Neil

Fig. 51. Bowfin, *Amia calva,* **p. 65.**
Photo–Patrick O'Neil

Fig. 52. Threadfin Shad, *Dorosoma petenense,* **p. 67.** *Photo–Patrick O'Neil*

Fig. 53. Rosyside Dace, *Clinostomus funduloides,* **p. 67.** *Photo–Patrick O'Neil*

Fig. 54. Tallapoosa Shiner, *Cyprinella gibbsi,* **p. 68.** *Photo–Patrick O'Neil*

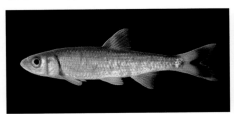

Fig. 55. Warpaint Shiner, *Luxilus coccogenis,* **p. 69.** *Photo–Patrick O'Neil*

Fig. 56. Orangefin Shiner, *Notropis ammophilus,* **p. 71.** *Photo–Patrick O'Neil*

Fig. 57. Rainbow Shiner, *Notropis chrosomus,* **p. 72.** *Photo–Patrick O'Neil*

Fig. 58. Southern Redbelly Dace, *Phoxinus erythrogaster,* **p. 74.** *Photo–Patrick O'Neil*

Fig. 59. Bluntnose Minnow, *Pimephales notatus,* **p. 74.** *Photo–Patrick O'Neil*

Fig. 60. Flagfin Shiner, *Pteronotropis signipinnis,* **p. 79.** *Photo–Patrick O'Neil*

Fig. 61. Southeastern Blue Sucker, *Cycleptus meridionalis,* **p. 80.** *Photo–Patrick O'Neil*

Fig. 62. Alabama Hog Sucker, *Hypentelium etowanum,* **p. 81.** *Photo–Patrick O'Neil*

Fig. 63. Black Buffalo, *Ictiobus niger,* **p. 81.** *Photo–Patrick O'Neil*

Fig. 64. River Redhorse, *Moxostoma carinatum,* **p. 81.** *Photo–Patrick O'Neil*

Fig. 65. Spotted Bullhead, *Ameiurus serracanthus,* **p. 82.** *Photo–Patrick O'Neil*

Fig. 66. Northern Studfish, *Fundulus catenatus,* **p. 86.** *Photo–Patrick O'Neil*

Fig. 67. Mottled Sculpin, *Cottus bairdii,* **p. 89.** *Photo–Patrick O'Neil*

Fig. 68. Yellow Bass, *Morone mississippiensis,* **p. 89.** *Photo–Patrick O'Neil*

Fig. 69. Shadow Bass, *Ambloplites ariommus,* **p. 90.** *Photo–Patrick O'Neil*

Fig. 70. Redeye Bass, *Micropterus coosae,* **p. 91.** *Photo–Patrick O'Neil*

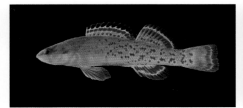

Fig. 71. Redspot darter, *Etheostoma artesiae,* **p. 92.** *Photo–Patrick O'Neil*

Fig. 72. Greenside Darter, *Etheostoma blennioides,* **p. 92.** *Photo–Patrick O'Neil*

Fig. 73. Rainbow Darter, *Etheostoma caeruleum,* **p. 93.** *Photo–Patrick O'Neil*

Fig. 74. Coosa Darter, *Etheostoma coosae,* **p. 93.** *Photo–Patrick O'Neil*

Fig. 75. Brown Darter, *Etheostoma edwini,* **p. 94.** *Photo–Patrick O'Neil*

Fig. 76. Harlequin Darter, *Etheostoma histrio,* **p. 94.** *Photo–Patrick O'Neil*

Fig. 77. Speckled Darter, *Etheostoma stigmaeum,* **p. 96.** *Photo–Patrick O'Neil*

Fig. 78. Freckled Darter, *Percina lenticula,* **p. 98.** *Photo–Patrick O'Neil*

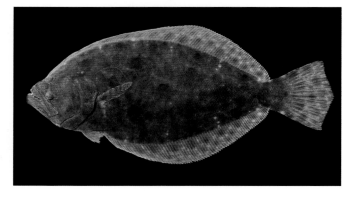

Fig. 79. Southern Flounder, *Paralichthys lethostigma,* **p. 100.** *Photo–Patrick O'Neil*

Fathead Minnow *Pimephales promelas*. A favorite bait fish, the "toughie" minnow is widespread due to bait-bucket introduction, but it is not particularly common in waters throughout the state. Lowest Conservation Concern.

Bullhead Minnow *Pimephales vigilax*. A main channel inhabitant in the Tennessee River drainage and Mobile River Basin. Reaches super-abundant numbers in some habitats. Lowest Conservation Concern.

Broadstripe Shiner *Pteronotropis euryzonus*. This uncommon shiner is an attractive associate of small, clear to blackwater Coastal Plain tributaries of the Chattahoochee River. **HIGH CONSERVATION CONCERN.**

Apalachee Shiner *Pteronotropis grandipinnis*. This newly redescribed relative of the broadstripe shiner is only found in the southeastern corner of the state in Chipola and Chattahoochee River tributaries. MODERATE CONSERVATION CONCERN.

Sailfin Shiner *Pteronotropis hypselopterus*. A widespread, locally abundant, coastal stream shiner of southern Alabama distinguished by its azure flanks. Most Choctawhatchee River populations were recently described as the orangetail shiner. Lowest Conservation Concern.

Orangetail Shiner *Pteronotropis merlini*. A newly described species found in upland reaches of the Choctawhatchee and Pea Rivers. Low Conservation Concern.

Flagfin Shiner *Pteronotropis signipinnis*. An extraordinarily colored coastal cyprinid preferring small tanin-stained streams, frequently with golden club, that drain forested wetlands in Mobile and Baldwin Counties and the lower Conecuh and Yellow Rivers. Lowest Conservation Concern. **(Fig. 60, p. 76)**

Bluenose Shiner *Pteronotropis welaka*. This magnificent shiner is widely scattered and uncommon across Alabama's Coastal Plain. Individuals prefer deep, soft-bottomed, weedy streams and spring runs. Their rarity is no doubt related to the difficulty of sampling their preferred habitat. **HIGH CONSERVATION CONCERN.**

Blacknose Dace *Rhinichthys atratulus*. This benthic fish prefers riffles and runs of small, upland headwaters of the Coosa, Black Warrior, and Tennessee Rivers. Lowest Conservation Concern.

Creek Chub *Semotilus atromaculatus*. The ruling predators in small headwater streams throughout the Mobile River Basin and Tennessee River drainage. Lowest Conservation Concern.

Dixie Chub *Semotilus thoreauianus*. Widespread but infrequently encountered in Mobile River Basin streams below the Fall Line. Common in Chattahoochee River tributaries near the Fall Line and also found in a few small tributaries in the lower Bear Creek system in Colbert County. Lowest Conservation Concern.

SUCKERS ~ FAMILY CATOSTOMIDAE

River Carpsucker *Carpiodes carpio*. Infrequently captured in larger tributaries and the main channel of the Tennessee River. Lowest Conservation Concern.

Quillback *Carpiodes cyprinus*. Prefers larger flowing rivers and impoundments generally below the Fall Line in the Mobile River Basin and in the Tennessee River drainage. Populations from the Escambia to the Chattahoochee Rivers represent an undescribed species. Lowest Conservation Concern.

Highfin Carpsucker *Carpiodes velifer*. Generally more common and abundant than the Quillback. Occupies Mobile Basin rivers and larger tributaries below the Fall Line. Found in the Tennessee River drainage but absent in the Chattahoochee. Populations in the Escambia to the Choctawhatchee Rivers represent an undescribed species. Lowest Conservation Concern.

White Sucker *Catostomus commersonii*. Prefer cooler, spring-fed headwaters and cave runs in the Tennessee River drainage around the Highland Rim. Lowest Conservation Concern.

Blue Sucker *Cycleptus elongatus*. An uncommon dweller in large rivers and streams of the Tennessee River Valley. Sampling in preferred habitat with appropriate gear will likely yield additional previously unknown locations. MODERATE CONSERVATION CONCERN.

Southeastern Blue Sucker *Cycleptus meridionalis*. This hardy sucker roams extensively throughout the lower Alabama and Tombigbee Rivers and the Mobile-Tensaw Delta. Low Conservation Concern. **(Fig. 61, p. 76)**

Creek Chubsucker *Erimyzon oblongus*. Inhabits low-gradient sandy streams throughout the Tennessee River drainage and Mobile River Basin. Less common above the Fall Line and absent in the upper Tallapoosa River. Lowest Conservation Concern.

Lake Chubsucker *Erimyzon sucetta*. Prefers weedy, silt-bottomed backwaters and streams throughout the Coastal Plain. Lowest Conservation Concern.

Sharpfin Chubsucker *Erimyzon tenuis*. Not commonly found in most of the state, somewhat limited to sandy and weedy streams in the Coastal Plain most frequently in Escatawpa, Perdido, and Mobile River tributaries. Lowest Conservation Concern.

Alabama Hog Sucker *Hypentelium etowanum*. This camouflaged sucker is perfectly adapted for concealment in rocky, gravelly streams in the Mobile River Basin, most frequently above the Fall Line, and in Fall Line tributaries to the Chattahoochee River. Lowest Conservation Concern. **(Fig. 62, p. 76)**

Northern Hog Sucker *Hypentelium nigricans*. Occurs in many habitat types throughout the Tennessee River drainage, from impoundments to small headwater streams. Lowest Conservation Concern.

Smallmouth Buffalo *Ictiobus bubalus*. The foundation of a significant fishery in main river channels of the Mobile River Basin and the Tennessee River drainage. Lowest Conservation Concern.

Bigmouth Buffalo *Ictiobus cyprinellus*. Restricted to the Tennessee River drainage, this large riverine sucker is occasionally encountered in impoundments and large rivers. Lowest Conservation Concern.

Black Buffalo *Ictiobus niger*. Found throughout impoundments and larger rivers and streams in the Tennessee River Valley. Larger adults have a deep blue color and local anglers have coined the name "blue rooters" to describe them. Lowest Conservation Concern. **(Fig. 63, p. 76)**

Spotted Sucker *Minytrema melanops*. Common in a variety of habitats throughout Alabama. Lowest Conservation Concern.

Silver Redhorse *Moxostoma anisurum*. This moderate-sized sucker resembles the river redhorse but lacks bright red fins, and is found in larger rivers and streams of the Tennessee River drainage. Presumed rarity of this species is likely due to inadequate sampling effort and gear. Lowest Conservation Concern.

Smallmouth Redhorse *Moxostoma breviceps*. Characterized by a small head, sickle-shaped dorsal fin, and bright red tail. Occurs in streams and impoundments of the Tennessee River drainage. Lowest Conservation Concern.

River Redhorse *Moxostoma carinatum*. This beautiful bronze sucker is known from moderate to large streams and impoundments in the Mobile River Basin, the Tennessee River drainage, and in the Conecuh River system. Lowest Conservation Concern. **(Fig. 64, p. 76)**

Black Redhorse *Moxostoma duquesneii*. A small stream sucker common above the Fall Line and in lower Alabama River tributaries. Lowest Conservation Concern.

Golden Redhorse *Moxostoma erythrurum*. More widespread in Mobile River Basin and Tennessee River drainage streams than the black redhorse. Lowest Conservation Concern.

Harelip Sucker *Moxostoma lacerum*. **Extinct** The only known collection in Alabama was from Cypress Creek, Lauderdale County, in 1889.

Blacktail Redhorse *Moxostoma poecilurum*. This orange-tailed sucker is widespread and common throughout the Mobile River Basin and coastal rivers. Lowest Conservation Concern.

Apalachicola Redhorse *Moxostoma* sp. cf. *poecilurum*. This undescribed redhorse is a common inhabitant of low-gradient streams and impoundments in the Chattahoochee River system. Low Conservation Concern.

Greater Jumprock *Scartomyzon lachneri*. Fairly common in Chattahoochee River tributaries and in impounded waters. Lowest Conservation Concern.

CATFISHES
ORDER SILURIFORMES

NORTH AMERICAN CATFISHES - FAMILY ICTALURIDAE

Snail Bullhead *Ameiurus brunneus*. This uncommon bullhead prefers deep, swift, streams and rivers with rock and sand bottoms in the Chattahoochee River drainage. Low Conservation Concern.

White Catfish *Ameiurus catus*. This ashy-colored white catfish is fairly widespread and occasionally abundant in the Chattahoochee River system with introduced populations scattered throughout the state. Low Conservation Concern.

Black Bullhead *Ameiurus melas*. Widespread but generally uncommon. Prefers low-gradient backwaters throughout the state. Lowest Conservation Concern.

Yellow Bullhead *Ameiurus natalis*. Can be found in varying habitats from streams and slow backwaters to swamps and oxbows across Alabama, and is the most widespread and common of Alabama's bullheads. Lowest Conservation Concern.

Brown Bullhead *Ameiurus nebulosus*. Occurs irregularly in smaller tributaries in a variety of habitats from quiet pools in backwaters and oxbows to streams, most frequently in the eastern half of the state. Lowest Conservation Concern.

Spotted Bullhead *Ameiurus serracanthus*. Alabama's rarest bullhead, this species is limited to the Chattahoochee River system in southeastern Alabama. MODERATE CONSERVATION CONCERN. **(Fig. 65, p. 77)**

Blue Catfish *Ictalurus furcatus*. A commercially valuable species found in larger streams and rivers throughout Alabama. Lowest Conservation Concern.

Channel Catfish *Ictalurus punctatus*. A favorite of anglers and the basis of a multi-million-dollar catfish aquaculture industry. Widespread and common in most Alabama rivers. Lowest Conservation Concern.

Elegant Madtom *Noturus elegans*. **Extirpated**. Formerly known from across the Tennessee River Valley, but substantial collecting effort the last 20 years has failed to locate this species in state waters.

Mountain Madtom *Noturus eleutherus*. Only known Alabama population of this riffle-dwelling madtom resides in the Elk River main channel near the Alabama-Tennessee state line. **HIGH CONSERVATION CONCERN.**

Slender Madtom *Noturus exilis*. Scattered throughout small, rocky streams and creeks in the Highland Rim of the Tennessee River drainage. Lowest Conservation Concern.

Black Madtom *Noturus funebris*. Occurs frequently in small streams of the Mobile River Basin below the Fall Line and in the Bear Creek system of the Tennessee River drainage. Also penetrates the Piedmont Uplands in the Tallapoosa River system. Lowest Conservation Concern.

Tadpole Madtom *Noturus gyrinus*. Restricted to the Coastal Plain, most frequently occurring in snags and undercut banks in western Mobile River Basin tributaries. Lowest Conservation Concern.

Speckled Madtom *Noturus leptacanthus*. Most common madtom in Alabama. Frequents snags and cover in most Coastal Plain streams and rivers penetrating upland areas in the Mobile River Basin. Lowest Conservation Concern.

Brindled Madtom *Noturus miurus*. This mottled, robust madtom occurs peripherally in the Bear Creek system, most commonly in Little Bear and Cedar Creeks. **HIGH CONSERVATION CONCERN.**

Frecklebelly Madtom *Noturus munitus*. Prefers stable gravel shoals in free-flowing rivers and larger streams in the Coastal Plain of Alabama. Currently known only from the lower Cahaba River and eastern tributaries to the upper Tombigbee River. The lower Alabama River population has apparently been extirpated by construction and maintenance of the Alabama River navigation system. **HIGH CONSERVATION CONCERN.**

Freckled Madtom *Noturus nocturnus*. This Coastal Plain species prefers rock and log snags in deeper runs of moderately swift streams and rivers generally in western drainage systems in Alabama. Lowest Conservation Concern.

Highlands Stonecat *Noturus* sp. cf. *flavus*. The Alabama distribution of this undescribed relative of the stonecat, *Noturus flavus*, is limited to the free-flowing main channel sections of the Elk River and Shoal Creek in the Tennessee Valley. **HIGH CONSERVATION CONCERN.**

Flathead Catfish *Pylodictis olivaris*. Occasional monsters (up to 36 kg [80 lb.]) of this widespread and common "yellow or appaloosa cat" are caught in larger rivers of the state. Juveniles and yearlings prefer riffle and shoal areas in flowing rivers. Lowest Conservation Concern.

PIKES AND MUDMINNOWS
ORDER ESOCIFORMES

PIKES - FAMILY ESOCIDAE

Redfin Pickerel *Esox americanus*. Commonly encountered in slow-moving, clear streams with aquatic vegetation throughout the Coastal Plain and occasionally above the Fall Line. Lowest Conservation Concern.

Muskellunge *Esox masquinongy*. **Exotic.** Has been stocked in the Tennessee and Tallapoosa River systems in past years.

Chain Pickerel *Esox niger*. This large predator, known for its respectable fight on a line, can be found in rivers and backwaters of impoundments throughout the state. Lowest Conservation Concern.

SMELTS, TROUTS, AND SALMONS
ORDER SALMONIFORMES

TROUTS AND SALMONS - FAMILY SALMONIDAE

Rainbow Trout *Oncorhynchus mykiss*. **Exotic.** Not native to Alabama, but stocked into selected waters. The tail race below Smith Lake Dam is the most popular rainbow trout fishery in the state.

Brown Trout *Salmo trutta*. **Exotic.** Past attempts at stocking this species in Alabama have been unsuccessful in producing self-sustaining populations.

TROUT PERCHES AND PIRATE PERCHES
ORDER PERCOPSIFORMES

PIRATE PERCH - FAMILY APHREDODERIDAE

Pirate Perch *Aphredoderus sayanus*. A widespread yet secretive species found throughout the Coastal Plain, preferring sheltered, hidden areas in backwaters, swamps,
sloughs, and streams. Lowest Conservation Concern.

CAVEFISHES
ORDER AMBLYOPSIFORMES

CAVEFISHES - FAMILY AMBLYOPSIDAE

Alabama Cavefish *Speoplatyrhinus poulsoni*. Limited to Key Cave, Lauderdale County,
this unique, troglobitic species has one of the most restricted distributions of any vertebrate species in Alabama. **Listed as *endangered* by the U.S. Fish and Wildlife
Service. HIGHEST CONSERVATION CONCERN.**

Southern Cavefish *Typhlichthys subterraneus*. Prefers pools in limestone cave environments in the Tennessee drainage and upper Coosa River system. Habitat is highly susceptible to degradation due to ground water of poor quality. MODERATE CONSER-
VATION CONCERN.

MULLETS
ORDER MUGILIFORMES

MULLETS - FAMILY MUGILIDAE

Striped Mullet *Mugil cephalus*. Invades larger coastal rivers and the main river trunks
of the Mobile River Basin upstream to the Fall Line. Lowest Conservation Concern.

SILVERSIDES
ORDER ATHERINIFORMES

NEW WORLD SILVERSIDES - FAMILY ATHERINOPSIDAE

Brook Silverside *Labidesthes sicculus*. This long and slender forage species commonly
occurs in larger streams and rivers in the Coastal Plain and in the Tennessee River
drainage, but is noticeably absent in the Coosa and Tallapoosa River systems. Lowest
Conservation Concern.

Mississippi Silverside *Menidia audens.* Recently recognized by R.D. Suttkus as occurring in Pickwick Reservoir and the upper Tombigbee River in Alabama. Lowest Conservation Concern.

Inland Silverside *Menidia beryllina.* Common in tributaries to Mobile Bay and the lower Mobile-Tensaw Delta, and occasional in the lower reaches of the Alabama River. Lowest Conservation Concern.

NEEDLEFISHES AND ALLIES

ORDER BELONIFORMES

NEEDLEFISHES - FAMILY BELONIDAE

Atlantic Needlefish *Strongylura marina.* A marine species that ascends main river channels of the Alabama and Tombigbee upstream to the Fall Line, penetrating well inland in other southeastern Alabama coastal rivers. Lowest Conservation Concern.

TOPMINNOWS, LIVEBEARERS, AND ALLIES

ORDER CYPRINODONTIFORMES

TOPMINNOWS - FAMILY FUNDULIDAE

Whiteline Topminnow *Fundulus albolineatus.* **Extinct.** Described from Spring Creek, Madison County, this species was last collected in 1889.

Stippled Studfish *Fundulus bifax.* Restricted to the Tallapoosa River and Sofkahatchee Creek of the Coosa River. Infrequently encountered in slow eddies along stream margins. MODERATE CONSERVATION CONCERN.

Western Starhead Topminnow *Fundulus blairae.* An infrequent and uncommon fish in the southwestern and central Coastal Plain of Alabama. Found in shoreline vegetation of overflow pools and backwaters of larger rivers and streams. Low Conservation Concern.

Northern Studfish *Fundulus catenatus.* This colorful and lively topminnow of the Tennessee River drainage prefers clear shallows near stream runs and riffles. Lowest Conservation Concern. **(Fig. 66, p. 77)**

Golden Topminnow *Fundulus chrysotus.* Limited to quiet ponds and vegetated backwaters of tributaries to the Mobile-Tensaw Delta, Mobile Bay, and the adjacent Coastal Lowlands. Low Conservation Concern.

Banded Topminnow *Fundulus cingulatus*. Occurs peripherally in Alabama. Known from a few scattered locations in Weeks Bay, along the Fort Morgan Peninsula, the Perdido River, and in the Escambia and Yellow Rivers at the Florida state line. Low Conservation Concern.

Marsh Killifish *Fundulus confluentus*. This uncommon killifish reaches its westernmost distribution limit in Baldwin County, Alabama, occurring in fresh to saline marshes in the Perdido River drainage and along the coastal shoreline. MODERATE CONSERVATION CONCERN.

Starhead Topminnow *Fundulus dispar*. Prefers pools in small, vegetated streams and backwaters along larger rivers. Known from scattered locations in lower Mobile River Basin. MODERATE CONSERVATION CONCERN.

Russetfin Topminnow *Fundulus escambiae*. Occurs in vegetated pools and shallow backwaters in streams and rivers of the lower Coastal Plain from Mobile River basin east to the Chattahoochee River. Lowest Conservation Concern.

Saltmarsh Topminnow *Fundulus jenkinsi*. Occurs infrequently in fresh to saline coastal marshes in the narrow coastal strip and barrier islands. MODERATE CONSERVATION CONCERN.

Blackstripe Topminnow *Fundulus notatus*. Locally abundant in western tributaries to the upper Tombigbee River, and known from scattered localities in the lower Mobile River Basin and Tennessee River drainage. Lowest Conservation Concern.

Bayou Topminnow *Fundulus nottii*. Prefers pooled blackwater streams with vegetation in the Tombigbee and Alabama Rivers below the Fall Line. Commonly found in streams draining the Southern Pine Hills and Coastal Lowlands. Lowest Conservation Concern.

Blackspotted Topminnow *Fundulus olivaceus*. Ubiquitous throughout Alabama in all types of aquatic habitats, but preferring stream and river margins. Lowest Conservation Concern.

Bayou Killifish *Fundulus pulvereus*. Occurs infrequently in bays and brackish waters of Mobile Bay, its tributaries, and barrier islands in Alabama. MODERATE CONSERVATION CONCERN.

Southern Studfish *Fundulus stellifer*. This brilliant studfish prefers pools and quiet areas of upland Coosa River streams, and a few tributaries in the Lime Hills region. Apparently extirpated in the Cahaba River system. Lowest Conservation Concern.

Pygmy Killifish *Leptolucania ommata*. Poorly known. Shallow, extensively vegetated overflow pools and backwaters in the Perdido River and Weeks Bay systems, and a handful of localities near the Gulf Coast, are the few places this diminutive fish is found in Alabama. Low Conservation Concern

Bluefin Killifish *Lucania goodei*. The vegetated shallows of Bazemores Mill Pond in Houston County are the only places this small killifish has been found in Alabama. MODERATE CONSERVATION CONCERN.

Rainwater Killifish *Lucania parva*. Poorly known. Found in the Mobile-Tensaw Delta, Mobile Bay, and nearshore marine areas. Occasionally encountered in overflow pools along the Chattahoochee River. Low Conservation Concern.

LIVEBEARERS - FAMILY POECILIIDAE

Western Mosquitofish *Gambusia affinis*. Common in most waters and occuring throughout the Tennessee River drainage and the northern half of the Mobile River Basin. Lowest Conservation Concern.

Eastern Mosquitofish *Gambusia holbrooki*. Also common throughout the coastal drainages from the Chattahoochee River west to the Mobile River Basin. Lowest Conservation Concern.

Least Killifish *Heterandria formosa*. One of the smallest fish in the world. Sporadically found in the lower Mobile River Basin and Mobile Bay tributaries and occasionally in tributaries along the Florida state line. Its rarity likely due to inadequate sampling in its preferred habitat of deep, blackwater streams with vegetated shorelines. Low Conservation Concern.

Sailfin Molly *Poecilia latipinna*. A common dweller in marine and estuarine areas and occasionally in freshwater lagoons in coastal zones. Lowest Conservation Concern.

PUPFISHES - FAMILY CYPRINODONTIDAE

Sheepshead Minnow *Cyprinodon variegatus*. A common resident of brackish and fresh waters around Mobile Bay and the lower Mobile-Tensaw Delta. Lowest Conservation Concern.

SCULPINS AND ALLIES
ORDER SCORPAENIFORMES

SCULPINS - FAMILY COTTIDAE

Mottled Sculpin *Cottus bairdii*. Uncommonly distributed across northern Alabama in the Fall Line Hills and Cumberland Plateau of the Tennessee River drainage. Lowest Conservation Concern. **(Fig. 67, p. 77)**

Banded Sculpin *Cottus carolinae*. Common above the Fall Line in the Mobile River Basin and also throughout the Tennessee River drainage; uncommon in the lower Alabama and Tombigbee River drainages. Prefers rocky riffles and shoals. Lowest Conservation Concern.

Tallapoosa Sculpin *Cottus* sp. cf. *carolinae*. This undescribed species is found in upland streams of the Tallapoosa River system. MODERATE CONSERVATION CONCERN.

Pygmy Sculpin *Cottus paulus*. This highly camouflaged sculpin is abundant in its only known location, Coldwater Spring and spring run in Calhoun County, the public water supply for the city of Anniston. **Listed as *threatened* by the U.S. Fish and Wildlife Service. HIGHEST CONSERVATION CONCERN**.

SUNFISHES, PERCHES, AND ALLIES
ORDER PERCIFORMES

TEMPERATE BASSES - FAMILY MORONIDAE

White Bass *Morone chrysops*. Originally native to the Tennessee River and coastal drainages, but now introduced throughout larger waters of the Mobile River Basin. Lowest Conservation Concern.

Yellow Bass *Morone mississippiensis*. Native to the Tennessee River and lower Mobile-Tensaw River Delta in Alabama with a few scattered sightings of stocked individuals in the Black Warrior and Cahaba Rivers. Recently discovered in the upper Coosa River in large numbers. Lowest Conservation Concern. **(Fig. 68, p. 77)**

Striped Bass *Morone saxatilis*. Both Gulf Coast and Atlantic strains of this prized game fish are found in Alabama. The hybrid striped bass (M. *chrysops* ♂ x *saxatilis* ♀), known as the palmetto bass, is stocked in larger waters throughout the state. MODERATE CONSERVATION CONCERN.

SUNFISHES - FAMILY CENTRARCHIDAE

Shadow Bass *Ambloplites ariommus*. One of Alabama's more strikingly colored sunfishes. Prefers rocks and vegetation in streams of most river systems south of the Tennessee River. Lowest Conservation Concern. **(Fig. 69, p. 77)**

Rock Bass *Ambloplites rupestris*. A panfish prized by fly fishers in the Tennessee River drainage and generally found only in streams of good quality and habitat condition. Lowest Conservation Concern.

Flier *Centrarchus macropterus*. Infrequently found in lowland areas throughout the Coastal Plain. Inhabits swamps, oxbows, overflow pools, and slow-moving streams. Lowest Conservation Concern.

Bluespotted Sunfish *Enneacanthus gloriosus*. This diminutive sunfish is uncommon in the state. Found only at scattered locations in the lower Tombigbee, Mobile-Tensaw River Delta and Mobile Bay tributaries, and the Escatawpa, Perdido, and Yellow Rivers. Low Conservation Concern.

Banded Sunfish *Enneacanthus obesus*. Common in Florida and along the Atlantic coast to New England, but known in Alabama only from the Perdido River system. MODERATE CONSERVATION CONCERN.

Redbreast Sunfish *Lepomis auritus*. Occurs in a variety of habitats in Alabama. Native to the Chattahoochee River, and perhaps parts of the Tallapoosa and Coosa Rivers, but introduced into the Black Warrior and Tennessee Rivers. Lowest Conservation Concern

Green Sunfish *Lepomis cyanellus*. This opportunistic species can be abundant in small headwater brooks, ponds, and polluted streams across the state. Lowest Conservation Concern.

Warmouth *Lepomis gulosus*. A heavy-bodied sunfish found throughout the state. Lowest Conservation Concern.

Orangespotted Sunfish *Lepomis humilis*. Brightly-colored as adults, these sunfish are sporadically encountered in the Mobile River Basin, but more frequently found in western tributaries to the Tombigbee River and in the Tennessee River drainage. Lowest Conservation Concern.

Bluegill *Lepomis macrochirus*. The ever popular "bream" to most anglers is stocked in ponds and found commonly and many times abundantly in all waters throughout the state. Lowest Conservation Concern.

Dollar Sunfish *Lepomis marginatus*. A brightly colored, short, and rounded sunfish found uncommonly in Coastal Plain streams across the state. Lowest Conservation Concern.

Longear Sunfish *Lepomis megalotis*. Brightly colored during the breeding season and widely found in all state waters where they prefer streams, creeks, and rivers. Lowest Conservation Concern.

Redear Sunfish *Lepomis microlophus*. This hardy sunfish occurs throughout the state, but is most frequently encountered in larger free-flowing waters. Stocked into ponds statewide. Lowest Conservation Concern.

Redspotted Sunfish *Lepomis miniatus*. Frequently found across the Alabama Coastal Plain and less common above the Fall Line, preferring lower gradient streams, swamps, and backwater sloughs. Lowest Conservation Concern.

Shoal Bass *Micropterus cataractae*. Restricted to Chattahoochee River tributaries, this uncommon species prefers riffles and shoals of moderate to fast-flowing streams near the Fall Line, rare in impounded waters. **HIGH CONSERVATION CONCERN.**

Redeye Bass *Micropterus coosae*. A prized upland game species found in small to medium-sized creeks and streams above the Fall Line in the Mobile River Basin and introduced into the Chattahoochee River. Rarely found in impounded waters. Lowest Conservation Concern. **(Fig. 70, p. 77)**

Smallmouth Bass *Micropterus dolomieu*. A Tennessee River native that occupies a wide array of habitats from small upland tributaries to the main Tennessee River channel. Lowest Conservation Concern.

Spotted Bass *Micropterus punctulatus*. A favorite of sport anglers that is located throughout the state from small upland creeks to reservoirs. Lowest Conservation Concern.

Largemouth Bass *Micropterus salmoides*. The premier southern sport fish found throughout the state in lakes, ponds, and reservoirs. Lowest Conservation Concern.

White Crappie *Pomoxis annularis*. Generally found in larger rivers and reservoirs. Prefers slack waters with extensive cover. Lowest Conservation Concern.

Black Crappie *Pomoxis nigromaculatus*. Found statewide. Prefers slack waters in reservoirs and rivers, but also enters large streams and creeks with clearer waters. Lowest Conservation Concern.

PERCHES - FAMILY PERCIDAE

Naked Sand Darter *Ammocrypta beanii*. This delicate, translucent sand dweller is at home in larger rivers and streams of the Mobile River Basin below the Fall Line and the Escatawpa River. Prefers shifting substrates of clean sand with some gravel. Lowest Conservation Concern.

Florida Sand Darter *Ammocrypta bifascia*. This larger cousin of the naked sand darter prefers shifting clean-sand shoals of coastal rivers and streams from the Perdido River east to the Choctawhatchee River in Alabama. Lowest Conservation Concern.

Southern Sand Darter *Ammocrypta meridiana*. A scaly version of the naked sand darter found in the Mobile River Basin below the Fall Line. Generally found in smaller streams and creeks compared with other Alabama sand darters. Lowest Conservation Concern.

Crystal Darter *Crystallaria asprella*. Construction of impoundments has significantly changed the character of large gravel and sand shoals in free-flowing rivers resulting in a substantial decline in this species' distribution, particularly in the Tombigbee River. Today, populations are widespread and abundant in the lower Tallapoosa and Cahaba Rivers, but scattered and unpredictable in the Conecuh and lower Alabama Rivers. MODERATE CONSERVATION CONCERN.

Redspot Darter *Etheostoma artesiae*. Occurs in riffles and pools of small to moderate-sized streams over a variety of substrates. Widespread throughout the Mobile River Basin. Lowest Conservation Concern. **(Fig. 71, p. 78)**

Warrior Darter *Etheostoma bellator*. An uncommon snubnose darter endemic to the upper Black Warrior in the lower Locust Fork and Mulberry Fork systems. MODER-ATE CONSERVATION CONCERN.

Locust Fork Darter *Etheostoma* sp. cf. *bellator*. An undescribed darter known historically from only a few tributaries of the upper Locust Fork system. **HIGH CONSERVATION CONCERN.**

Sipsey Darter *Etheostoma* sp. cf. *bellator*. An undescribed relative of the Warrior darter distributed in clear streams of the Sipsey Fork system upstream of Lewis Smith Reservoir, but absent from Hubbard Creek. **HIGH CONSERVATION CONCERN.**

Greenside Darter *Etheostoma blennioides*. Restricted to large creeks and flowing rivers of the Tennessee River Valley. Alabama's largest *Etheostoma* occupies cobble and gravel areas with algae and aquatic moss. Lowest Conservation Concern. **(Fig. 72, p. 78)**

Blenny Darter *Etheostoma blennius*. This unique darter of the Tennessee River system is found in swift riffles and shoals of gravel, rubble, and cobble in northwestern Alabama. Low Conservation Concern.

Slackwater Darter *Etheostoma boschungi*. Tawny-colored males distinguish this Tennessee River species that is restricted to upland reaches of Cypress Creek, Swan Creek, and the upper Flint River. **Listed as *threatened* by the U.S. Fish and Wildlife Service. HIGHEST CONSERVATION CONCERN.**

Holiday Darter *Etheostoma brevirostrum*. This festively colored snubnose darter is found in the upper reaches of Shoal Creek, a cool, clear tributary to Choccolocco Creek of the Coosa River system. **HIGHEST CONSERVATION CONCERN.**

Rainbow Darter *Etheostoma caeruleum*. Widespread and common in gravel and cobble riffles throughout the Tennessee River drainage in the state. Lowest Conservation Concern. **(Fig. 73, p. 78)**

Bluebreast Darter *Etheostoma camurum*. Occupies cobble and slab riffles and shoals, and reaches the very southern extent of its distribution in the last free-flowing section of the Elk River in Alabama. **HIGH CONSERVATION CONCERN.**

Vermilion Darter *Etheostoma chermocki*. Limited to upper Turkey Creek in the Locust Fork system. Can be abundant but is very restricted in distribution. **Listed as *endangered* by the U.S. Fish and Wildlife Service. HIGHEST CONSERVATION CONCERN.**

Bluntnose Darter *Etheostoma chlorosomum*. Restricted to the Mobile River Basin below the Fall Line, where it prefers swampy and low gradient backwaters of the Coastal Plain. Lowest Conservation Concern.

Lipstick Darter *Etheostoma chuckwachatte*. Limited almost exclusively to the Northern Piedmont Upland in the Tallapoosa River system in riffles of medium to large streams with moderate to swift current. **HIGH CONSERVATION CONCERN.**

Ashy Darter *Etheostoma cinereum*. **Extirpated.** Occupies clear pools and eddies of large upland streams, but this darter has not been collected in the Alabama portion of the Tennessee River in more than 150 years.

Coastal Darter *Etheostoma colorosum*. This common and widespread species occurs in log snags and shoreline habitat of coastal streams from the Perdido River to the Choctawhatchee River. Lowest Conservation Concern.

Coosa Darter *Etheostoma coosae*. Endemic to the Coosa River system where it embraces cover near riffles and raceways in streams and small, spring-fed creeks. Lowest Conservation Concern. **(Fig. 74, p. 78)**

Crown Darter *Etheostoma corona*. Restricted to the Cypress Creek system in the Tennessee River where it is widespread and abundant in headwater creeks and smaller streams. Lowest Conservation Concern.

Fringed Darter *Etheostoma crossopterum.* Aptly named for its ragged dorsal fin, this drab darter is uncommon in the Shoal Creek and Six Mile Creek systems in the Tennessee Valley. MODERATE CONSERVATION CONCERN.

Choctawhatchee Darter *Etheostoma davisoni.* This straw-colored darter is a pool resident of sandy-bottomed streams in southeastern Alabama. Lowest Conservation Concern.

Coldwater Darter *Etheostoma ditrema.* A spring and stream form of this imperiled species have recently been recognized. Both ecological forms occur scattered throughout the Coosa River system. **HIGH CONSERVATION CONCERN.**

Tuskaloosa Darter *Etheostoma douglasi.* Fairly common in the middle reaches of the Locust Fork and the upper Sipsey Fork, but rather uncommon throughout the remainder of its distribution in the upper Black Warrior River. MODERATE CONSERVATION CONCERN.

Blackside Snubnose Darter *Etheostoma duryi.* Widespread and common in small to medium-sized streams throughout the Tennessee River drainage. Lowest Conservation Concern.

Brown Darter *Etheostoma edwini.* Found in lower Coastal Plain streams among aquatic vegetation and root mats, this species is distributed from the Perdido to the Chattahoochee River in southern Alabama. Lowest Conservation Concern. **(Fig. 75, p. 78)**

Fantail Darter *Etheostoma flabellare.* Shallow gravel and cobble riffles in the Tennessee River Valley are home to this commonly occurring darter. Lowest Conservation Concern.

Swamp Darter *Etheostoma fusiforme.* True to its common name, this darter frequents low-gradient, slow-flowing streams and backwaters known only from a few locations in Alabama's Coastal Plain. Lowest Conservation Concern.

Harlequin Darter *Etheostoma histrio.* Scattered throughout Alabama's Coastal Plain, this darter occupies a variety of habitats from small swift streams with gravel and snag shoals to deep flowing rivers. Lowest Conservation Concern. **(Fig. 76, p. 78)**

Blueside Darter *Etheostoma jessiae.* The beautiful azure markings befit the common name of this species found at scattered locations in the Tennessee River Valley and commonly in the Paint Rock River system. Low Conservation Concern.

Greenbreast Darter *Etheostoma jordani.* Moderate to swift riffles of cobble, gravel, and slab rock in the Coosa, Cahaba, and lower Tallapoosa Rivers are favored by this darter. Lowest Conservation Concern.

Stripetail Darter *Etheostoma kennicotti*. A light tan-colored darter infrequently encountered in upland stream pools of the Tennessee River system, but is rather common in the Paint Rock River system. Lowest Conservation Concern.

Tombigbee Darter *Etheostoma lachneri*. This Tombigbee River endemic is widespread and common throughout the Coastal Plain, but noticeably absent in streams draining the Black Belt. Lowest Conservation Concern.

Brighteye Darter *Etheostoma lynceum*. Although common in Mississippi and west Tennessee, this darter is very rare in Alabama, reaching the easternmost part of its distribution in the Escatawpa River system in Mobile and Washington Counties. **HIGHEST CONSERVATION CONCERN.**

Lollipop Darter *Etheostoma neopterum*. Its common name refers to the fleshy knobs on the dorsal fin of this rare Tennessee River species. Known only from the Shoal Creek system in Lauderdale County. **HIGHEST CONSERVATION CONCERN.**

Blackfin Darter *Etheostoma nigripinne*. A common stream dweller in the Tennessee River drainage found in a variety of aquatic habitats in the Highland Rim and Fall Line Hills. Lowest Conservation Concern.

Johnny Darter *Etheostoma nigrum*. Common below the Fall Line in the Mobile River Basin, usually not extending south beyond the Lime Hills region, and found at scattered locations in the Tennessee River drainage. Lowest Conservation Concern.

Watercress Darter *Etheostoma nuchale*. Deep, slow-moving backwaters of a few springs in Jefferson County are the entire known distribution of this highly restricted and rare species. **Listed as *endangered* by the U.S. Fish and Wildlife Service. HIGHEST CONSERVATION CONCERN.**

Goldstripe Darter *Etheostoma parvipinne*. Occurs widely, though scattered, throughout Alabama's Coastal Plain, inhabiting aquatic vegetation, woody debris, mud, and silt in small, sluggish streams and spring seeps. Lowest Conservation Concern.

Rush Darter *Etheostoma phytophilum*. This rare khaki-colored spring-run dweller is found in the upper Black Warrior drainage in the Locust Fork system and a few tributaries to Clear Creek of the Sipsey Fork. **HIGHEST CONSERVATION CONCERN.**

Cypress Darter *Etheostoma proeliare*. Prefers backwater, vegetated pools of sluggish Coastal Plain streams and swamps in the Tombigbee, Black Warrior, and lower Alabama River drainages. A few locations have been documented in the Conecuh River system. Lowest Conservation Concern.

Alabama Darter *Etheostoma ramseyi*. Found predominantly in Alabama River tributaries draining the Coastal Plain, with some localities in the Cahaba River above the Fall Line. Lowest Conservation Concern.

Redline Darter *Etheostoma rufilineatum*. The presence of this common species in Tennessee River collections indicates good, stable stream habitats. Lowest Conservation Concern.

Rock Darter *Etheostoma rupestre*. Generally confined to rocky, gravelly shoals and riffles in the Mobile River Basin principally below the Fall Line, but penetrating upland streams in the Cahaba, Coosa, and Black Warrior Rivers. Lowest Conservation Concern.

Snubnose Darter *Etheostoma simoterum*. Widely distributed in clear tributary streams of the Tennessee River drainage. Lowest Conservation Concern.

Speckled Darter *Etheostoma stigmaeum*. One of Alabama's more common species, found throughout the Mobile River Basin, Conecuh River system, and in upper Bear Creek in the Tennessee River drainage. Lowest Conservation Concern. **(Fig. 77, p. 78)**

Gulf Darter *Etheostoma swaini*. Widespread, preferring clear streams and rivers of the Coastal Plain with debris snags, rubble, and gravel. Lowest Conservation Concern.

Tallapoosa Darter *Etheostoma tallapoosae*. Fancies small Piedmont streams in the Tallapoosa River system. Low Conservation Concern.

Trispot Darter *Etheostoma trisella*. **Extirpated**. Last taken in Alabama in 1958, it was known from only two locations. Sampling efforts in Georgia have discovered additional populations, therefore upper Coosa River tributaries in Alabama may still harbor extant populations.

Tuscumbia Darter *Etheostoma tuscumbia*. Localized, but sometimes abundant, at selected limestone springs in the Highland Rim of northern Alabama in the Tennessee River drainage. **HIGH CONSERVATION CONCERN.**

Boulder Darter *Etheostoma wapiti*. The only population of this rare darter in Alabama inhabits the Elk River near the Tennessee state line. **Listed as *endangered* by the U.S. Fish and Wildlife Service. HIGHEST CONSERVATION CONCERN.**

Banded Darter *Etheostoma zonale*. This emerald-colored darter frequents swift riffles and shoals with vegetation in streams and rivers scattered over the Tennessee River Valley. Low Conservation Concern.

Backwater Darter *Etheostoma zonifer*. Small, turbid streams and backwaters of Black Belt streams are home to this darter. Lowest Conservation Concern.

Bandfin Darter *Etheostoma zonistium*. The brilliant orange underside of males distinguishes this uncommon inhabitant of small Tennessee River streams in the extreme northwestern part of Alabama. **HIGH CONSERVATION CONCERN.**

Blueface Darter *Etheostoma* sp. cf. *zonistium*. This rare cousin of the bandfin darter is found in Hubbard Creek of the upper Sipsey Fork and upstream of Upper Bear Creek Reservoir in the Tennessee River drainage. **HIGH CONSERVATION CONCERN.**

Yellow Perch *Perca flavescens*. An introduced species in the Tennessee, Coosa, and Chattahoochee Rivers, but the population in Mobile-Tensaw tributaries is thought to be native. Low Conservation Concern.

Goldline Darter *Percina aurolineata*. Swift cobble and gravel shoals, and undercut banks in the Cahaba River near the Fall Line, are home to this uncommon darter. **Listed as *threatened* by the U.S. Fish and Wildlife Service. HIGHEST CONSERVATION CONCERN.**

Southern Logperch *Percina austroperca*. Occurs in sandy streams and rivers of southern Alabama from the Escambia River to the Choctawhatchee River. MODERATE CONSERVATION CONCERN.

Coal Darter *Percina brevicauda*. This diminutive darter is endemic to the Mobile River Basin occurring in the Locust Fork and Cahaba Rivers, and one tributary to the Coosa River. **HIGH CONSERVATION CONCERN.**

Blotchside Logperch *Percina burtoni*. A rare darter that reaches the southernmost part of its distribution in clear headwater tributaries to the Paint Rock River in the Tennessee Valley. Historically known from Shoal Creek tributaries. **HIGHEST CONSERVATION CONCERN.**

Logperch *Percina caprodes*. Individuals are found in waters ranging from reservoirs to headwater creeks throughout the Tennessee River drainage. Lowest Conservation Concern.

Gilt Darter *Percina evides*. Infrequent in the Tennessee River Valley preferring rocky and gravelly shoals in larger, flowing streams and rivers. **HIGH CONSERVATION CONCERN.**

Mobile Logperch *Percina kathae*. Common in the Mobile River Basin. Most often encountered above the Fall Line in a variety of habitats from reservoirs to small streams. Lowest Conservation Concern.

Freckled Darter *Percina lenticula*. This uncommon giant of darters lives in deep, swift areas of flowing rivers and large streams in the Coastal Plain of the Mobile River Basin. MODERATE CONSERVATION CONCERN. **(Fig. 78, p. 78)**

Blackside Darter *Percina maculata*. Infrequently found in stream pools in the Mobile River Basin and Tennessee River drainage. Lowest Conservation Concern.

Blackbanded Darter *Percina nigrofasciata*. Alabama's most ubiquitous and common darter is found in a multitude of waters throughout the state, excluding the Tennessee River drainage. Lowest Conservation Concern.

Bronze Darter *Percina palmaris*. Larger upland streams of the Tallapoosa and upper Coosa River systems are preferred by this distinctive darter. Lowest Conservation Concern.

Slenderhead Darter *Percina phoxocephala*. Common north and west of Alabama but only occurs peripherally in the Bear Creek system of the Tennessee River drainage. **HIGHEST CONSERVATION CONCERN.**

Dusky Darter *Percina sciera*. Has an unusual distribution, occurring commonly in shoals and riffles of larger streams and rivers of the Tennessee River drainage and the upper Tombigbee River and occasionally taken in lower Alabama River tributaries. Lowest Conservation Concern.

River Darter *Percina shumardi*. Prefers shoals of gravel, rubble, and cobble in free-flowing large rivers and streams of the Mobile River Basin and Tennessee River drainage. Impoundments have reduced populations of this darter. Lowest Conservation Concern.

Gulf Logperch *Percina suttkusi*. Uncommon inhabitants of larger streams and rivers in the Mobile River Basin Coastal Plain. Lowest Conservation Concern.

Snail Darter *Percina tanasi*. This most famous of darters is known only from one location in Alabama, the Paint Rock River system of the Tennessee River drainage. **Listed as *threatened* by the U.S. Fish and Wildlife Service. HIGHEST CONSERVATION CONCERN.**

Saddleback Darter *Percina vigil*. Inhabits swift gravel and sand shoals of flowing streams and rivers in the Alabama Coastal Plain. A few historical collections are known from the Tennessee River drainage. Lowest Conservation Concern.

Muscadine Darter *Percina* sp. cf. *macrocephala*. A fairly common endemic of the Tallapoosa River found in riffles and shoals with large rubble, and in deep runs over sand and gravel. MODERATE CONSERVATION CONCERN.

Warrior Bridled Darter *Percina* sp. cf. *macrocephala*. A rare undescribed species found only in Sipsey Fork upstream of Lake Lewis Smith. **HIGHEST CONSERVATION CONCERN.**

Halloween Darter *Percina* sp. A rare darter known in Alabama only from the lower reaches of Uchee and Little Uchee Creeks. Occurs in riffles of high-gradient streams. **HIGHEST CONSERVATION CONCERN.**

Sauger *Sander canadense*. This prized sport fish occurs commonly in larger streams and reservoirs in the Tennessee River drainage. Lowest Conservation Concern.

Walleye *Sander vitreus*. Occurs at scattered localities throughout the Mobile River Basin and some populations are locally common or abundant. MODERATE CONSERVATION CONCERN.

DRUMS AND CROAKERS - FAMILY SCIAENIDAE

Freshwater Drum *Aplodinotus grunniens*. "Gaspergou" are found in practically all large rivers and reservoirs in the state, but few records are known from coastal rivers in southeastern Alabama. Lowest Conservation Concern.

Silver Perch *Bairdiella chrysoura*. Occasionally enters fresh water in coastal areas. Lowest Conservation Concern.

Spotted Seatrout *Cynoscion nebulosus*. This favored sport fish migrates seasonally into the Mobile-Tensaw River Delta. Lowest Conservation Concern.

Atlantic Croaker *Micorpogonias undulatus*. A common estuarine resident and occasional inhabitant of fresh coastal rivers. Lowest Conservation Concern.

Red Drum *Sciaenops ocellatus*. A large estuarine and marine sciaenid occasionally encountered in freshwater. Lowest Conservation Concern.

PYGMY SUNFISHES - FAMILY ELASSOMATIDAE

Spring Pygmy Sunfish *Elassoma alabamae*. This rare Tennessee River endemic is known historically and recently from less than a handful of spring locations in Limestone and Lauderdale Counties. **HIGHEST CONSERVATION CONCERN.**

Everglades Pygmy Sunfish *Elassoma evergladei*. More common east of Alabama but does occur sporadically in the lower Coastal Plain and more frequently in streams of lower Baldwin County. Low Conservation Concern.

Banded Pygmy Sunfish *Elassoma zonatum*. Swamps and backwater areas of small Coastal Plain streams are choice habitats for this fairly common species. Also occurs in a few drainages above the Fall Line. Lowest Conservation Concern.

CICHLIDS - FAMILY CICHLIDAE

Blue Tilapia *Oreochromis aureus*. **Exotic**. A cultured species, escapees of which are occasionally encountered in state waters.

SLEEPERS - FAMILY ELEOTRIDAE

Fat Sleeper *Dormitator maculatus*. Found in brackish waters and occasionally in freshwater tidal creeks and sloughs around Mobile Bay. Low Conservation Concern.

Largescaled Spinycheek Sleeper *Eleotris amblyopsis*. Restricted to low salinity backwaters around Mobile Bay. Low Conservation Concern.

FLOUNDERS
ORDER PLEURONECTIFORMES

SAND FLOUNDERS - FAMILY PARALICHTHYIDAE

Southern Flounder *Paralichthys lethostigma*. Common in bays along the coast, the Mobile-Tensaw Delta, and penetrates the Alabama and Tombigbee Rivers upstream to Claiborne and Coffeeville Dams, respectively. Lowest Conservation Concern. **(Fig. 79, p. 78)**

AMERICAN SOLES - FAMILY ACHIRIDAE

Hogchoker *Trinectes maculatus*. Like the flounder, found in bay tributaries and in the lower Alabama and Tombigbee Rivers upstream to the first dams. They also penetrate upstream in the Conecuh and Choctawhatchee Rivers. Lowest Conservation Concern.

AMPHIBIANS AND REPTILES

Barking Treefrog
Hyla gratiosa

INTRODUCTION

Many of Alabama's amphibians and reptiles continue to fare poorly. The 1983 committee noted declines in several ground-dwelling species, especially Coastal Plain reptiles, and that trend continues. Suspected major causes of these declines include absence of fire, conversion of natural habitats to other uses, and predation by exotic fire ants. Other causes may include deliberate killing, overcollecting, road mortality, pesticides and herbicides, and siltation of streams. The southern hognose snake may now be extirpated from Alabama, and several species are for the first time assigned a high-priority conservation status. Examples include the southeastern five-lined skink, eastern and speckled kingsnakes, and eastern coral snake. Formerly common species now elevated to moderate conservation concern include the six-lined racerunner, oak toad, corn snake, and eastern hognose snake.

The committee repeatedly noted that declining forms often were members of a suite of species suffering because of their adaptation to an ancestral habitat of open longleaf pine forest characterized by a diverse herbaceous groundcover. These habitats are for the most part either already lost, or not adequately managed with frequent fire. Fire-maintained longleaf pine forest is probably the single most important habitat to the greatest number of Alabama's imperiled terrestrial amphibians and reptiles, including the gopher tortoise, Florida and black pine snakes, gopher frog, and flatwoods salamander.

While many species are "protected" from collecting and direct persecution, readers should be aware that the state has not traditionally regulated habitat destruction. For example, it is illegal to remove a gopher tortoise from its habitat, yet nothing prevents the bulldozing of a thousand acres of the same habitat, so long as eradicating wildlife is not the primary objective (applies to 17 counties; such an action would be a felony in the three counties where the gopher tortoise is federally protected). Many states require mitigation for destruction of ecologically important uplands, but Alabama does not.

Established exotic amphibians and reptiles have not yet caused the problems that are reported for the other groups. Fortunately, none recorded to date is particularly invasive or competitive with native species in Alabama, but we should be ever watchful for less benign arrivals. It is feared that if the brown tree snake (*Boiga irregularis*), which devasted the bird life of Guam, became established in the Southeast, it would be virtually impossible to eradicate.

Alabama remains a state with potential for new discoveries and/or clarification of taxonomic questions. It has at least three salamander species (two *Eurycea*, one *Siren*) that are currently being described, and others may still be found. Five amphibians presently known only from neighboring states potentially occur here, and searches for their presence should be undertaken. The Pigeon Mountain salamander (*Plethodon petraeus*) and Georgia blind salamander (*Haideotriton wallacei*) both occur just across the Georgia border. A search for the former should be conducted on Lookout Mountain, and the latter may occur in subterranean aquatic habitats associated with the Ocala Limestone formation in the Dougherty Plain of extreme southeastern Alabama. Two Mississippi species, the northern crawfish frog (*Rana areolata circulosa*) and possibly extinct Catahoula salamander (*Plethodon ainsworthi*), could potentially be in the Coastal Plain of western Alabama, a region that has not received sufficient attention from herpetologists. A population of dwarf siren (*Pseudobranchus* sp.) was recently documented from the Escambia (Conecuh) River drainage in Florida, and this secretive form should be sought in suitable habitats of extreme southern Alabama.

Much remains to be learned about Alabama's herpetofauna. Because occurrence and distribution data for many species are scarce or lacking, some status designations had to be based on subjective impressions. Fortunately, it is becoming increasingly feasible for anyone to gather and electronically transmit data, even photo vouchers, and the Alabama Herpetological Atlas Project (AHAP) enables a statewide network of volunteers to report their observations so that the status and management needs of our herpetofauna will be better understood in the future. Readers are encouraged to submit sightings to AHAP at www.ahap.org.

The annotations that follow represent our best assessment of the status of 73 native amphibians (30 frogs, 43 salamanders) and 93 reptiles (12 lizards, 49 snakes, 31 turtles, and an alligator), which include 13 subspecies (of five reptiles) that the committee felt merited separate treatment. Five established exotic species, one frog and four lizards, also are documented within the state.

Priority designations were based on each species' population in Alabama, without regard to status elsewhere. Thus, a species whose distribution barely reaches the state may be classified as Priority 1, 2, or 3, even though it may be secure in adjacent states. The committee followed the scientific nomenclature of Crother (2000). However, the selection of common names was guided by traditional usage, and frequently differed from those proposed in that document.

I thank the other 16 committee members for the dedicated effort each put into this project. I am most indebted and grateful to Robert H. Mount, previous chair of this committee, editor of the 1984 and 1986 publications, and author of *The Reptiles and Amphibians of Alabama*. His long-term naturalist's perspective has been invaluable, and much of what follows in this section is derived extensively from his work.

Mark A. Bailey

COMMITTEE

Mr. Mark A. Bailey, Conservation Southeast Inc., Shorter, AL, Chairperson/Compiler

Mr. Matthew J. Aresco, Department of Biological Science, Florida State University, Tallahassee, FL

Dr. George R. Cline, Biology Department, Jacksonville State University, Jacksonville, AL

Dr. George W. Folkerts, Department of Biological Sciences, Auburn University, AL

Mr. James C. Godwin, Alabama Natural Heritage Program, The Nature Conservancy, Huntingdon College, Montgomery, AL

Dr. Craig Guyer, Department of Biological Sciences, Auburn University, AL

Dr. Mark H. Hughes, International Paper Company, Bainbridge, GA

Mr. John B. Jensen, Nongame-Endangered Wildlife Program, Georgia Department of Natural Resources, Forsyth, GA

Dr. Ken R. Marion, Biology Department, University of Alabama at Birmingham, AL

Mr. D. Bruce Means, Coastal Plains Institute and Land Conservancy, Tallahassee, FL

Mr. Paul E. Moler, Wildlife Research Laboratory, Florida Fish and Wildlife Conservation Commission, Gainesville, FL

Dr. Robert H. Mount, Department of Biological Sciences (retired), Auburn University, AL

Dr. David H. Nelson, Department of Biology, University of South Alabama, Mobile, AL

Dr. Megan G. Peterson, Division of Science and Mathematics, Birmingham-Southern College, Birmingham, AL

Mr. Eric C. Soehren, Alabama Department of Conservation and Natural Resources, State Lands Division, Natural Heritage Section, Montgomery, AL

Dr. Dan W. Speake, Alabama Cooperative Fish and Wildlife Research Unit, U.S. Geological Survey, and School of Forestry and Wildlife Sciences (retired), Auburn University, AL

Dr. Thane Wibbels, Biology Department, University of Alabama at Birmingham, AL

AMPHIBIANS
CLASS AMPHIBIA
FROGS AND TOADS
ORDER ANURA

"TRUE" TOADS - FAMILY BUFONIDAE

American Toad *Bufo americanus*. Fairly common in northeastern Alabama above Fall Line Hills. Breeds in temporary woodland pools January to May. Encountered most frequently late winter to early spring near deciduous forest. Lowest Conservation Concern.

Fowler's Toad *Bufo fowleri*. Common statewide in a variety of habitats, including disturbed areas. Breeds March to August, often in more permanent aquatic sites than other toads. Alabama's most commonly encountered and widely distributed toad; often seen on roads. Lowest Conservation Concern.

Oak Toad *Bufo quercicus*. Uncommon to fairly common south of Blackland Prairie. Found locally in Coosa River Valley of Ridge and Valley, where it has not been verified for many years. Breeds April to July in temporary pools. Inhabits areas of sandy soils, especially fire-maintained pine flatwoods, where it may be absent from some areas of seemingly suitable habitat. MODERATE CONSERVATION CONCERN. (Fig. 80, p. 113)

Southern Toad *Bufo terrestris*. Common in southern and western portions of Alabama, occupying all of Coastal Plain and western portions of Southwestern Appalachians. Breeds March to June in small ponds and woodland pools. Exploits a variety of habitats. Often seen on roads. Lowest Conservation Concern. (Fig. 81, p. 113)

TREEFROGS AND ALLIES - FAMILY HYLIDAE

Northern Cricket Frog *Acris crepitans crepitans*. Common above Fall Line Hills and locally common in Coastal Plain. Occurs essentially statewide. Breeds March through August in a wide variety of aquatic habitats, especially margins of permanent water bodies with sparse vegetation. Low Conservation Concern. (Fig. 82, p. 113)

Southern Cricket Frog *Acris gryllus gryllus*. Common in Coastal Plain, locally common above Fall Line Hills, absent from northeastern and extreme northern Alabama. Breeds March through August in, and near, temporary water bodies, preferring weedy shorelines, wet meadows, and similar habitats. Lowest Conservation Concern.

Pine Barrens Treefrog *Hyla andersonii*. Threatened. Known from fewer than 20 isolated locations in southern Escambia, Covington, and Geneva Counties as part of a disjunct population shared with the Florida Panhandle. Breeds March to August in fire-maintained shrub bogs. Habitat quality and quantity declining, especially on private lands. **HIGH CONSERVATION CONCERN.**

Bird-voiced Treefrog *Hyla avivoca*. Common in Coastal Plain to which it is apparently restricted. If valid, one unverified record from St. Clair County in Ridge and Valley ecoregion would represent a northern disjunct population. Breeds April through July in forested swamps, beaver ponds, and floodplains. Lowest Conservation Concern.

Cope's Gray Treefrog *Hyla chrysoscelis*. Common statewide. Breeds April through August in temporary to semi-permanent pools. Found in a variety of habitats, most frequently in association with deciduous forest. Lowest Conservation Concern.

Green Treefrog *Hyla cinerea*. Common nearly statewide, but rare or absent from portions of Interior Plateau and northern portions of Southwestern Appalachians, Ridge and Valley, and Piedmont. Breeds April to August in permanent aquatic habitats with emergent vegetation. Lowest Conservation Concern.

Pine Woods Treefrog *Hyla femoralis*. Locally common in Coastal Plain, where most frequently encountered in Dougherty Plain and Southern Pine Plains and Hills. Disjunct populations in Ridge and Valley have not been verified in many years. Breeds April to August in temporary pools and ponds. Typically inhabits pine-dominated forests in areas of sandy soils. Lowest Conservation Concern.

Barking Treefrog *Hyla gratiosa*. Fairly common in Coastal Plain, scarcer in other regions, where suitable habitats often are limited and distribution more localized. Occurs essentially statewide. Breeds March through July, usually in temporary ponds or fishless semi-permanent ponds. Low Conservation Concern. **(Fig. 83, p. 113)**

Squirrel Treefrog *Hyla squirella*. Common in Coastal Plain, less common and local in Ridge and Valley and extreme southern Piedmont. Breeds April to August in temporary pools and ponds, exploits a variety of habitats, and often encountered around buildings. Lowest Conservation Concern.

Mountain Chorus Frog *Pseudacris brachyphona*. Fairly common from Fall Line Hills northward, absent from most of Coastal Plain. Breeds December to April in shallow temporary pools in wooded areas, most often in hilly terrain. Lowest Conservation Concern.

Northern Spring Peeper *Pseudacris crucifer crucifer*. Common statewide. Breeds January to April in ponds, pools, and swamps in, or near, wooded areas. Rarely encountered during warmer months. Lowest Conservation Concern. **(Fig. 84, p. 113)**

Upland Chorus Frog *Pseudacris feriarum feriarum*. Common nearly statewide; absent from extreme southern Alabama except along Conecuh and Chattahoochee Rivers, where its distribution barely extends into Florida. Breeds December to April in temporary pools in woods and fields. Lowest Conservation Concern.

Southern Chorus Frog *Pseudacris nigrita nigrita*. Locally common in Dougherty Plain and Southern Pine Plains and Hills. Also occurs in eastern portion of Southern Hilly Gulf Coastal Plain. Breeds February to May, usually in grassy temporary wetlands in, or near, areas of sandy soils. Lowest Conservation Concern.

Little Grass Frog *Pseudacris ocularis*. Rare and peripheral in Dougherty Plain. This tiniest of North American frogs, found from Florida to Virginia, barely reaches extreme southeastern Alabama. Known from only four localities in southeastern Houston County. Breeds late winter to late summer in shallow, grassy cypress ponds and roadside ditches. **HIGH CONSERVATION CONCERN**.

Ornate Chorus Frog *Pseudacris ornata*. Uncommon to locally common in Coastal Plain east of Cahaba and Alabama Rivers. Occurs west of Mobile Bay in southern Mississippi. Expected in Mobile and Washington Counties of Alabama. Breeds from December to March in shallow, temporary pools. Choruses indicate possible presence of other winter-breeding amphibians of conservation concern, such as gopher frogs and flatwoods salamanders. MODERATE CONSERVATION CONCERN. (**Fig. 85, p. 113**)

LEPTODACTYLID FROGS - FAMILY LEPTODACTYLIDAE

Greenhouse Frog *Eleutherodactylus planirostris*. **Exotic**. Apparently confined to coastal areas of Baldwin and Mobile Counties, where it prefers lawn edges, gardens, and greenhouses to "natural" habitats.

NARROW-MOUTHED TOADS AND ALLIES - FAMILY MICROHYLIDAE

Eastern Narrow-mouthed Toad *Gastrophryne carolinensis*. Common statewide. A secretive burrowing frog that breeds April to September in vegetated margins of lakes, ponds, and ditches. Lowest Conservation Concern.

SPADEFOOT TOADS AND ALLIES - FAMILY PELOBATIDAE

Eastern Spadefoot *Scaphiopus holbrookii*. Locally common statewide. A secretive burrowing frog that may breed at any season following heavy rains. Capable of reproducing in pools that hold water only two to three weeks. Susceptible to destruction of breeding habitat, which may not be readily recognized as wetland. Low Conservation Concern.

"TRUE" FROGS - FAMILY RANIDAE

Gopher Frog *Rana capito*. Endangered. Principally a Coastal Plain longleaf pine forest inhabitant, where 10 historic records exist. Subspecific allocation of Alabama populations is problematic; formerly considered *R. c. sevosa*, dusky gopher frog (see Mississippi gopher frog). Highly terrestrial, but breeds late January to March in open temporary ponds. Alabama's five extant breeding sites are in Escambia and Covington Counties. The only Ridge and Valley breeding pond (Shelby County) was drained for a subdivision in 1997, and a Barbour County breeding pond was destroyed by road construction. **HIGHEST CONSERVATION CONCERN.**

American Bullfrog *Rana catesbeiana*. Common statewide. A large, familiar, highly aquatic frog. Breeds March to August in lakes, ponds, and many streams. Lowest Conservation Concern. (**Fig. 86, p.113**)

Bronze Frog/Green Frog *Rana clamitans* ssp. Common statewide, this highly aquatic and familiar frog is bronze (*R. c. clamitans*) in southern and green (*R. c. melanota*) in northern Alabama. Breeds April to August. Prefers swamps, small streams, and other aquatic habitats. Lowest Conservation Concern.

Pig Frog *Rana grylio*. Locally common in Lower Coastal Plain and southernmost tier of counties of Dougherty Plain and Southern Pine Plains and Hills. A large, highly aquatic frog of permanent, open water bodies with emergent vegetation. Breeds April to August. Lowest Conservation Concern.

Mississippi Gopher Frog *Rana sevosa*. Endangered/***Possibly extirpated***. Recently described (2001) as western component of what had been considered *R. capito sevosa* (dusky gopher frog) from Mobile Bay to Louisiana. Currently known from a single population in Mississippi, but also recorded from Gulf Coast Flatwoods of Alabama (mouth of Dog River). Similar in appearance and habitat requirements to gopher frog. Secretive and difficult to survey. **Listed as *endangered* by the U.S. Fish and Wildlife Service. HIGHEST CONSERVATION CONCERN.**

River Frog *Rana heckscheri*. Peripheral and rare in southern portion of Southern Pine Plains and Hills, and potentially in Dougherty Plain of southernmost tier of counties. Common in Florida and Georgia. Documented in Alabama from four old records. **HIGHEST CONSERVATION CONCERN.**

Pickerel Frog *Rana palustris*. Fairly common to uncommon and locally distributed in all regions above Fall Line, with disjunct populations in Lime Hills and Southern Pine Plains and Hills of Coastal Plain (Monroe and Conecuh Counties). Frequently encountered in, and near, cave entrances, but exploits other cool-water habitats. Breeds in winter and early spring. A Conecuh County population, associated with a limestone cave, has not been confirmed in over two decades. Low Conservation Concern. (**Fig. 87, p. 114**)

Southern Leopard Frog *Rana sphenocephala*. Common statewide. Fairly aquatic but ranges away from water when foraging. Often seen on roads. Breeds mostly December through March in woodland pools, swamps, ponds, and other wetlands. Lowest Conservation Concern.

Wood Frog *Rana sylvatica*. Rare and local in distribution. Documented from twelve locations in eastern Ridge and Valley and upper Piedmont from Mount Cheaha, in Talledega County, south to Horseshoe Bend in Tallapoosa County. A highly terrestrial frog of deciduous forests. Breeds January to February in woodland pools. Thought to be declining, but status not investigated in over two decades. MODERATE CONSERVATION CONCERN. (**Fig. 88, p. 114**)

SALAMANDERS
ORDER CAUDATA

MOLE SALAMANDERS - FAMILY AMBYSTOMATIDAE

Flatwoods Salamander *Ambystoma cingulatum*. Endangered. Historically known from five sites in low pine flatwoods of Southern Coastal Plain, Dougherty Plain, and Southern Pine Plains and Hills. Highly secretive and burrowing. Not documented in Alabama in over two decades despite surveys from 1992 to 1995. May persist in scattered remnants of intact habitat, which continue to decline through fire suppression, development, and conversion of forest type. **HIGHEST CONSERVATION CONCERN**.

Spotted Salamander *Ambystoma maculatum*. Uncommon to fairly common statewide except southern Coastal Plain and much of southern portions of Dougherty Plain and southern Pine Plains and Hills. Believed to be declining. Found predominantly in low hardwood forest where it breeds in woodland pools in winter. Low Conservation Concern. (**Fig. 89, p. 114**)

Marbled Salamander *Ambystoma opacum*. Fairly common and similar to spotted salamander in distribution, habits, and habitat requirements. Low Conservation Concern.

Mole Salamander *Ambystoma talpoideum*. Locally common to uncommon in Coastal Plain, with scattered populations known from Interior Plateau. Populations also known from southwestern Appalachians a few miles east of Georgia border, and expected in adjacent portions of northeastern Alabama. A burrowing salamander that breeds in winter in woodland pools. Low Conservation Concern.

Small-mouthed Salamander *Ambystoma texanum*. Poorly known in Interior Plateau and western two-thirds of Coastal Plain, where it may be largely confined to floodplains of rivers and larger streams. Extends eastward along Alabama River to Montgomery County. A winter-breeding, burrowing salamander; uses floodplain pools as breeding sites. Few records available from Alabama, where populations may be disjunct. MODERATE CONSERVATION CONCERN.

Eastern Tiger Salamander *Ambystoma tigrinum tigrinum*. Uncommon to rare in all major regions except possibly the Piedmont, from which records are lacking. Seldom encountered except at temporary ponds and woodland pools during winter breeding season, which may be December to March. Populations disjunct, and habitat requirements poorly understood. MODERATE CONSERVATION CONCERN. **(Fig. 90, p. 114)**

AMPHIUMAS - FAMILY AMPHIUMIDAE

Two-toed Amphiuma *Amphiuma means*. Uncommonly encountered in Coastal Plain, from Blackland Prairie southward. A large, eel-like salamander of weedy ponds and swamps. Seldom seen due to highly aquatic and burrowing habits. Low Conservation Concern.

One-toed Amphiuma *Amphiuma pholeter*. Rare, poorly known, and peripheral. Known from one locality each in Southern Coastal Plain and Southern Pine Plains and Hills. Potentially occurs in southern portion of Dougherty Plain. Inhabits deep liquid organic muck of alluvial soils along streams. **HIGH CONSERVATION CONCERN**.

Three-toed Amphiuma *Amphiuma tridactylum*. Uncommon in western portion of Coastal Plain, in Tombigbee, Black Warrior, and Alabama River drainages. Similar in habitat preferences to two-toed amphiuma. Low Conservation Concern.

GIANT SALAMANDERS - FAMILY CRYPTOBRANCHIDAE

Eastern Hellbender *Cryptobranchus alleganiensis alleganiensis*. Rare and possibly endangered in Interior Plateau and adjacent Southwestern Appalachians in Tennessee River drainage. A very large aquatic salamander of free-flowing rivers and streams. In Alabama, now confined to a few free-flowing Tennessee River tributaries. **HIGHEST CONSERVATION CONCERN**.

LUNGLESS SALAMANDERS - FAMILY PLETHODONTIDAE

Green Salamander *Aneides aeneus*. Rare to uncommon in Appalachian Plateau and Fall Line Hills and Transition Hills of extreme northwestern Alabama. Inhabits sandstone cliffs, bluffs, rock faces, and climbs trees. Populations thought to have declined throughout. **HIGH CONSERVATION CONCERN**.

Seepage Salamander *Desmognathus aeneus*. Rare and possibly threatened in western portion of Fall Line Hills from northern Hale County to southern Marion County, and eastern portion of Ridge and Valley and adjacent Piedmont. Highly secretive and dependent on shaded seepage areas in moist ravines of deciduous forest, where it lives beneath leaf litter. **HIGH CONSERVATION CONCERN**.

Apalachicola Dusky Salamander *Desmognathus apalachicolae*. Locally common in southeastern portion of Coastal Plain in Choctawhatchee and lower Chattahoochee River drainages. Occurs along edges of small seepage streams at bottoms of wooded ravines. Susceptible to siltation and pollution. Lowest Conservation Concern.

Southern Dusky Salamander *Desmognathus auriculatus*. Rapidly declining and possibly endangered due to unknown causes. In Alabama, known only from a few localities in southernmost tier of counties where it occurs in mucky areas in gum swamps, sphagnum bogs, and forested sluggish stream floodplains. **HIGHEST CONSERVATION CONCERN**.

Spotted Dusky Salamander *Desmognathus conanti*. Fairly common to common statewide except where absent in extreme southern portion of Dougherty Plain and Southern Pine Plains and Hills. Alabama populations were formerly considered to be northern dusky salamander, *D. fuscus*. Some Coastal Plain populations may represent an undescribed species. Inhabits a variety of damp habitats, especially ravine streams, springs, and seepage areas. Commonly called "spring lizard." Low Conservation Concern.

Seal Salamander *Desmognathus monticola*. Northern populations fairly common; southern populations uncommon to rare and may be declining. Northern distribution includes upper Appalachian Plateau Escarpment, Ridge and Valley, and Piedmont. Disjunct Coastal Plain populations known from one site in Fall Line Hills near Tennessee River, Autauga County, and several sites in Buhrstone/Lime Hills. Inhabits cool, shaded ravines with small permanent to semi-permanent streams. Low Conservation Concern.

Ocoee Salamander *Desmognathus ocoee*. Common, but extremely limited in distribution in northeastern portion of Southwestern Appalachians. Until recently (1996), Alabama populations were considered to be mountain dusky salamander, *D. ochrophaeus*. Known from fewer than 10 localities in Alabama. Inhabits cliff faces and damp talus areas, especially in mist zones of waterfalls. MODERATE CONSERVATION CONCERN.

Southern Two-lined Salamander *Eurycea cirrigera*. Common, essentially statewide. Inhabits a variety of shaded aquatic habitats, including springs, edges of small rocky streams, and (in Coastal Plain) floodplain pools. Lowest Conservation Concern.

Three-lined Salamander *Eurycea guttolineata*. Common throughout Coastal Plain, Piedmont, and Ridge and Valley, as well as portions of Southwestern Appalachians and Interior Plateau south of Tennessee River. Found in similar shaded habitats as two-lined salamander, including forested floodplains. Lowest Conservation Concern.

Long-tailed Salamander *Eurycea longicauda*. Fairly common north of Tennessee River in Interior Plateau and Southwestern Appalachians. Found near springs, seeps, and streams, often taking shelter under rocks. Lowest Conservation Concern.

Cave Salamander *Eurycea lucifuga*. Fairly common to common in Interior Plateau, Southwestern Appalachians, and Ridge and Valley. Most frequently encountered in, and around, caves and areas with karst topography. Lowest Conservation Concern. (**Fig. 91, p. 114**)

Dwarf Salamander complex *Eurycea quadridigitata* (includes two undescribed species). Until distributions and habitat requirements of two undescribed forms are better defined, descriptions are tenuous. Fairly common in much of Coastal Plain except northwestern portion. Found in damp pine woods, edges of floodplains and swamps, and forested seeps and ravines. MODERATE CONSERVATION CONCERN.

Tennessee Cave Salamander *Gyrinophilus palleucus palleucus*. Rare in Interior Plateau and Cumberland Plateau of Southwestern Appalachians. Restricted to limestone caves containing water. Approximately 20 Alabama localities, all in Tennessee River drainage. **HIGH CONSERVATION CONCERN**

Spring Salamander *Gyrinophilus porphyriticus* ssp. Uncommon in all regions above Fall Line Hills except for Interior Plateau where it is apparently absent. Somewhat spotty distribution. Includes three intergrading subspecies, *G. p. porphyriticus* (northern spring salamander), *G. p. duryi* (Kentucky spring salamander), and *G. p. dunni* (Carolina spring salamander). Found in, and near, caves, springs, and seeps. Low Conservation Concern.

Four-toed Salamander *Hemidactylium scutatum*. Uncommon statewide, but possibly less secure in Coastal Plain, where it may be more locally distributed in disjunct populations. Secretive and infrequently encountered. Inhabits wet forested areas with sphagnum, often in stream floodplains. Alabama distribution and ecology poorly understood. Low Conservation Concern.

Red Hills Salamander *Phaeognathus hubrichti*. Threatened, but may be locally common under optimal conditions. Entire global distribution confined to five Alabama counties in Buhrstone/Lime Hills ("Red Hills"). Secretive, inhabits burrows on forested bluff and ravine slopes. Eliminated from many formerly inhabited sites by habitat disturbance. **Designated the official state amphibian by the Alabama Legislature. Listed as *threatened* by the U.S. Fish and Wildlife Service. HIGH CONSERVATION CONCERN.**

Slimy Salamander complex (three species). Formerly considered a single species, *Plethodon glutinosus*, these very similar species now known to be genetically distinct. At

Fig. 80. Oak Toad, *Bufo quercicus*, **p. 105.**
Photo–John Jensen

Fig. 81. Southern Toad, *Bufo terrestris*,
p. 105. *Photo–Mark Bailey*

Fig. 82. Northern Cricket Frog, *Acris
crepitans crepitans*, **p. 105.** *Photo–John Jensen*

Fig. 83. Barking Treefrog, *Hyla gratiosa*,
p. 106. *Photo–Mark Bailey*

Fig. 84. Northern Spring Peeper,
Pseudacris crucifer crucifer, **p. 106.**
Photo–John Jensen

Fig. 85. Ornate Chorus Frog, *Pseudacris
ornata,* **p. 107.** *Photo–John Jensen*

Fig. 86. American Bullfrog,
Rana catesbeiana, **p. 108.**
Photo–Mark Bailey

Fig. 87. Pickerel Frog, *Rana palustris,*
p. 108. *Photo—John Jensen*

Fig, 88. Wood Frog, *Rana sylvatica,*
p. 109. *Photo—John Jensen*

Fig. 89. Spotted Salamander,
Ambystoma maculatum, **p. 109.**
Photo—Mark Bailey

Fig. 90. Eastern Tiger Salamander,
Ambystoma tigrinum tigrinum, **p. 110.**
Photo—John Jensen

Fig. 91. Cave Salamander, *Eurycea*
lucifuga, **p. 112.** *Photo—John Jensen*

Fig. 92. Southern Red-backed
Salamander, *Plethodon serratus,* **p. 117.**
Photo—John Jensen

Fig. 93. Gulf Coast Mud Salamander,
Pseudotriton montanus flavissimus, **p. 117.**
Photo—John Jensen

Fig. 94. Northern Red Salamander,
Pseudotriton ruber ruber, **p. 117.**
Photo—John Jensen

Fig. 95. American Alligator, *Alligator mississippiensis,* **p. 119.** *Photo–Malcolm Pierson*

Fig. 97. Eastern Fence Lizard, *Sceloporus undulatus,* **p. 120.** *Photo–Mark Bailey*

Fig. 96. Eastern Glass Lizard, *Ophisaurus ventralis,* **p. 119.** *Photo–Eric Soehren*

Fig. 98. Scarlet Snake, *Cemophora coccinea,* **p. 121.** Photo–John Jensen

Fig. 99. Black Racer, *Coluber constrictor ssp.,* **p. 121.** Photo–John Jensen

Fig. 100. Mud Snake, *Farancia abacura ssp.,* **p. 122.** *Photo–John Jensen*

Fig. 101. Eastern Coachwhip, *Masticophis flagellum flagellum,* **p. 124.** *Photo–John Jensen*

Fig. 102. Queen Snake, *Regina septemvittata,* **p. 126.** *Photo–John Jensen*

Fig. 103. DeKay's Brown Snake, *Storeria dekayi ssp.,* **p. 126.** *Photo–John Jensen*

Fig. 104. Eastern Garter Snake, *Thamnophis sirtalis sirtalis,* **p. 127.** *Photo–Mark Bailey*

Fig. 105. Copperhead, *Agkistrodon contortrix ssp.,* **p. 127.** *Photo–Mark Bailey*

Fig. 106. Eastern Chicken Turtle, *Deirochelys reticularia reticularia,* **p. 129.** *Photo–John Jensen*

Fig. 107. Escambia Map Turtle, *Graptemys ernsti,* **p. 130.** *Photo–Mark Bailey*

Fig. 108. Eastern Box Turtle, *Terrapene carolina ssp.,* **p. 131.** *Photo–Mark Bailey*

Fig. 109. Eastern Spiny Softshell, *Apalone spinifera aspera,* **p. 132.** *Photo–John Jensen*

least one representative found in every Alabama county. Identification based on appearance is impossible. Found in wide variety of habitats, often in rotting logs and under rocks. The following distribution descriptions are approximate.

Northern Slimy Salamander *Plethodon glutinosus*. Common. Eastern Alabama, from Southwestern Appalachians south to Fall Line Hills. Lowest Conservation Concern.

Southeastern Slimy Salamander *Plethodon grobmani*. Common. Coastal Plain east of Alabama River. Lowest Conservation Concern.

Mississippi Slimy Salamander *Plethodon mississippi*. Common. Coastal Plain west and north of Alabama River, including western portions of adjacent Southwestern Appalachians and Interior Plateau. Lowest Conservation Concern.

Southern Red-backed Salamander *Plethodon serratus*. Poorly known. Documented from a few localities in upper Ridge and Valley near Anniston. May occur in adjacent Talladega Uplands of the Piedmont. Easily confused with southern zigzag and Webster's salamanders. MODERATE CONSERVATION CONCERN. (**Fig. 92, p. 114**)

Southern Zigzag Salamander *Plethodon ventralis*. Common. Until 1997, Alabama populations were known as northern zigzag salamander, *P. dorsalis*. Found in Interior Plateau and Southwestern Appalachians. Inhabits damp, rocky deciduous forest. Lowest Conservation Concern.

Webster's Salamander *Plethodon websteri*. Found in all regions above Fall Line Hills except Interior Plateau. Similar in habits and appearance to southern zigzag salamander. A disjunct Coastal Plain population reported from Buhrstone/Lime Hills has not been confirmed in many years. Lowest Conservation Concern.

Gulf Coast Mud Salamander *Pseudotriton montanus flavissimus*. Uncommon and secretive. Alabama distribution poorly understood, but most records are in Ridge and Valley, Piedmont, and Coastal Plain. Inhabits mucky seeps along stream floodplains, and is rarely encountered above surface. Low Conservation Concern. (**Fig. 93, p. 114**)

Northern Red Salamander *Pseudotriton ruber ruber*. Fairly common above Fall Line Hills. Intergrades with southern red salamander in upper portions of Coastal Plain. Inhabits stream margins and springs in forested areas. Low Conservation Concern. (**Fig. 94, p. 114**)

Southern Red Salamander *Pseudotriton ruber vioscai*. Uncommon to rare. Believed to be declining. Southern portion of Dougherty Plain and Southern Pine Plains and Hills of Coastal Plain. Intergrades with northern red salamander north of this region. Associated with springs, seeps, and other damp habitats. MODERATE CONSERVATION CONCERN.

WATERDOGS AND MUDPUPPIES - FAMILY PROTEIDAE

Black Warrior Waterdog *Necturus alabamensis*. Threatened. Restricted to upper Black Warrior River Basin in Southwestern Appalachians. Occurs only in Alabama. A permanently aquatic salamander of medium to large rocky streams. Surveys of 59 potential streams in the 1990s yielded this species at only 14 of 113 sites. Status in reservoirs unknown. Rarely encountered except during winter and early spring when may be found in submerged leaf beds. Susceptible to water quality degradation. **Currently a candidate for federal listing. HIGH CONSERVATION CONCERN.**

Gulf Coast Waterdog *Necturus beyeri*. Uncommon to common in suitable habitats. Widespread in Mobile Bay drainage of Coastal Plain. Occurs in lower densities in Ridge and Valley and Piedmont, possibly due to habitat limitations. Similar in habits to Black Warrior waterdog, but may be less dependent on rocks and crevices for shelter. Low Conservation Concern.

Common Mudpuppy *Necturus maculosus*. Uncommon. Restricted to Tennessee River drainage of Interior Plateau, Transition Hills of extreme northwestern Coastal Plain, and Southwestern Appalachians. Occurs in Tennessee River, its impoundments, and medium to large tributaries. Low Conservation Concern.

Unnamed Waterdog *Necturus* sp. cf. *beyeri*. A poorly known but locally common mudpuppy of lesser Gulf drainages from Mobile Bay eastward. Absent from greater Mobile Bay drainage. May ultimately be referable to *N. lodingi*. Low Conservation Concern.

NEWTS - FAMILY SALAMANDRIDAE

Eastern Newt *Notophthalmus viridescens* ssp. Fairly common statewide in all regions. Includes subspecies *N. v. viridescens* (red-spotted newt), *N. v. louisianensis* (central newt), and intergrades. Inhabits a variety of aquatic and terrestrial habitats, depending on life cycle. Larvae and adults are aquatic, and juveniles (efts) are terrestrial. Lowest Conservation Concern.

SIRENS - FAMILY SIRENIDAE

Lesser Siren *Siren intermedia*. Common. Widespread in Coastal Plain. Includes subspecies *S. i. intermedia* (eastern lesser siren), *S. i. nettingi* (western lesser siren), and intergrades. May include more than one species. An aquatic eel-like salamander of ponds, swamps, and sluggish streams. Lowest Conservation Concern.

Greater Siren *Siren lacertina*. Poorly known. Known from only one location in Alabama, a pond in Southern Hilly Gulf Coastal Plain of Henry County. A large aquatic eel-like salamander of ponds, oxbows, and sluggish streams. MODERATE CONSERVATION CONCERN.

Undescribed Siren *Siren* sp. Poorly known. A large undescribed siren of extreme southern Coastal Plain. Known in Alabama from two localities in Southern Pine Plains and Hills: Fish River, Baldwin County and Lake Jackson, Covington County. Likely similar in habits to Greater Siren. MODERATE CONSERVATION CONCERN.

REPTILES
CLASS REPTILIA

CROCODILIANS
ORDER CROCODYLIA
ALLIGATORS - FAMILY ALLIGATORIDAE

American Alligator *Alligator mississippiensis*. Fairly common in many Coastal Plain lakes, rivers, and associated aquatic habitats, and common in Mobile-Tensaw Delta. Generally absent above Fall Line Hills except for an introduced Tennessee River population near Wheeler National Wildlife Refuge. Although still absent from portions of historic distribution, alligators have rebounded remarkably from low numbers since 1960s due to federal and state protection. Low Conservation Concern. **(Fig. 95, p. 115)**

LIZARDS
ORDER SQUAMATA, SUBORDER LACERTILIA
GLASS LIZARDS - FAMILY ANGUIDAE

Slender Glass Lizard *Ophisaurus attenuatus*. Uncommon to rare essentially statewide, this legless lizard is infrequently encountered and believed to be declining. Most known occurrences are from above Fall Line Hills. Generally associated with relatively dry, open habitats. MODERATE CONSERVATION CONCERN.

Mimic Glass Lizard *Ophisaurus mimicus*. Uncommon to rare, secretive, and possibly threatened throughout. A recently described (1987) legless lizard of southeastern coastal flatwoods. Three documented occurrences from southern portion of Alabama's Dougherty Plain and Southern Pine Plains and Hills. Preferred pine flatwoods habitat now much reduced. **HIGH CONSERVATION CONCERN.**

Eastern Glass Lizard *Ophisaurus ventralis*. Uncommon to rare in Coastal Plain, Ridge and Valley, and Piedmont. Formerly common in Coastal Plain, now appears to have experienced a marked decline and is rare to absent in many areas. Typically encountered in mesic habitats and under debris. MODERATE CONSERVATION CONCERN. **(Fig. 96, p. 115)**

GECKOES - FAMILY GEKKONIDAE

Mediterranean House Gecko *Hemidactylus turcicus*. **Exotic**. Found locally in, and near, buildings of urban areas, especially in southern half of state. Nocturnal, and may be seen feeding on insects near lights after dark.

Indo-Pacific Gecko *Hemidactylus garnotii*. **Exotic**. Similar in distribution and habits to *H. turcicus*. Parthenogenetic (unisexual).

SPINY LIZARDS AND ALLIES - FAMILY PHRYNOSOMATIDAE

Texas Horned Lizard *Phrynosoma cornutum*. **Exotic**. Reportedly established along the coast in some localities. May occur in relatively open, sandy areas.

Eastern Fence Lizard *Sceloporus undulatus*. Common and statewide in occurrence. Prefers dry, open woodlands and rocky areas. A conspicuous lizard that basks in open areas and runs when approached. Includes subspecies *S. u. undulatus* (southern fence lizard) and *S. u. hyacinthinus* (northern fence lizard). Low Conservation Concern. **(Fig. 97, p. 115)**

ANOLES - FAMILY POLYCHRIDAE

Green Anole *Anolis carolinensis*. Common and statewide in occurrence, but relatively scarce in extreme northern portion. A climbing lizard that inhabits a variety of vegetated habitats, including residential areas. Many know this conspicuous color-changing lizard as "chameleon." Lowest Conservation Concern.

Brown Anole *Anolis sagrei*. **Exotic**. Recently reported from a few locations in extreme southern Alabama, this Caribbean species is well established in Florida. Similar in habits to *A. carolinensis*.

SKINKS - FAMILY SCINCIDAE

Coal Skink *Eumeces anthracinus* ssp. Rare and infrequently encountered. Widely distributed, but limits of distribution incompletely known. Most records from Coastal Plain, but also documented from Southwestern Appalachians and Ridge and Valley. Inhabits hilly terrain in mixed pine-hardwood forest, usually near water. Likely inhabits pitcher plant bogs in southern Alabama, as do nearby populations in Florida Panhandle. Some Alabama populations are *E. a. pluvialis* (southern coal skink) while others are intergradient with *E. a. anthracinus* (northern coal skink). **HIGH CONSERVATION CONCERN.**

Northern Mole Skink *Eumeces egregius similis*. Uncommon. Known from east of the Tombigbee and Black Warrior Rivers in the Coastal Plain, Piedmont, and Ridge and Valley. Alabama's only red-tailed skink, this secretive burrowing lizard is rarely seen above ground. Thought to be declining. Low Conservation Concern.

Common Five-lined Skink *Eumeces fasciatus*. Common and statewide in a variety of mesic habitats. Frequently encountered, often in, or near, rotting logs and stumps, rocks, and trash piles. Lowest Conservation Concern.

Southeastern Five-lined Skink *Eumeces inexpectatus*. Formerly common statewide but believed to be declining and potentially threatened, especially in southern Alabama. Reasons for downward trend unknown. Prefers relatively open dry forestlands. Easily confused with common five-lined skink. **HIGH CONSERVATION CONCERN.**

Broad-headed Skink *Eumeces laticeps*. Common statewide and frequently encountered in areas with rotting logs, stumps, and tree cavities. Alabama's largest and most arboreal skink. Low Conservation Concern.

Ground Skink *Scincella lateralis*. Fairly common statewide, but population densities have declined markedly in the past quarter century. Inhabits most terrestrial forested habitats. Low Conservation Concern.

RACERUNNERS - FAMILY TEIIDAE

Eastern Six-lined Racerunner *Cnemidophorus sexlineatus sexlineatus*. Uncommon to locally fairly common statewide. Most frequently encountered in southern portions of Alabama, but considerably less common than in the past. A fast-moving conspicuous resident of a variety of dry, open habitats, especially areas of sandy soils. Decline could be related to decreased burning. MODERATE CONSERVATION CONCERN.

SNAKES
ORDER SQUAMATA, SUBORDER SERPENTES
COLUBRID SNAKES - FAMILY COLUBRIDAE

Worm Snake *Carphophis amoenus* ssp. Fairly common. Known from most regions except portions of Coastal Plain, Piedmont, and Ridge and Valley. A secretive small woodland snake of mesic deciduous forest. Includes subspecies *C. a. amoenus* (Eastern worm snake) and *C. a. helenae* (midwest worm snake). Lowest Conservation Concern.

Scarlet Snake *Cemophora coccinea*. Fairly common statewide. A small secretive snake of forested habitat types, especially areas with loose, well-drained soils. Often mistaken for coral snakes or scarlet kingsnakes due to colorful banded pattern. Thought to be declining throughout much of its distribution. Lowest Conservation Concern. **(Fig. 98, p. 115)**

Black Racer *Coluber constrictor* ssp. Common statewide, but declining in many areas. A familiar diurnal species that occurs in virtually all terrestrial habitats. Most frequently encountered in open forest and forest edges, and along brushy margins of aquatic habitats. Includes subspecies *C. c. constrictor* (northern black racer) and *C. c. priapus* (southern black racer). Low Conservation Concern. **(Fig. 99, p. 115)**

Ring-necked Snake *Diadophis punctatus* ssp. Fairly common statewide, but less abundant than in the past. A frequently encountered small woodland snake. Alabama populations are intergradient combinations involving two or all of three subspecies, *D. p. punctatus* (southern ring-necked snake), *D. p. edwardsi* (northern ring-necked snake) and *D. p. stictogenys* (Mississippi ring-necked snake). Lowest Conservation Concern.

Eastern Indigo Snake *Drymarchon couperi*. Endangered/**Possibly extirpated**. Historically reported from Southern Pine Plains and Hills in Mobile, Baldwin, and Covington Counties in extreme southern Alabama, but not documented from natural populations in state since 1954. Recent reports *may* be from several experimental introductions in late 1970s and 1980s. Further investigation into possibly extant natural populations is needed, especially in Mobile County. **Listed as *threatened* by the U.S. Fish and Wildlife Service. HIGHEST CONSERVATION CONCERN**.

Corn Snake *Elaphe guttata guttata*. Uncommon to locally fairly common statewide. While still fairly common in northern Alabama, Coastal Plain populations have declined precipitously. Somewhat arboreal, but less so than related rat snakes. Corn snakes nest in loose soil or organic debris, are mainly nocturnal, and are found in a variety of terrestrial habitats that support sizeable small rodent populations. MODER-ATE CONSERVATION CONCERN.

Rat Snake *Elaphe obsoleta* ssp. Fairly common statewide. This large arboreal snake, known to many as "chicken snake," has not declined like corn snakes. Rat snakes may nest high in tree cavities, a position that may reduce mortality from fire ants and other ground-foraging predators. Occurs in most terrestrial habitats, and occasionally may be found in, or near, forested suburbs. Populations in extreme northeastern Alabama are *E. o. obsoleta* (black rat snake), while others, except intergrades, are *E. o. spiloides* (gray rat snake). Lowest Conservation Concern.

Mud Snake *Farancia abacura* ssp. Uncommon to fairly common throughout Coastal Plain, wherever suitable habitat is found. Also known from Interior Plateau near Tennessee River. A large and secretive semi-aquatic snake of beaver swamps, ponds, floodplains, and sluggish streams. Includes two intergrading subspecies, *F. a. abacura* (eastern mud snake) and *F. a. reinwardti* (western mud snake). Low Conservation Concern. **(Fig. 100, p. 115)**

Rainbow Snake *Farancia erytrogramma erytrogramma*. Rare and possibly threatened. Seldom encountered in known distribution, which includes Coastal Plain and possibly adjacent regions above Fall Line Hills. Recorded from fewer than 10 locations in Alabama. A large semi-aquatic burrowing snake of rivers, large creeks, and occasionally ponds. **HIGH CONSERVATION CONCERN**.

Eastern Hog-nosed Snake *Heterodon platirhinos*. Uncommon to rare in many places where formerly common. Statewide in distribution. Often called "spreading adder," this familiar snake is apparently declining for unknown reasons. Typically inhabits fields, open woods, and disturbed areas. MODERATE CONSERVATION CONCERN.

Southern Hog-nosed Snake *Heterodon simus*. Endangered/**Possibly extirpated**. Known from portions of Coastal Plain and Ridge and Valley. A small secretive snake of sandy woods, fields, and other upland habitats. Although at least 10 records exist, none are known since 1975. Reasons for apparent decline unknown. Southern hognose snakes are declining throughout their distribution, but still occur in parts of southern Georgia, South Carolina, and Florida, and may persist in very low numbers in Alabama. **HIGHEST CONSERVATION CONCERN.**

Prairie Kingsnake *Lampropeltis calligaster calligaster.* Peripheral and uncommon in Interior Plateau, and possibly Appalachian Plateau north of Tennessee River. Known from Madison County, and may occur in Limestone and Jackson Counties. A secretive and poorly known burrowing snake of open woodlands and grassy areas. **HIGH CONSERVATION CONCERN.**

Mole Kingsnake *Lampropeltis calligaster rhombomaculata.* Uncommon to rare in Coastal Plain, uncommon elsewhere. Thought to occur statewide, but records are lacking from substantial areas. A secretive burrowing snake of woods and fields. Occasionally found above ground after dark, especially after rains. MODERATE CONSERVATION CONCERN.

Eastern Kingsnake *Lampropeltis getula getula.* Rare to uncommon, and possibly threatened. Found in south-central and eastern portion of Coastal Plain and adjacent Piedmont. Also known from Dauphin Island. A large, diurnal, conspicuous grounddwelling snake of most terrestrial habitats. Formerly one of Alabama's most commonly encountered snakes, it and speckled kingsnake have declined markedly for reasons not well understood. **HIGH CONSERVATION CONCERN.**

Speckled Kingsnake *Lampropeltis getula holbrooki.* Rare to uncommon, and possibly threatened. Coastal Plain inhabitant, except for those portions occupied by eastern and black kingsnakes. Attains its greatest population densities in Blackland Prairie. This subspecies is similar in both habits and conservation status to eastern kingsnake. **HIGH CONSERVATION CONCERN.**

Black Kingsnake *Lampropeltis getula nigra.* Fairly common above Fall Line Hills in northern Alabama. Similar in habits to eastern and speckled kingsnakes, but apparently has not declined to extent of Coastal Plain forms of *L. getula.* Low Conservation Concern.

Scarlet Kingsnake *Lampropeltis triangulum elapsoides.* Uncommon to fairly common. Presumed statewide in distribution, but many areas lack records. Secretive and rarely seen except in spring. Along with scarlet snake, sometimes confused with the coral snake due to its similar colorful banded pattern. Low Conservation Concern.

Red Milk Snake *Lampropeltis triangulum syspila.* Uncommon and infrequently encountered in northwestern portion of Appalachian Plateau. Inhabits woodland, often near rocky areas. A secretive snake usually found in, and under, rotting logs, and occasionally seen on roads at night. Intergrades eastward with eastern milk snake. MODERATE CONSERVATION CONCERN.

Eastern Milk Snake *Lampropeltis triangulum triangulum*. Uncommon and infrequently encountered in eastern portions of Appalachian Plateau, including Lookout Mountain. Similar in habits and habitat preference to red milk snake, with which it intergrades westward in DeKalb and Jackson Counties. MODERATE CONSERVATION CONCERN.

Eastern Coachwhip *Masticophis flagellum flagellum*. Formerly common, now declining and generally rare to uncommon, especially in northern Alabama. A large conspicuous snake of sparse grassy woods and fields from Tennessee River to coastal dunes. While some northern populations are feared extirpated, a few areas of scrubby or frequently burned Coastal Plain habitats still support fair numbers. MODERATE CONSERVATION CONCERN. **(Fig. 101, p. 115)**

Gulf Saltmarsh Snake *Nerodia clarkii clarkii*. Uncommon to fairly common in suitable habitat, which is limited. This coastal water snake has specialized habitat requirements and has declined due to destruction and degradation of salt marshes in both Baldwin and Mobile Counties. Formerly considered a subspecies of *N. fasciata*. MODERATE CONSERVATION CONCERN.

Mississippi Green Water Snake *Nerodia cyclopion*. Peripheral and fairly common in Southern Coastal Plain from Tensaw Delta westward. A large snake of forested swamps, oxbows, and sluggish, tree-lined streams, where it may be found as far as 97 kilometers (60 miles) inland from coastal areas. Less frequently encountered in lower Mobile Bay area, where forest gives way to marsh and grass flats. MODERATE CONSERVATION CONCERN.

Plain-bellied Water Snake *Nerodia erythrogaster* ssp. Common statewide. A large snake of most permanently aquatic habitats, especially swamps, sluggish streams, and weedy lakes and ponds. Chiefly nocturnal. Includes two intergrading subspecies, *N. e. erythrogaster* (red-bellied water snake) and *N. e. flavigaster* (yellow-bellied water snake). Lowest Conservation Concern.

Southern Water Snake *Nerodia fasciata* ssp. Common across southern portions of Coastal Plain. Inhabits most permanently aquatic habitats, especially sinkhole ponds and streams with abundant vegetation. Includes subspecies *N. f. fasciata* (banded water snake), *N. f. confluens* (broad-banded water snake), and *N. f. pictiventris* (Florida water snake) and intergrades. Lowest Conservation Concern.

Florida Green Water Snake *Nerodia floridana*. Peripheral and locally common in Southern Coastal Plain from Mobile Bay eastward in Baldwin County. Similar in appearance to Mississippi green water snake, but inhabits marshes and wet prairie habitats instead of forested wetlands. Not known more than 48 kilometers (30 miles) inland from coastal areas, and susceptible to local extirpations from hurricanes. MODERATE CONSERVATION CONCERN.

Diamond-backed Water Snake *Nerodia rhombifer*. Fairly common to common in western portions of Coastal Plain, extending eastward along Tennessee and Tallapoosa drainages to Macon County. A heavy-bodied large snake of river sloughs, lakes, and swamps. Low Conservation Concern.

Midland Water Snake *Nerodia sipedon pleuralis*. Common statewide, except southernmost portions of Coastal Plain, where apparently confined to immediate vicinity of Conecuh, Yellow, and Choctawhatchee Rivers. A conspicuous inhabitant of ponds, lakes, and streams, and the most frequently encountered water snake in the northern two-thirds of Alabama. Lowest Conservation Concern.

Brown Water Snake *Nerodia taxispilota*. Fairly common in southeastern portion of Coastal Plain. Most frequently encountered in streams and stream impoundments. Large and active by day, it basks conspicuously and is frequently subject to human persecution. Low Conservation Concern.

Rough Green Snake *Opheodrys aestivus*. Uncommon to fairly common statewide. Formerly more common, this familiar slender and docile snake is found in a variety of heavily vegetated terrestrial habitats, including overhanging branches around lakes and streams. Reasons for apparent decline unknown. Low Conservation Concern.

Black Pine Snake *Pituophis melanoleucus lodingi*. Rare and possibly endangered in southern Pine Plains and Hills region west of Mobile Bay. Also known from Buhrstone/Lime Hills of Clarke County. Apparently extirpated from large area around Mobile. Intergrades east of Mobile Bay with Florida pine snake. A large snake of dry, periodically burned open pine or mixed pine-scrub oak forest with abundant ground-cover vegetation. **Currently a candidate for federal listing. HIGHEST CONSERVATION CONCERN**.

Northern Pine Snake *Pituophis melanoleucus melanoleucus*. Rare and possibly threatened. Populations may be disjunct and very localized in Ridge and Valley, Appalachian Plateau, and Interior Plateau. A large upland snake of relatively open, periodically burned pine or mixed pine-hardwood forest and adjacent clearings in sandy or gravelly uplands. **HIGH CONSERVATION CONCERN**.

Florida Pine Snake *Pituophis melanoleucus mugitus*. Threatened in southern portion of Coastal Plain east of Mobile Bay. Also known from Southern Hilly Gulf Coastal Plain region of Russell County in extreme eastern Alabama. Individuals from Escambia and Baldwin Counties are intergradient with black pine snake, and a Fall Line Hills population in Elmore County appears to be intergradient with northern pine snake. A large snake of open, periodically burned pine forest with abundant groundcover. Frequently associated with burrows of gopher tortoise and southeastern pocket gopher. **HIGH CONSERVATION CONCERN.**

Glossy Crayfish Snake *Regina rigida sinicola*. Fairly common in Coastal Plain, except extreme northwestern portions. A small secretive snake of ponds and swamps. Believed to be stable throughout most of its distribution. Lowest Conservation Concern.

Queen Snake *Regina septemvittata*. Fairly common to uncommon. Nearly statewide, but apparently absent from Coastal Plain west of Tombigbee River, and from southern portions of Baldwin County. Believed to be declining, especially in southern Alabama. A small slender water snake of streams and stream impoundments, often seen basking on limbs overhanging water. MODERATE CONSERVATION CONCERN. **(Fig. 102, p. 116)**

Pine Woods Snake *Rhadinaea flavilata*. Peripheral and rare in southern Coastal Plain and southern Pine Plains and Hills of southwestern Alabama, where known from only a few localities in Mobile, Washington, and Baldwin Counties. A small secretive snake of damp pine flatwoods; occasionally appears in residential areas. MODERATE CONSERVATION CONCERN.

North Florida Swamp Snake *Seminatrix pygaea pygaea*. Peripheral and rare in extreme southern Coastal Plain. Known from three Covington County localities and one locality west of Conecuh River in Escambia County that represents the northwestern limit of the known United States' distribution. A small secretive snake of swamps and weedy ponds. **HIGH CONSERVATION CONCERN.**

DeKay's Brown Snake *Storeria dekayi* ssp. Common essentially statewide, but lack of records from much of southeastern Coastal Plain may reflect actual scarcity or absence there. One of Alabama's most common snakes north of Buhrstone/Lime Hills. Often encountered around human dwellings and erroneously called "ground rattler." Includes three intergrading subspecies, *S. d. dekayi* (northern brown snake), *S. d. limnetes* (marsh brown snake), and *S. d. wrightorum* (midland brown snake). Lowest Conservation Concern. **(Fig. 103, p. 116)**

Northern Red-bellied Snake *Storeria occipitomaculata occipitomaculata*. Fairly common statewide. A small, secretive ground-dwelling snake of mesic forested habitats where soils are moderately heavy. Often found under logs, rocks, and other objects. Believed to be declining in many areas. Lowest Conservation Concern.

Southeastern Crowned Snake *Tantilla coronata*. Fairly common statewide, but thought to be declining. A small, secretive ground-dwelling snake of dry woodland ridges and hillsides. Often found under rocks, logs, and in rotting stumps. Low Conservation Concern.

Eastern Ribbon Snake *Thamnophis sauritus sauritus*. Fairly common statewide, but not as frequently encountered as in the past. A semi-aquatic snake of marshes, beaver swamps, lake and stream margins, and wet meadows. Low Conservation Concern.

Eastern Garter Snake *Thamnophis sirtalis sirtalis*. Fairly common statewide. Very generalized in habitat preferences, and found in most terrestrial habitat types. Frequently encountered, especially in northern Alabama. Low Conservation Concern. **(Fig. 104, p. 116)**

Rough Earth Snake *Virginia striatula*. Fairly common across most of Alabama, and present in all regions except Interior Plateau. Absent from northeastern portions of Appalachian Plateau and Ridge and Valley. Inhabits relatively drier woodlands than smooth earth snake. More commonly encountered in Coastal Plain, and believed to have declined in recent decades. Lowest Conservation Concern.

Smooth Earth Snake *Virginia valeriae* ssp. Common statewide. Usually inhabits more mesic woodlands than rough earth snake, but both may occur together, and are very similar in appearance. Most Alabama populations are *V. v. valeriae* (eastern smooth earth snake), but western populations may show influence of intergradation with *V. v. elegans* (western smooth earth snake). Lowest Conservation Concern.

CORAL SNAKES - FAMILY ELAPIDAE

Eastern Coral Snake *Micrurus fulvius*. Rare and possibly threatened. A colorful, venomous snake principally occurring in Coastal Plain from Buhrstone/Lime Hills southward, but also known from disjunct localities in southern Ridge and Valley (Bibb and St. Clair Counties) and Piedmont (Coosa County). Spends much time underground, emerging to forage in early morning and late afternoon. Inhabits a variety of terrestrial habitats having loose, friable soils. Few recent observations may indicate that this secretive species has declined in Alabama. Two more common and similarly patterned nonvenomous snakes, scarlet kingsnakes and scarlet snakes, are frequently mistaken for eastern coral snakes. **HIGH CONSERVATION CONCERN.**

PIT VIPERS - FAMILY VIPERIDAE

Copperhead *Agkistrodon contortrix* ssp. Common statewide. Most frequently encountered venomous snake in Alabama. Inhabits a wide variety of upland habitats. May be increasing in parts of Coastal Plain, especially where fire is suppressed. Includes subspecies *A. c. contortrix* (southern copperhead) and *A. c. mokeson* (northern copperhead). Lowest Conservation Concern. **(Fig. 105, p. 116)**

Cottonmouth *Agkistrodon piscivorus* ssp. Common statewide. Occurs in most aquatic habitats, but reaches greatest abundance in Coastal Plain swamps. The only venomous aquatic snake in North America. Includes subspecies *A. p. piscivorus* (eastern cottonmouth), *A. p. conanti* (Florida cottonmouth), and *A. p. leucostoma* (western cottonmouth). Lowest Conservation Concern.

Eastern Diamondback Rattlesnake *Crotalus adamanteus*. Uncommon to rare and possibly threatened. Alabama's largest venomous snake. Exploits a variety of upland habitats from extreme southern portion of Southern Hilly Gulf Coastal Plain to Gulf Coast, favoring relatively dry pine flatwoods and longleaf pine-turkey oak sandhills. Overwinters in stump holes and gopher tortoise burrows, where it is vulnerable to "gassing" by snake hunters. Infrequently encountered where formerly common, and now absent from many areas of historic occurrence. **HIGH CONSERVATION CONCERN.**

Timber Rattlesnake *Crotalus horridus*. Fairly common to uncommon statewide, except for extreme southern Alabama. Commonly called canebrake or velvet-tail rattlesnake. A large venomous snake of upland and lowland forested habitats, especially in sparsely settled areas. Declining or absent from many formerly inhabited areas because of direct persecution, habitat fragmentation, and gradual loss of deciduous and mixed forest types, but still apparently secure in some areas. Low Conservation Concern.

Pigmy Rattlesnake *Sistrurus miliarius* ssp. Uncommon to rare. Statewide in distribution, but rarely encountered in recent years except in extreme southern Alabama. Believed to be declining. Inhabits a variety of upland habitats. Often called "ground rattler" by those who recognize it. Includes subspecies *S. m. miliarius* (Carolina pigmy rattlesnake), *S. m. barbouri* (dusky pigmy rattlesnake), and *S. m. streckeri* (western pigmy rattlesnake). MODERATE CONSERVATION CONCERN.

TURTLES
ORDER TESTUDINES
SEA TURTLES - FAMILY CHELONIIDAE

Loggerhead Sea Turtle *Caretta caretta*. Rare and endangered along Gulf Coast. Most frequently encountered sea turtle in Alabama's waters, and only one that regularly nests on Alabama beaches. Mainly carnivorous, but some vegetation is consumed. **Listed as *threatened* by the U.S. Fish and Wildlife Service. HIGHEST CONSERVATION CONCERN.**

Green Sea Turtle *Chelonia mydas*. Rare and endangered along Gulf Coast. Nesting in Alabama is rare. Small numbers of this herbivorous species, most often subadults, occur in state waters, but feeding areas of submerged grass beds are limited in Alabama.

Listed as *threatened* by the U.S. Fish and Wildlife Service. **HIGHEST CONSER-VATION CONCERN.**

Kemp's Ridley Sea Turtle *Lepidochelys kempii.* Rare and endangered along Gulf Coast. Although virtually entire population nests in Mexico and southern Texas, at least two nests have been documented in Alabama. An occasional visitor to Alabama waters, where it is sometimes caught in shrimp nets. Mostly carnivorous. **Listed as *endangered* by the U.S. Fish and Wildlife Service. HIGHEST CONSERVATION CONCERN.**

SNAPPING TURTLES - FAMILY CHELYDRIDAE

Common Snapping Turtle *Chelydra serpentina serpentina.* Common statewide. A large aquatic turtle of a wide variety of permanently aquatic habitats. Lowest Conservation Concern.

Alligator Snapping Turtle *Macrochelys temminckii.* Uncommon to rare in streams south of Tennessee River, and very rare in Tennessee River system. Most numerous in Coastal Plain. Inhabits rivers, oxbows, and sloughs, and occasionally occurs in medium-sized creeks. A very large turtle that is recovering from historic commercial harvest for food. **HIGH CONSERVATION CONCERN.**

LEATHERBACK SEA TURTLES - FAMILY DERMOCHELYIDAE

Leatherback Sea Turtle *Dermochelys coriacea.* Rare and endangered along Gulf Coast. An occasional visitor to Alabama waters, but not known to nest in state. Largest of sea turtles, feeding primarily on jellyfish. **Listed as *endangered* by the U.S. Fish and Wildlife Service. HIGHEST CONSERVATION CONCERN.**

EMYDID TURTLES - FAMILY EMYDIDAE

Painted Turtle *Chrysemys picta* ssp. Common to fairly common in Tennessee, Chattahoochee, and Mobile Bay drainages except portions of Black Warrior and Cahaba Rivers. Includes three intergrading subspecies, *C. p. picta* (eastern painted turtle), *C. p. dorsalis* (southern painted turtle), and *C. p. marginata* (midland painted turtle). Lowest Conservation Concern.

Eastern Chicken Turtle *Deirochelys reticularia reticularia.* Uncommon to locally common. Occurs throughout Coastal Plain and a portion of Ridge and Valley, where it is less frequently encountered. A turtle of semi-permanent shallow ponds, swamps, and borrow pits. Often moves on land, where it aestivates and sometimes overwinters under leaves. Low Conservation Concern. **(Fig. 106, p. 116)**

Barbour's Map Turtle *Graptemys barbouri.* Uncommon to fairly common in large streams of southeastern Alabama, where restricted to Chattahoochee and Choctawhatchee River systems. The Choctawhatchee River population only recently was discovered (1997). Greatest numbers occur along stream stretches with exposed limestone and abundant snags for basking. **HIGH CONSERVATION CONCERN.**

Escambia Map Turtle *Graptemys ernsti*. Fairly common to common, but limited to Escambia (Conecuh), Yellow, and Choctawhatchee River drainages. Relatively recently (1992) separated as species distinct from similar Alabama map turtle, *G. pulchra*. Occurs both in main channels of larger streams and in smaller tributaries. MODERATE CONSERVATION CONCERN. **(Fig. 107, p. 116)**

Northern Map Turtle *Graptemys geographica*. Uncommon to locally common in Interior Plateau, Appalachian Plateau, and Ridge and Valley. Absent from Coastal Plain, but occurs in Tennessee River system as well as upper Mobile Bay drainage (Black Warrior, Cahaba, and Coosa River systems). Inhabits rivers as well as smaller creeks. Low Conservation Concern.

Black-knobbed Sawback *Graptemys nigrinoda* ssp. Fairly common in Coastal Plain reaches of Alabama, Tombigbee, Black Warrior, Cahaba, Coosa, and Tallapoosa Rivers, but not as common as in past. Endemic to Alabama, except for a small portion of distribution in Mississippi. Includes subspecies *G. n. nigrinoda* (northern black-knobbed sawback) and *G. n. delticola* (southern black-knobbed sawback). MODERATE CONSERVATION CONCERN.

Ouachita Map Turtle *Graptemys ouachitensis*. Fairly common in Tennessee River reservoirs of northern Alabama. A large turtle of low-gradient streams and impoundments. Often seen basking in large numbers during spring. Lowest Conservation Concern.

Alabama Map Turtle *Graptemys pulchra*. Fairly common throughout Mobile Bay drainage. Mostly confined to Alabama, but ranges into Mississippi along Tombigbee River and into Georgia along Coosa River. Occurs both in main channels of larger streams and smaller tributaries. Low Conservation Concern.

Mississippi Diamondback Terrapin *Malaclemys terrapin pileata*. Rare and possibly endangered in coastal marshes of Mobile and Baldwin Counties. Formerly much more common, but declining due to variety of factors, including habitat degradation and mortality in crab traps. **HIGHEST CONSERVATION CONCERN.**

Alabama Red-bellied Turtle *Pseudemys alabamensis*. Endangered. Restricted to extreme lower portion of Mobile Bay drainage in Mobile and Baldwin Counties. Primarily a freshwater species, but may occur in moderately brackish water with abundant vegetation. **Designated the official state reptile by the Alabama Legislature. Listed as *endangered* by the U.S. Fish and Wildlife Service. HIGHEST CONSERVATION CONCERN.**

River Cooter *Pseudemys concinna concinna*. Common and statewide in rivers, lakes, and larger streams. Subspecific allocation of Alabama's populations is problematic. Lowest Conservation Concern.

Florida Cooter *Pseudemys concinna floridana*. Somewhat peripheral, and fairly common in southern portion of Coastal Plain. Taxonomic status questionable; many authorities consider it a full species, *P. floridana*. Occurs in vegetated lakes and ponds, as well as oxbows and vegetated margins of large sluggish streams. Lowest Conservation Concern.

Eastern Box Turtle *Terrapene carolina* ssp. Common to locally uncommon or rare statewide. While they have declined over past two decades, box turtles still are frequently encountered (especially after rains) in, or near, forested areas. Often seen on roads. Includes subspecies *T. c. carolina* (eastern box turtle) with influence of *T. c. major* (Gulf Coast box turtle) and *T. c. triunguis* (three-toed box turtle). Low Conservation Concern. **(Fig. 108, p. 116)**

Pond Slider *Trachemys scripta* ssp. Common statewide. Inhabits ponds, lakes, rivers, creeks, and swamps. Shows high tolerance to pollution. Includes two intergrading subspecies, *T. s. scripta* (yellow-bellied pond slider), *T. s. elegans* (red-eared pond slider), and possibly a third, *T. s. troosti* (Cumberland pond slider). Lowest Conservation Concern.

MUD AND MUSK TURTLES - FAMILY KINOSTERNIDAE

Eastern Mud Turtle *Kinosternon subrubrum* ssp. Common statewide in virtually all aquatic habitats except free-flowing creeks and rivers. Often wanders on land and is frequently seen crossing roads. Includes *K. s. subrubrum* (eastern mud turtle) and *K. s. hippocrepis* (Mississippi mud turtle), and intergrades between the two. Lowest Conservation Concern.

Razor-backed Musk Turtle *Sternotherus carinatus*. Peripheral in Escatawpa River and its tributaries in Mobile County. Possibly occurs in Red Creek in Washington County. Long known from Mississippi, it was first documented from Alabama in 1994. **HIGH CONSERVATION CONCERN.**

Flattened Musk Turtle *Sternotherus depressus*. Threatened. Restricted to upper Black Warrior River Basin in Southwestern Appalachians. Occurs only in Alabama. A small bottom-dwelling turtle of rocky rivers and large creeks. Extirpated from many formerly occupied streams. Although most habitat is degraded, a few sizeable populations remain in certain free-flowing streams with good water quality. Some reservoir habitats also are inhabited. **Listed as *threatened* by the U.S. Fish and Wildlife Service. HIGH CONSERVATION CONCERN.**

Loggerhead Musk Turtle *Sternotherus minor ssp*. Common essentially statewide, except for upper Black Warrior River system. A bottom-dwelling small turtle of creeks and rivers. Includes subspecies *S. m. minor* (loggerhead musk turtle) and *S. m. peltifer* (stripe-necked musk turtle) and intergrades. Low Conservation Concern.

Stinkpot *Sternotherus odoratus*. Common statewide in a variety of sluggish-water environments. More tolerant of habitat degradation than other members of its genus. Lowest Conservation Concern.

TORTOISES - FAMILY TESTUDINIDAE

Gopher Tortoise *Gopherus polyphemus*. Threatened. Greatly reduced from historic abundance; locally common in only a few protected areas. A large burrowing land turtle of open sandy areas in Coastal Plain south of Blackland Prairie, and extreme eastern Fall Line Hills. **Western population (Louisiana; Mississippi; and Mobile, Washington, and Choctaw Counties in Alabama) listed as *threatened* by the U.S. Fish and Wildlife Service. HIGH CONSERVATION CONCERN.**

SOFTSHELL TURTLES - FAMILY TRIONYCHIDAE

Florida Softshell *Apalone ferox*. Peripheral. Known from only a few localities in southern Baldwin County and extreme southern Coastal Plain in the Yellow and Choctawhatchee River systems. Inhabits sluggish streams, lakes, and ponds. MODERATE CONSERVATION CONCERN.

Midland Smooth Softshell *Apalone mutica mutica*. Common. Inhabits Tennessee Valley creeks, rivers, and impoundments. Low Conservation Concern.

Gulf Coast Smooth Softshell *Apalone mutica calvata*. Common. Coastal Plain portions of Mobile Bay drainage. Inhabits creeks, rivers, and impoundments in western portion of Coastal Plain. Low Conservation Concern.

Eastern Spiny Softshell *Apalone spinifera aspera*. Fairly common. Inhabits streams and lakes of Tennessee River drainage. Low Conservation Concern. **(Fig. 109, p. 116)**

Gulf Coast Spiny Softshell *Apalone spinifera spinifera*. Fairly common. Inhabits streams and lakes south of Tennessee River. Low Conservation Concern.

BIRDS

Great Egret
Ardea albea

INTRODUCTION

Bird watching has become a popular pastime for many people in the state and country. Not only do birds offer tremendous recreational, economic, and psychological benefit, they are often great indicators of environmental health. Decreasing populations and threats to certain species may indicate an ecosystem in peril. To ignore the warning signs may eventually be detrimental to our own species. To ensure that Alabama birdlife remains healthy and disparate, a diversity of healthy ecosystems in the state must be maintained and protected. The primary purpose of this checklist is to educate the reader about the birds that breed, overwinter, and migrate through our beautiful state. It is hoped that an increasing awareness of Alabama's birdlife will stimulate a greater appreciation and protection of Alabama's natural resources so that future generations will have an opportunity to enjoy and benefit from them.

The checklist is composed of 420 species that comprise the official Alabama Ornithological Society (AOS) state list (AOS 1999, McConnell 2001, D. Cooley, pers. comm). A total of 178 species are known breeders including approximately 158 species that regulary breed in the state. Additionally, 174 species regularly winter, and 80 species migrate through Alabama. The list also contains 38 accidental, three extinct, two extirpated, and four exotic species.

The scientific classification, common names, and order in which the species are presented follow AOU (1998) and Banks et al. (2002). The relative abundance, seasonal occurrence, and reproductive status designations were determined using Jackson (2001), Imhof (1976), and the personal observations of Bird Committee members and the participants in the Second Alabama Nongame Wildlife Conference at Auburn University, July 23-24, 2002. Species habitat information was based on AOU (1998), Holliman et al. (1984), Imhof (1976), and the personal observations of the Bird Committee members.

Historically, bird sightings in Alabama have been recorded for specific bird reporting geographic regions (Imhof 1976, Jackson 2001) and we follow that tradition in this checklist (see figure). The use of geographic regions allows for species information to be applied at a more local level. The Gulf Coast

Region is composed of two counties and has the greatest diversity of birdlife in the state. The Inland Coastal Plain is the largest reporting region (34 counties) and contains numerous ecoregions (e.g., Fall Line Hills, Blackland Prairie, Southeastern Floodplains and Low Terraces, Southern Pine Plains and Hills). The Mountain Region (24 counties) is a combination of three major ecoregions: the Southwestern Appalachians, the Ridge and Valley, and the transitional Piedmont. The Tennessee Valley (eight counties) is at the northern end of the state, contains significant inland water, and is composed primarily of the Interior and Cumberland Plateaus (Imhof 1976, Griffith et al. 2001).

Bird reporting geographic regions.

The approach of the Bird Committee in assigning conservation status designations was a global one, i.e., the committee was most interested in identifying those species or subspecies that are showing signs of eventual extinction throughout their distribution, rather than just extirpation from the state. Thus, some species assigned a high conservation priority designation may actually be fairly common in Alabama, but their protection here is of utmost importance because Alabama provides critical breeding, wintering, or migratory habitats necessary for their overall success. Conversely, some species assigned a low conservation priority designation may be uncommon or rare in Alabama, but their protection here is of little consequence to their overall success because Alabama provides little to satisfy their needs. This is a different approach than has been followed by the other groups in this book, but is warranted because of the unusually high degree of mobility that birds display.

The conservation designations prioritize species as to their need of conservation attention. Conservation priority designations for most breeding and wintering species (247 species) were based on Partners in Flight data (PIF 2001) and the judgment of the Bird Committee members. In addition, the participants of the Second Alabama Nongame Wildlife Conference provided information that helped the Bird Committee make its final designations. In most cases, data for four vulnerability parameters (i.e., relative abundance, distribution, threats to habitat, and population trend) were examined by the Bird Committee. If data for a species demonstrated vulnerability in all four parameters, a species was considered of Highest Conservation Concern (seven species). Species of High Conservation Concern were those that showed vulnerability in three parameters (19 species). Species of Moderate Conservation Concern (56 species) showed vulnerability in two parameters, or in one parameter and an uncertainty in another (e.g., population trend). Species of Low (115 species) and Lowest Conservation Concern (50) were those that had demonstrated vulnerability or uncertainty in one parameter, or in no parameters, respectively.

Abundance, geographical, and seasonal descriptors used in the annotations can be found on pages 10 and 11.

Thomas M. Haggerty

COMMITTEE

Dr. Thomas M. Haggerty, Department of Biology, University of North Alabama, Florence, AL, Chairperson/Compiler

Mr. Dwight Cooley, Wheeler National Wildlife Refuge Complex, U.S. Fish and Wildlife Service, Decatur, AL

Dr. Geoff Hill, Department of Biological Sciences, Auburn University, AL

Dr. Greg D. Jackson, Alabama Ornithological Society Records Curator, Birmingham, AL

Dr. Paul Kittle, Department of Biology, University of North Alabama, Florence, AL

Dr. Ralph E. Mirarchi, School of Forestry and Wildlife Sciences, Auburn University, AL

Mr. Eric C. Soehren, Alabama Department of Conservation and Natural Resources, State Lands Division, Natural Heritage Section, Montgomery, AL

Dr. James W. Tucker, Jr., Archbold Biological Station, Lake Placid, FL

BIRDS

CLASS AVES

LOONS

ORDER GAVIIFORMES

LOONS - FAMILY GAVIIDAE

Red-throated Loon *Gavia stellata*. Rare in fall, winter, and spring in all regions. Found on lakes, bays, and in the Gulf.

Pacific Loon *Gavia pacifica*. Rare in winter and spring in all regions. Found on lakes, bays, and in the Gulf.

Common Loon *Gavia immer*. Common in winter in Tennessee Valley and Gulf Coast regions, but uncommon to rare in Inland Coastal Plain and Mountain regions. Rare to occasional in summer in all regions. Found on lakes, bays, and in the Gulf. MODERATE CONSERVATION CONCERN. **(Fig. 110, p. 163)**

GREBES

ORDER PODICIPEDIFORMES

GREBES - FAMILY PODICIPEDIDAE

Pied-billed Grebe *Podilymbus podiceps*. Breeder. Common to uncommon in spring, rwinter, and fall, but uncommon to occasional in summer in all regions. Found on lakes, marshy ponds, and rarely in salt water. Low Conservation Concern. **(Fig. 111, p. 163)**

Horned Grebe *Podiceps auritus*. Fairly common in winter in Tennessee Valley and Gulf Coast regions, but uncommon to rare in Mountain and Inland Coastal Plain regions. Found on lakes, bays, and in the Gulf. MODERATE CONSERVATION CONCERN.

Red-necked Grebe *Podiceps grisegena*. Occasional in winter, especially in Tennessee Valley and Gulf Coast regions. Found on lakes, large ponds with reedy borders, bays, and estuaries.

Eared Grebe *Podiceps nigricollis*. Uncommon to rare in winter, spring, and fall in Gulf Coast region. Rare in winter, spring, and fall in other regions. Found on lakes, bays, and in the Gulf. Low Conservation Concern.

Western Grebe *Aechmophorus occidentalis*. Occasional in winter, spring, and fall. Found on sloughs, lakes, and in the Gulf.

ALBATROSSES, SHEARWATERS, PETRELS, AND ALLIES

ORDER PROCELLARIIFORMES

SHEARWATERS, FULMARS - FAMILY PROCELLARIIDAE

Cory's Shearwater *Calonectris diomedea*. Rare to uncommon in summer and fall in Gulf Coast region. Pelagic. Found in the Gulf.

Greater Shearwater *Puffinus gravis*. Occasional in summer, fall, and early winter in Gulf Coast region. Mostly pelagic. Found in the Gulf

Sooty Shearwater *Puffinus griseus*. Occasional in Gulf Coast region. Mostly pelagic. Found in the Gulf.

Audubon's Shearwater *Puffinus lherminieri*. Occasional in Gulf Coast region. Pelagic. Found in the Gulf.

STORM PETRELS - FAMILY HYDROBATIDAE

Wilson's Storm-Petrel *Oceanites oceanicus*. Fairly common in summer in Gulf Coast region. Pelagic. Found in the Gulf.

Leach's Storm-Petrel *Oceanodroma leucorhoa*. Rare in summer. Pelagic. Found in the Gulf.

Band-rumped Storm-Petrel *Oceanodroma castro*. Fairly common in summer. Pelagic. Found in the Gulf.

TROPICBIRDS, PELICANS, FRIGATEBIRDS, AND ALLIES

ORDER PELECANIFORMES

TROPICBIRDS - FAMILY PHAETHONTIDAE

White-tailed Tropicbird *Phaethon lepturus*. Accidental. Hypothetical.

Red-billed Tropicbird *Phaethon aethereus*. Accidental.

BOOBIES AND GANNETS - FAMILY SULIDAE

Masked Booby *Sula dactylatra*. Rare during all seasons. Pelagic. Found in the Gulf and along outer coast.

Brown Booby *Sula leucogaster*. Occasional during spring, summer, and fall. Found in the Gulf and along outer coast.

Northern Gannet *Morus bassanus*. Common in winter. Fairly common to uncommon in spring and fall. Rare in summer. Found in the Gulf and along outer coast.

PELICANS - FAMILY PELECANIDAE

American White Pelican *Pelecanus erythrorhynchos*. Fairly common on Gulf Coast in winter, but uncommon in spring, summer, and fall. Uncommon to rare inland in winter and during migration. Found on lakes, bays, marshes. Low Conservation Concern. **(Fig. 112, p. 163)**

Brown Pelican *Pelecanus occidentalis*. Breeder. Common on Gulf Coast. Occasional inland. Found on salt water bays and in the Gulf. Low Conservation Concern. **(Fig. 113, p. 163)**

CORMORANTS - FAMILY PHALACROCORACIDAE

Neotropic Cormorant *Phalacrocorax brasilianus*. Accidental.

Double-crested Cormorant *Phalacrocorax auritus*. Occasional breeder. Common in all regions in fall, winter, and spring. Fairly common to uncommon in summer. Found on lakes, rivers, bays, and in the Gulf. Lowest Conservation Concern. **(Fig. 114, p. 163)**

Great Cormorant *Phalacrocorax carbo*. Occasional in winter on Gulf Coast. Found on bays and in the Gulf.

ANHINGAS - FAMILY ANHINGIDAE

Anhinga *Anhinga anhinga*. Breeder. Fairly common to uncommon in Inland Coastal Plain and Gulf Coast regions in spring, summer, and fall, but rare in winter. Occasional in Tennessee Valley and Mountain regions in spring, summer, and fall. Found on ponds, lakes, marshy areas, and in heavily timbered swamps, oxbows, bottomlands, and riverine systems. Low Conservation Concern.

FRIGATEBIRDS - FAMILY FREGATIDAE

Magnificent Frigatebird *Fregata magnificens*. Uncommon in summer and fall, and rare in spring in Gulf Coast region. Found in the Gulf and Mississippi Sound.

HERONS, STORKS, IBISES, FLAMINGOS, AND ALLIES

ORDER CICONIIFORMES

HERONS AND BITTERNS - FAMILY ARDEIDAE

American Bittern *Botaurus lentiginosus*. Uncommon in winter, spring, and fall in Gulf Coast region. Rare inland in fall, winter, and spring. Found in marshes and along shrubby swamp borders. MODERATE CONSERVATION CONCERN.

Least Bittern *Ixobrychus exilis*. Breeder. Uncommon to fairly common during spring, summer, and fall in Gulf Coast region, but rare in winter. Uncommon to rare inland during spring, summer, and fall. Found in marshes and along shrubby swamp borders. **HIGH CONSERVATION CONCERN.**

Great Blue Heron *Ardea herodias*. Breeder. Common throughout state in all seasons. Feeds in shallow water of ponds, lakes, and rivers. Low Conservation Concern. **(Fig. 115, p. 163)**

Great Egret *Ardea alba*. Breeder. Common throughout year on Inland Coastal Plain and Gulf Coast regions. Common to fairly common in spring, summer, and fall in Tennessee Valley and Mountain regions, but uncommon to rare in winter. Feeds in shallow water. Low Conservation Concern.

Snowy Egret *Egretta thula*. Breeder. Common throughout year in Gulf Coast region. Rare to uncommon in spring and early summer in Inland Coastal Plain region, but fairly common in late summer and early fall. Rare to uncommon during spring, summer, and fall in Tennessee Valley and Mountain regions. Feeds in shallow water. Low Conservation Concern.

Little Blue Heron *Egretta caerulea*. Breeder. Common in summer, but uncommon in other seasons in Inland Coastal Plain and Gulf Coast regions. Rare to uncommon in spring to mid-summer in Mountain and Tennessee Valley regions, but fairly common in late summer and early fall. Feeds in shallow water. Low Conservation Concern.

Tricolored Heron *Egretta tricolor*. Breeder. Fairly common to common in all seasons in Gulf Coast region. Rare during spring, summer, and fall in Inland Coastal Plain and Tennessee Valley regions. Feeds in shallow water. Low Conservation Concern. **(Fig. 116, p. 163)**

Reddish Egret *Egretta rufescens*. Breeder. Fairly common in spring, summer, and fall in Gulf Coast region. Feeds in shallow brackish and salt water, mostly on mudflats. **HIGH CONSERVATION CONCERN.**

Cattle Egret *Bubulcus ibis*. Breeder. Common in spring, summer, and early fall in Inland Coastal Plain and Gulf Coast regions, and rare in winter. Uncommon in

Mountain region in summer, but rare during spring and fall. Fairly common in summer and early fall in Tennessee Valley region, but rare to uncommon in spring and late fall. Feeds mainly in fields with cattle. Lowest Conservation Concern. **(Fig. 117 p. 163)**

Green Heron *Butorides virescens*. Breeder. Common in spring, summer, and fall in all regions. Rare in winter in Mountain, Inland Coastal Plain, and Gulf Coast regions. Feeds mostly at water's edge. MODERATE CONSERVATION CONCERN.

Black-crowned Night-Heron *Nycticorax nycticorax*. Breeder. Uncommon in all regions throughout year. Feeds mostly at water's edge. MODERATE CONSERVATION CONCERN.

Yellow-crowned Night-Heron *Nyctanassa violacea*. Breeder. Fairly common in the spring, summer, and fall in Gulf Coast region, but rare in winter. Uncommon in spring, summer, and fall in other regions, but occasional in winter. Feeds at water's edge or in wet meadows. MODERATE CONSERVATION CONCERN.

IBISES AND SPOONBILLS - FAMILY THRESKIORNITHIDAE

White Ibis *Eudocimus albus*. Breeder. Fairly common in spring, summer, and fall in Gulf Coast region, but uncommon in winter. Uncommon in spring, summer, and fall in Inland Coastal Plain and occasional in winter. Rare in summer in Tennessee Valley and Mountain regions and occasional in spring and fall. Feeds in shallow water. MODERATE CONSERVATION CONCERN. **(Fig. 118, p. 163)**

Glossy Ibis *Plegadis falcinellus*. Breeder. Uncommon in Gulf Coast region in spring, summer, and fall, but occasional in other regions during those seasons. Found in marshes, on mudflats, and along shores of large bodies of water. Low Conservation Concern.

White-faced Ibis *Plegadis chihi*. Historical breeder. Occasional in spring, summer, and fall mainly in Gulf Coast region. Found in marshes, on mudflats, and along shores of large bodies of water.

Roseate Spoonbill *Platalea ajaja*. Occasional in summer and fall, mostly in Gulf Coast and Inland Coastal Plain regions. Feeds in shallow water.

STORKS - FAMILY CICONIIDAE

Wood Stork *Mycteria americana*. Possible breeder. Fairly common in late summer and early fall, but occasional to rare in spring and late fall in Inland Coastal Plain region. Occasional in spring, summer, and fall in other regions. Feeds in shallow water. **Listed as *endangered* by the U.S. Fish and Wildlife Service. HIGH CONSERVATION CONCERN.**

VULTURES - FAMILY CATHARTIDAE

Black Vulture *Coragyps atratus*. Breeder. Fairly common in late spring, summer, and fall, but uncommon in winter and early spring in Tennessee Valley region. Common throughout year in other regions. Found in agricultural and livestock areas. Lowest Conservation Concern.

Turkey Vulture *Cathartes aura*. Breeder. Common in all seasons and regions. Found in wooded as well as open areas. Lowest Conservation Concern. **(Fig. 119, p. 164)**

SCREAMERS, SWANS, GEESE, AND DUCKS

ORDER ANSERIFORMES

SWANS, GEESE, AND DUCKS - FAMILY ANATIDAE

Black-bellied Whistling-Duck *Dendrocygna autumnalis*. Accidental.

Fulvous Whistling-Duck *Dendrocygna bicolor*. Historical breeder. Rare in spring, summer, and fall in Gulf Coast region. Occasional in late fall, winter, and early spring in other regions. Prefers dense marshes and adjacent waters.

Greater White-fronted Goose *Anser albifrons*. Uncommon in fall and winter in Tennessee Valley and Inland Coastal Plain regions. Rare on Gulf Coast in fall and winter. Found in freshwater and brackish marshes, agricultural fields, and on ponds. Lowest Conservation Concern.

Snow Goose *Chen caerulescens*. Fairly common to uncommon in winter and fall in Tennessee Valley and Mountain regions, but rare in summer. Uncommon to rare in winter, spring, and fall in other regions. Found in freshwater and brackish marshes, agricultural fields, and on lakes. Low Conservation Concern.

Ross's Goose *Chen rossii*. Rare in winter, early spring, and late fall in all regions. Found in freshwater and brackish marshes, agricultural fields, and on lakes.

Canada Goose *Branta canadensis*. Breeder. Common in winter in Tennessee Valley region, but fairly common to rare in spring, summer, and fall. Uncommon in all seasons in Mountain region. Fairly common in winter, spring, and fall in Inland Coastal Plain, but uncommon in spring, summer, and fall. Rare in winter and fall in Gulf Coast region. Found in freshwater and brackish marshes, agricultural fields, and on lakes. Breeding birds have been established from introduced resident populations. Lowest Conservation Concern.

Brant *Branta bernicla*. Occasional in fall and winter in Tennessee Valley, Mountain, and Gulf Coast regions. Often associates with snow geese. Found in freshwater and brackish marshes, agricultural fields, and on lakes.

Tundra Swan *Cygnus columbianus*. Rare in winter and fall in Tennessee Valley region, but occasional in spring. Occasional in winter and fall in other regions. Prefers shallow freshwater and brackish marshes with dense growths of underwater vegetation. Low Conservation Concern.

Wood Duck *Aix sponsa*. Breeder. Common in all seasons and regions. Found in wooded swamps, beaver ponds, bottomlands, creeks, and on lakes. Low Conservation Concern.

Gadwall *Anas strepera*. Occasional breeder. Common in winter, fairly common to uncommon in spring and fall, and rare in summer in all regions. Found in shallow freshwater and brackish-water ponds with abundant aquatic vegetation. Lowest Conservation Concern.

Eurasian Wigeon *Anas penelope*. Occasional in winter, spring, and fall mostly in the Tennessee Valley region. Associates with American wigeon. Found in shallow freshwater and brackish-water ponds with abundant aquatic vegetation.

American Wigeon *Anas americana*. Common in winter, spring, and fall, and occasional in summer in all regions. Found in shallow freshwater and brackish-water ponds with abundant aquatic vegetation. Low Conservation Concern.

American Black Duck *Anas rubripes*. Local breeder. Common in winter, uncommon in spring and fall, and rare in summer in Tennessee Valley region. Rare in fall, winter, and spring in Mountain and Inland Coastal Plain regions. Occasional in winter, spring, and fall in Gulf Coast region. Found in freshwater and brackish-water marshes and on lakes. **HIGH CONSERVATION CONCERN**.

Mallard *Anas platyrhynchos*. Breeder. Common in winter, fairly common in spring and fall, and uncommon in summer in all regions. Found in shallow water of ponds, lakes, marshes, and flooded fields. Breeding birds are probably domesticated birds or birds released by sportsman's clubs. Low Conservation Concern.

Mottled Duck *Anas fulvigula*. Breeder. Fairly common in spring, summer, and fall and uncommon in winter in Gulf Coast region (mostly Mobile County). Found in freshwater and brackish marshes and ponds. MODERATE CONSERVATION CONCERN.

Blue-winged Teal *Anas discors*. Occasional breeder. Common to fairly common in spring and fall in Tennessee Valley and Mountain regions, but rare in summer and rare to occasional in winter. Common to fairly common in spring and fall, uncommon to rare in winter in Inland Coastal Plain and Gulf Coast regions. Found in shallow freshwater and brackish water ponds, sloughs, marshes, and mudflats. Low Conservation Concern. **(Fig. 120, p. 164)**

Cinnamon Teal *Anas cyanoptera*. Accidental.

Northern Shoveler *Anas clypeata*. Occasional breeder. Common in winter, spring, and fall in all regions, and occasional in summer in Tennessee Valley region. Found in freshwater and brackish water ponds, swamps, and on lakes. Lowest Conservation Concern.

White-cheeked Pintail *Anas bahamensis*. Accidental.

Northern Pintail *Anas acuta*. Common in winter, spring, and fall in all regions. Fairly common to rare in spring and fall in all regions. Occasional in summer in Tennessee Valley and Gulf Coast regions. Found in freshwater and brackish marshes, agricultural fields, and shallow portions of lakes, ponds, and rivers. Low Conservation Concern. **(Fig. 121, p. 164)**

Green-winged Teal *Anas crecca*. Common to fairly common in winter, spring, and fall in all regions. Occasional in summer in Tennessee Valley. Found in shallow freshwater and brackish water marshes, and on lakes and mudflats. Lowest Conservation Concern.

Canvasback *Aythya valisineria*. Fairly common in winter and uncommon to rare in spring and fall in Tennessee Valley region. In other regions, uncommon in winter, spring, and fall, and occasional in spring and summer. Found on shallow lakes, ponds, marshes, and estuaries. MODERATE CONSERVATION CONCERN.

Redhead *Aythya americana*. Uncommon in winter, spring, and fall, and occasional in summer in all regions. Found on lakes, rivers, and bays in fresh, brackish, or salt water. MODERATE CONSERVATION CONCERN.

Ring-necked Duck *Aythya collaris*. Common in winter, early spring, and late fall, and uncommon to rare in other seasons in all regions. Found in shallow, wooded, freshwater ponds, swamps, and lakes. Lowest Conservation Concern.

Greater Scaup *Aythya marila*. Uncommon to rare in winter, spring, and fall in Gulf Coast and Tennessee Valley regions. Occasional in winter and spring in Inland Coastal Plain and Mountain regions. Found on relatively deep lakes, rivers, and bays. Low Conservation Concern.

Lesser Scaup *Aythya affinis*. Common in winter, spring, and fall in Tennessee Valley and Gulf Coast regions, and occasional in summer. Fairly common in winter, spring, and fall in Mountain and Inland Coastal Plain regions, and occasional in summer. Found on lakes, rivers, and bays. Low Conservation Concern.

King Eider *Somateria spectabilis*. Accidental. Hypothetical.

Harlequin Duck *Histrionicus histrionicus*. Accidental.

Surf Scoter *Melanitta perspicillata*. Rare in winter, spring, and fall in Tennessee Valley, Mountain, and Gulf Coast regions. Found primarily in offshore waters and less commonly on lakes.

White-winged Scoter *Melanitta fusca*. Rare to occasional in winter, spring, and late fall in all regions. Found primarily in offshore waters and less commonly on lakes.

Black Scoter *Melanitta nigra*. Rare in winter, spring, and fall in Gulf Coast region. Occasional in fall and winter in Tennessee Valley and Mountain regions. Found primarily in offshore waters and less commonly on lakes.

Oldsquaw *Clangula hyemalis*. Rare in winter, spring, and late fall in Gulf Coast and Tennessee Valley regions. Occasional in winter, spring, and late fall in Mountain and Inland Coastal Plain regions. Found on deeper bays and lakes.

Bufflehead *Bucephala albeola*. Common in winter, early spring, and late fall in Tennessee Valley and Gulf Coast regions. Uncommon in winter, spring, and fall in Inland Coastal Plain and Mountain regions. Found on lakes, bays, and slow-moving rivers. MODERATE CONSERVATION CONCERN.

Common Goldeneye *Bucephala clangula*. Fairly common in winter, spring, and late fall in Tennessee Valley and Gulf Coast regions, but occasional in summer. Uncommon in winter and rare in spring and fall in Mountain region. Rare in winter and occasional in spring in Inland Coastal Plain. Found on lakes, bays, and slow-moving rivers. Low Conservation Concern.

Hooded Merganser *Lophodytes cucullatus*. Occasional breeder. Fairly common in winter, spring, and fall, and rare in summer in all regions. Found primarily on wooded freshwater ponds, lakes, and slow water river systems, less commonly in marshes and bays. MODERATE CONSERVATION CONCERN.

Common Merganser *Mergus merganser*. Rare in winter and rare to occasional in spring and fall in primarily the Tennessee Valley region. Found on freshwater lakes and rivers. Low Conservation Concern.

Red-breasted Merganser *Mergus serrator*. Common in winter, uncommon in spring and fall, and occasional in summer in Gulf Coast region. In Tennessee Valley region, fairly common in winter and fall, uncommon in spring, and occasional in summer. In Mountain and Inland Coastal Plain regions, uncommon to rare in winter, rare in spring and fall, and occasional in summer. Found on estuaries, bays, shallow coastal waters, lakes, and deep slow-moving rivers. Lowest Conservation Concern.

Ruddy Duck *Oxyura jamaicensis*. Common in winter and fairly common to rare in fall and spring in Tennessee Valley region. In other regions, fairly common in winter, fairly common to rare in spring and fall, and occasional in summer. Found on freshwater ponds, lakes, slow-moving rivers, estuaries, and bays. Low Conservation Concern.

OSPREY, KITES, EAGLES, HAWKS, AND FALCONS
ORDER FALCONIFORMES

OSPREY, KITES, EAGLES, AND HAWKS - FAMILY ACCIPITRIDAE

Osprey *Pandion haliaetus*. Breeder. Fairly common in spring, summer, and fall in Gulf Coast region, and uncommon in winter. In other regions, uncommon in spring and fall, and rare in winter and summer. Found on lakes, rivers, and bays. Low Conservation Concern. **(Fig. 122, p. 164)**

Swallow-tailed Kite *Elanoides forficatus*. Breeder. Uncommon and local in summer, and rare in early fall in Inland Coastal Plain and Gulf Coast regions. Occasional in spring and summer in Tennessee Valley and Mountain regions. Found in wooded swamps, mature floodplain forests, and oxbows. **HIGH CONSERVATION CONCERN.**

White-tailed Kite *Elanus leucurus*. Occasional in winter and fall in Gulf Coast and Inland Coastal Plain regions. Found in grasslands, cultivated fields, and on partially cleared lands.

Mississippi Kite *Ictinia mississippiensis*. Breeder. Fairly common in spring, summer, and fall in Inland Coastal Plain and Gulf Coast regions. Rare and local in spring, summer, and early fall in Tennessee Valley. In Mountain region, occasional in spring, summer, and fall. Found in river swamps and floodplain forests. Low Conservation Concern.

Bald Eagle *Haliaeetus leucocephalus*. Breeder. Uncommon in winter, spring, and fall in Tennessee Valley region, and rare in summer. In other regions, rare throughout year. Found primarily around lakes, rivers, and bays. **Listed as *threatened* by the U.S. Fish and Wildlife Service.** MODERATE CONSERVATION CONCERN. **(Fig. 123, p. 164)**

Northern Harrier *Circus cyaneus*. Fairly common in winter, spring, and fall in all regions. Found in cultivated fields, marshes, meadows, and grasslands. **HIGH CONSERVATION CONCERN.**

Sharp-shinned Hawk *Accipiter striatus*. Breeder. Common in Gulf Coast region in fall, uncommon in winter and spring. In Tennessee Valley and Mountain regions, fairly common in fall and uncommon in winter, spring, and summer. In Inland Coastal Plain, uncommon in winter, spring, and fall, and rare in summer. Found in forests, open woodlands, and wooded suburbs. MODERATE CONSERVATION CONCERN.

Cooper's Hawk *Accipiter cooperii*. Breeder. Fairly common in fall in Gulf Coast region, uncommon in winter and spring, and rare in summer. In other regions, uncommon in winter, spring, and fall, and rare in summer. Found in open woodlands and wooded suburbs. Low Conservation Concern.

Northern Goshawk *Accipiter gentilis*. Accidental.

Red-shouldered Hawk *Buteo lineatus*. Breeder. Fairly common in all seasons and regions. Found in moist woodlands and swamps. Low Conservation Concern.

Broad-winged Hawk *Buteo platypterus*. Breeder. Common in fall, fairly common in spring and summer, and occasional in winter in all regions. Found in deciduous woodlands; during migration can be seen flying overhead from any habitat type. MODERATE CONSERVATION CONCERN.

Swainson's Hawk *Buteo swainsoni*. Rare in fall and occasional in winter in primarily Gulf Coast region.

Red-tailed Hawk *Buteo jamaicensis*. Breeder. Common in winter, fairly common in spring and fall, and uncommon in summer in Gulf Coast region. In other regions, common in winter and fairly common in spring, summer, and fall. Found in open country and woodland edges. Low Conservation Concern.

Ferruginous Hawk *Buteo regalis*. Accidental. Hypothetical.

Rough-legged Hawk *Buteo lagopus*. Rare in winter and rare to occasional in spring primarily in the Tennessee Valley region. Found in grasslands and open cultivated areas. MODERATE CONSERVATION CONCERN.

Golden Eagle *Aquila chrysaetos*. Rare in winter, spring, and fall in all regions. Found in open country and mixed habitats. MODERATE CONSERVATION CONCERN.

FALCONS - FAMILY FALCONIDAE

Crested Caracara *Caracara plancus*. Accidental.

American Kestrel *Falco sparverius*. Breeder. Common in winter, common to fairly common in spring and fall, and rare in summer in inland regions. In Gulf Coast region, common in winter and common to uncommon in spring and fall. Found in open fields and woodland edges. Southeastern subspecies (*F. s. paulus*) has declined dramatically. **HIGH CONSERVATION CONCERN.**

Merlin *Falco columbarius*. Fairly common to uncommon in fall, rare in winter, and uncommon to rare in spring in Gulf Coast region. In other regions, rare in winter and fall, and rare to occasional in spring and early summer. Found along coastal dunes and shorelines, and in marshes, grasslands, and cultivated fields. MODERATE CONSERVATION CONCERN.

Peregrine Falcon *Falco peregrinus*. Historical breeder. Fairly common in fall, and rare in winter and spring in Gulf Coast region. In other regions, rare in winter, spring, and fall. Found in open country habitats, such as coastal dunes, shorelines, marshes, grasslands, cultivated fields, and cities. MODERATE CONSERVATION CONCERN.

Prairie Falcon *Falco mexicanus*. Accidental.

GALLINACEOUS BIRDS

ORDER GALLIFORMES

GROUSE AND TURKEYS - FAMILY PHASIANIDAE

Ruffed Grouse *Bonasa umbellus*. Breeder. Occasional to rare and very local in northeast corner of state. Found in deciduous and mixed woodlands. MODERATE CONSERVATION CONCERN.

Wild Turkey *Meleagris gallopavo*. Breeder. Fairly common in all seasons and regions. Found in forested and partially forested habitats. Low Conservation Concern.

QUAIL - FAMILY ODONTOPHORIDAE

Northern Bobwhite *Colinus virginianus*. Breeder. Common to fairly common in all seasons and regions. Found on farms, along woodland edges, and in brushy open country habitats and old fields. Low Conservation Concern.

CRANES, RAILS, AND ALLIES

ORDER GRUIFORMES

RAILS - FAMILY RALLIDAE

Yellow Rail *Coturnicops noveboracensis*. Occasional in winter, spring, and fall mostly in Inland Coastal Plain and Gulf Coast regions. Found in drier, grassy portions of marshes, open edges of wet fields, and, rarely, in salt marshes. HIGH CONSERVATION CONCERN.

Black Rail *Laterallus jamaicensis*. Possible breeder. Rare in spring and occasional in other seasons in Gulf Coast region. Found in coastal marshes. HIGH CONSERVATION CONCERN.

Clapper Rail *Rallus longirostris*. Breeder. Common in all seasons in Gulf Coast region. Found in salt water and brackish marshes around the mouths of coastal rivers and creeks. MODERATE CONSERVATION CONCERN. (Fig. 124, p. 164)

King Rail *Rallus elegans*. Breeder. Uncommon in all seasons in Gulf Coast regions and Inland Coastal Plain regions. In Mountain and Tennessee Valley regions, rare to uncommon in spring, summer, and fall. Found in brackish water, freshwater, and, less often, in saltwater marshes. MODERATE CONSERVATION CONCERN.

Virginia Rail *Rallus limicola*. Historical breeder. Uncommon in winter, and uncommon to rare in spring and fall in Inland Coastal Plain and Gulf Coast regions. In Mountain and Tennessee Valley regions, rare in winter, spring, and fall. Found in brackish water, freshwater, and less often salt water marshes. Low Conservation Concern.

Sora *Porzana carolina*. Fairly common in winter, spring, and fall in Gulf Coast region. In Mountain and Inland Coastal Plain regions, uncommon in winter and uncommon to rare in spring and fall. In Tennessee Valley region, uncommon to rare in spring and fall. Found in freshwater and saltwater marshes, and wet grassy fields. Low Conservation Concern. **(Fig. 125, p. 164)**

Purple Gallinule *Porphyrio martinica*. Breeder. Uncommon in summer and uncommon to rare in spring and fall in Inland Coastal Plain and Gulf Coast regions. Occasional in spring in Mountain and Tennessee Valley regions. Found in freshwater marshes, swamps, and ponds. MODERATE CONSERVATION CONCERN. **(Fig. 126, p. 164)**

Common Moorhen *Gallinula chloropus*. Breeder. Fairly common in spring, summer, and fall, and uncommon in winter in Gulf Coast region. In Inland Coastal Plain, uncommon in summer and uncommon to rare in spring and fall. In Tennessee Valley and Mountain regions, rare in spring, summer, and fall. Found in freshwater marshes, swamps, and ponds. Low Conservation Concern.

American Coot *Fulica americana*. Occasional breeder. Common in winter, common to uncommon in spring and fall, and rare in summer in all regions. Found on rivers, ponds, lakes, and in swamp and delta areas. Low Conservation Concern.

LIMPKINS - FAMILY ARAMIDAE

Limpkin *Aramus guarauna*. Accidental.

CRANES - FAMILY GRUIDAE

Sandhill Crane *Grus canadensis*. Historical breeder. Uncommon in winter and rare in spring and fall in Gulf Coast region. In other regions, uncommon to rare in winter, early spring, and fall. Found in open grasslands, marshes, and corn fields. **Mississippi subspecies (*G. c. pulla*), which is the most likely to breed in Alabama, listed as *endangered* by the U.S. Fish and Wildlife Service.** MODERATE CONSERVATION CONCERN. **(Fig. 127, p. 164)**

Whooping Crane *Grus americana*. Accidental. Hypothetical.

SHOREBIRDS, GULLS, AUKS, AND ALLIES
ORDER CHARADRIIFORMES

PLOVERS AND LAPWINGS - FAMILY CHARADRIIDAE

Black-bellied Plover *Pluvialis squatarola*. Common in winter, spring, and fall, and rare in summer in Gulf Coast region. In Mountain and Inland Coastal Plain regions, rare in spring and fall. In Tennessee Valley region, uncommon in fall and rare in spring. Found on beaches, wet savannas, shores of ponds and lakes, flooded fields, and extensive short-grass areas. Low Conservation Concern.

American Golden-Plover *Pluvialis dominica*. Fairly common in spring and uncommon to rare in fall in all regions. Found in short grasslands, flooded fields, and on mudflats and beaches.

Snowy Plover *Charadrius alexandrinus*. Breeder. Uncommon to rare and local in all seasons in Gulf Coast region. Found on beaches and sandflats. **HIGHEST CONSERVATION CONCERN**.

Wilson's Plover *Charadrius wilsonia*. Breeder. Rare and local in spring, summer, and fall in Gulf Coast region. Found on sandy beaches and tidal mudflats. **HIGHEST CONSERVATION CONCERN**.

Semipalmated Plover *Charadrius semipalmatus*. Common in spring and fall, fairly common in winter, and uncommon to rare in summer in Gulf Coast region. In other regions, fairly common in spring and fall, and occasional in early winter. Found on mudflats and tidal flats. MODERATE CONSERVATION CONCERN.

Piping Plover *Charadrius melodus*. Fairly common in winter, spring, and fall, and rare in late summer in Gulf Coast region. In other regions, occasional in spring and rare in fall. Found on sandy beaches, dunes, and tidal flats. **Listed as *threatened* by the U.S. Fish and Wildlife Service. HIGHEST CONSERVATION CONCERN.**

Killdeer *Charadrius vociferus*. Breeder. Common in all regions and seasons. Found on short-grass fields, mudflats, and shores. Lowest Conservation Concern.

Mountain Plover *Charadrius montanus*. Accidental.

OYSTERCATCHERS - FAMILY HAEMATOPODIDAE

American Oystercatcher *Haematopus palliatus*. Breeder. Fairly common in Gulf Coast region (mostly Mobile County) in all seasons. Found on beaches, shellflats, and mudflats. **HIGH CONSERVATION CONCERN**.

STILTS AND AVOCETS - FAMILY RECURVIROSTRIDAE

Black-necked Stilt *Himantopus mexicanus*. Breeder. Common in spring, summer, and fall, and rare in winter in Gulf Coast region. In other regions, occasional in spring, summer, and fall. Found in shallow lakes, grassy marshes, pools, flooded fields, and on mudflats. Low Conservation Concern.

American Avocet *Recurvirostra americana*. Possible breeder. Fairly common in winter, spring, and fall, and rare in summer in Gulf Coast region. In other regions, occasional in spring and late summer, and rare in fall. Found in marshes, and on ponds, shallow lakes, shorelines, and flats. Low Conservation Concern.

SNIPE, WOODCOCK, AND SANDPIPERS - FAMILY SCOLOPACIDAE

Greater Yellowlegs *Tringa melanoleuca*. Common in winter, spring, and fall, rare in early summer, and uncommon in late summer in Gulf Coast region. In Tennessee Valley, fairly common in winter and spring, common in fall, and uncommon in summer. In Mountain and Inland Coastal Plain regions, fairly common in spring and fall, uncommon in winter and late summer. Found along shorelines of shallow ponds and lakes, marsh edges, in flooded fields, and on mudflats. Low Conservation Concern.

Lesser Yellowlegs *Tringa flavipes*. Common in spring and fall, uncommon in winter and late summer, and rare in early summer in Gulf Coast region. In other regions, common in spring and fall, rare in winter, uncommon to rare in summer. Found along shorelines of shallow ponds and lakes, marsh edges, in flooded fields, and on mudflats. Low Conservation Concern.

Solitary Sandpiper *Tringa solitaria*. Common in spring, late summer, and fall in all regions. Found along lake borders, stream banks, ponds, and marsh edges.

Willet *Catoptrophorus semipalmatus*. Breeder. Common in all seasons in Gulf Coast region. In other regions, rare in spring, late summer, and fall. Found on mudflats, beaches, and in marshes. Low Conservation Concern.

Spotted Sandpiper *Actitis macularia*. Historical breeder. Common in spring, late summer, and fall, and uncommon to rare in winter in Gulf Coast region. In other regions, common in spring, late summer, and fall, and rare in winter. Found along pond and lake margins, stream banks, and on mudflats. MODERATE CONSERVATION CONCERN.

Upland Sandpiper *Bartramia longicauda*. Fairly common in fall, uncommon in spring and summer in Gulf Coast and Inland Coastal Plain regions. In Mountain and Tennessee Valley regions, uncommon to rare in spring, fall, and summer. Found in short-grass areas, in cultivated fields, and on flats.

Whimbrel *Numenius phaeopus*. Uncommon in spring and fall, and occasional in winter in Gulf Coast region. In other regions, occasional in late winter, early spring, and fall. Found on beaches and mudflats, and in marshes and flooded fields.

Long-billed Curlew *Numenius americanus*. Uncommon in winter, spring, and fall, and rare in late summer in Gulf Coast region. Found in short-grass areas and marshes, and on mudflats and beaches.

Hudsonian Godwit *Limosa haemastica*. Occasional in spring and fall in Gulf Coast and Tennessee Valley regions. Found in meadows, grain fields, flooded fields, and on mudflats.

Marbled Godwit *Limosa fedoa*. Uncommon in spring and fall, rare in winter, and occasional in late summer in Gulf Coast region. In other regions, occasional in spring and fall. Found in pastures, pools, and on mudflats. MODERATE CONSERVATION CONCERN

Ruddy Turnstone *Arenaria interpres*. Common in winter and spring, fairly common in late summer, and rare in early summer in Gulf Coast region. In other regions, rare in spring and fall. Found along rocky shores, jetties, and on mudflats and beaches. MODERATE CONSERVATION CONCERN

Red Knot *Calidris canutus*. Rare in winter, spring, and late summer, and occasional in early summer in Gulf Coast region. In other regions, occasional in fall. Found on mudflats and along sandy shores. Low Conservation Concern.

Sanderling *Calidris alba*. Common in winter, spring, and fall, fairly common in late summer, and rare in early summer in Gulf Coast region. In other regions, occasional to rare in spring, and rare to uncommon in late summer and fall. Found on sandy beaches and mudflats, and along pond edges and lakeshores. Low Conservation Concern.

Semipalmated Sandpiper *Calidris pusilla*. Common in spring, fairly common to common in late summer and fall, and occasional in early summer in Gulf Coast region. In other regions, fairly common in spring and fall, and uncommon in late summer. Found on beaches, mudflats, and along pond edges and lakeshores.

Western Sandpiper *Calidris mauri*. Common in winter, spring, and fall; rare in early summer; and fairly common in late summer in Gulf Coast regions. In other regions, occasional to rare in winter, rare in spring, uncommon in late summer, and fairly common in fall. Found on beaches, mudflats, and along pond edges and lakeshores. MODERATE CONSERVATION CONCERN

Least Sandpiper *Calidris minutilla*. Fairly common in winter, common in spring and fall, occasional in early summer, and uncommon in late summer in Gulf Coast region. In other regions, common in spring, fairly common in fall, uncommon in winter and late summer, and occasional in early summer. Found on beaches, mudflats, and along pond edges and lakeshores. Low Conservation Concern.

White-rumped Sandpiper *Calidris fuscicollis.* Fairly common in spring and early summer, and rare in fall in Gulf Coast region. In other regions, fairly common in spring and early summer, rare in fall, and occasional in late summer. Found along marshy edges, in grassy areas, along pond edges and lakeshores, and on mudflats.

Baird's Sandpiper *Calidris bairdii.* Rare in spring and fall, and occasional in late summer in all regions. Found along marshy edges, pond edges, and lakeshores, and on grassy areas and mudflats.

Pectoral Sandpiper *Calidris melanotos.* Common in fall, fairly common in spring, uncommon in late summer, and occasional in winter in Gulf Coast region. In other regions, common in spring and fall, and uncommon in late summer. Found in wet meadows, flooded fields, on mudflats, and along shores of ponds, pools, and lakes.

Sharp-tailed Sandpiper *Calidris acuminata.* Accidental.

Purple Sandpiper *Calidris maritima.* Accidental.

Dunlin *Calidris alpina.* Common in winter, spring, and fall, and occasional in early summer in Gulf Coast regions. In Tennessee Valley, common in fall, and fairly common in spring and winter. In Inland Coastal Plain, uncommon in fall, and rare in winter and spring. In Mountain region, uncommon in fall, and occasional in winter and spring. Found on mudflats, beaches, and along pools. Low Conservation Concern.

Curlew Sandpiper *Calidris ferruginea.* Accidental.

Stilt Sandpiper *Calidris himantopus.* Common in spring, late summer and fall, and rare in winter in Gulf Coast region. In Tennessee Valley and Inland Coastal Plain regions, uncommon in fall, and rare in spring and summer. In Mountain region, rare in late summer and fall, and occasional in spring. Found in marshes and pools and on mudflats.

Buff-breasted Sandpiper *Tryngites subruficollis.* Fairly common in fall, and uncommon in spring in Gulf Coast region. In other regions, uncommon in fall and occasional in spring. Found in dry, short grasslands, pastures, plowed fields, and on mudflats.

Ruff *Philomachus pugnax.* Accidental.

Short-billed Dowitcher *Limnodromus griseus.* Common in winter, spring, late summer, and fall, and occasional in early summer in Gulf Coast region. In Tennessee Valley region, uncommon in fall, rare in spring, and occasional in summer. In Mountain and Inland Coastal Plain regions, uncommon in fall, rare in late summer, and occasional in spring. Found on mudflats, along pond and lakeshores, and in flooded fields. MODERATE CONSERVATION CONCERN.

Long-billed Dowitcher *Limnodromus scolopaceus*. Common in spring and fall, and occasional in winter in Gulf Coast region. In other regions, rare in fall and early winter, and occasional in spring and late summer. Found on mudflats, along pond and lakeshores, and in flooded fields.

Common Snipe *Gallinago gallinago*. Common in winter, spring, and fall, occasional to rare in summer in all regions. Found in marshes and wet grassy areas. Low Conservation Concern.

Eurasian Woodcock *Scolopax minor*. Accidental. Hypothetical. Historical record from 1889.

American Woodcock *Scolopax minor*. Breeder. Fairly common in fall and winter, and occasional in spring and summer in Gulf Coast region. Uncommon in winter, spring, and fall, and rare in summer in other regions. Found in moist shrubby woods, floodplains, thickets, and swamps. **HIGH CONSERVATION CONCERN**.

Wilson's Phalarope *Phalaropus tricolor*. Fairly common in fall, uncommon in spring and late summer, and occasional in winter and early summer in Gulf Coast region. In Tennessee Valley, rare in spring, late summer, and fall. In Mountain and Inland Coastal Plain regions, rare in fall and occasional in spring. Found on ponds and mudflats, along lake margins and marsh edges, and in flooded fields and salt marshes.

Red-necked Phalarope *Phalaropus lobatus*. Occasional inland and rare in spring and fall in all regions. Pelagic. Found in the Gulf, on bays, along pond margins, and in open marshes.

Red Phalarope *Phalaropus fulicarius*. Rare in winter, spring, and fall offshore. Onshore and inland, occasional to rare in late summer, fall, and occasional in winter. Pelagic. Found in the Gulf, and on lakes, bays, ponds, and in marshes.

JAEGERS, SKUAS, GULLS, AND TERNS - FAMILY LARIDAE

Pomarine Jaeger *Stercorarius pomarinus*. Rare to uncommon in all seasons offshore. Onshore and inland, occasional in winter, spring, and fall. Pelagic. Found in the Gulf, on bays, and on large lakes.

Parasitic Jaeger *Stercorarius parasiticus*. Rare in winter, spring, summer, and early fall in Gulf Coast region. Found in the Gulf and on bays.

Long-tailed Jaeger *Stercorarius longicaudus*. Accidental. Hypothetical.

Laughing Gull *Larus atricilla*. Breeder. Common in all seasons in Gulf Coast region. In other regions, rare in all seasons. Found in the Gulf and marshes and on beaches, lakes, and rivers. Lowest concervation concern.

Franklin's Gull *Larus pipixcan*. Rare in winter and fall, occasional in spring in Gulf Coast region. Inland (mostly Tennessee Valley), rare in spring, fall, and winter. Found in marshes and on lakes and rivers.

Little Gull *Larus minutus*. Occasional in winter, spring, and fall in all regions. Found on beaches, bays, rivers, lakes, ponds, and in marshes and flooded fields.

Bonaparte's Gull *Larus philadelphia*. Common in winter, spring, and fall in Gulf Coast and Tennessee Valley regions. Uncommon in winter, spring, and fall in Inland Coastal Plain and Mountain regions. Found on bays, lakes, and rivers. Lowest Conservation Concern.

Ring-billed Gull *Larus delawarensis*. Common in winter, spring, and fall, and rare in summer in Gulf Coast and Tennessee Valley regions. In Mountain and Inland Coastal Plain regions, fairly common in winter, spring and fall, and occasional in summer. Found in the Gulf, and on bays, beaches, rivers, lakes, irrigated and plowed fields, and garbage dumps. Lowest Conservation Concern. **(Fig. 128, p. 164)**

California Gull *Larus californicus*. Accidental.

Herring Gull *Larus argentatus*. Occasional breeder. Common in winter, spring, and fall, and rare in summer in Gulf Coast and Tennessee Valley regions. In Mountain and Inland Coastal Plain regions, uncommon in winter and spring, and rare to uncommon in fall. Found in the Gulf and on bays, beaches, rivers, lakes, and garbage dumps. Low Conservation Concern.

Thayer's Gull *Larus thayeri*. Accidental. Hypothetical.

Iceland Gull *Larus glaucoides*. Accidental.

Lesser Black-backed Gull *Larus fuscus*. Rare in winter, spring, and fall in Gulf Coast and Tennessee Valley regions. Found in the Gulf and on bays, beaches, lakes, and rivers.

Glaucous Gull *Larus hyperboreus*. Rare in winter, spring, and fall in Gulf Coast and Tennessee Valley regions. Found in the Gulf, and on bays, beaches, lakes, and rivers.

Great Black-backed Gull *Larus marinus*. Rare in winter, spring, and fall in Gulf Coast region. In Tennessee Valley region, occasional in winter and spring. Found in the Gulf, and on bays, beaches, lakes, and large rivers. Lowest Conservation Concern.

Sabine's Gull *Xema sabini*. Accidental.

Black-legged Kittiwake *Rissa tridactyla*. Rare in winter and spring, and occasional to rare in fall in Gulf Coast and Tennessee Valley regions. Found in the Gulf, and on large lakes.

Gull-billed Tern *Sterna nilotica*. Breeder. Fairly common in spring, summer, and fall, and rare in winter in Gulf Coast region. Found in the Gulf and salt marshes, and on bays and beaches. Low Conservation Concern.

Caspian Tern *Sterna caspia*. Breeder. Fairly common in all seasons in Gulf Coast region. In Tennessee Valley, uncommon in spring and fall, and rare in summer. In Mountain and Inland Coastal Plain regions, rare in fall, and occasional in winter, spring, and summer. Found in the Gulf and on large lakes, large rivers, bays, and beaches. Low Conservation Concern.

Royal Tern *Sterna maxima*. Breeder. Common in all seasons in Gulf Coast region. In Mountain and Inland Coastal Plain regions, occasional in fall. Found in the Gulf and on bays and beaches. Low Conservation Concern.

Sandwich Tern *Sterna sandvicensis*. Breeder. Common in spring, summer, and fall, and rare to occasional in winter in Gulf Coast region. Found in the Gulf and on bays and beaches. Low Conservation Concern.

Roseate Tern *Sterna dougallii*. Accidental.

Common Tern *Sterna hirundo*. Breeder. Fairly common in fall, common in spring and summer, and rare in winter in Gulf Coastal Plain region. In other regions, rare in spring and fall, and occasional in summer. Found in the Gulf and on bays, beaches, lakes, and rivers. Low Conservation Concern.

Forster's Tern *Sterna forsteri*. Occasional breeder. Common in winter, spring, and fall in Gulf Coast region, and uncommon to rare in summer. In Tennessee Valley, fairly common to uncommon in spring and fall, uncommon in winter, and rare to uncommon in summer. In Mountain and Inland Coastal Plain regions, uncommon to rare in winter, spring, late summer, and fall. Found in marshes and the Gulf and on bays, beaches, rivers, lakes, and ponds. Low Conservation Concern.

Least Tern *Sterna antillarum*. Breeder. Common in spring, summer, and fall, and occasional in winter in Gulf Coast region. In Tennessee Valley region, rare in spring, late summer, and fall. In Mountain region, rare in fall, occasional in spring, and occasional to rare in summer. In Inland Coastal Plain, occasional in fall. Found in the Gulf and on bays, beaches, rivers, lakes, and ponds. MODERATE CONSERVATION CONCERN.

Bridled Tern *Sterna anaethetus*. Uncommon in spring, summer, and fall offshore. Occasional onshore after storms. Pelagic. Found in the Gulf.

Sooty Tern *Sterna fuscata*. Rare in summer and fall, and occasional in spring in Gulf Coast region (mostly offshore). Occasional inland in fall due to storms. Pelagic. Found in the Gulf and along barrier islands.

Black Tern *Chlidonias niger*. Common in summer and fall, fairly common in spring, and occasional in winter in Gulf Coast region. In other regions, uncommon in fall, and rare in spring and summer. Pelagic. Found in freshwater marshes and in the Gulf, on bays, lakes, rivers, ponds, and in flooded fields.

Brown Noddy *Anous stolidus*. Accidental.

Black Skimmer *Rynchops niger*. Breeder. Common in all seasons in Gulf Coast region. In other regions, occasional in fall due to storms. Found in the Gulf and on bays and beaches. Low Conservation Concern. **(Fig. 129, p. 165)**

PIGEONS AND DOVES
ORDER COLUMBIFORMES

DOVES AND PIGEONS - FAMILY COLUMBIDAE

Rock Dove *Columba livia*. **Exotic**. Breeder. Common in all seasons and regions. Found in cities and on farms, bridges, and cliffs.

Band-tailed Pigeon *Columba fasciata*. Accidental. Hypothetical.

Eurasian Collared-Dove *Streptopelia decaocto*. **Exotic**. Breeder. Common in all seasons in Gulf Coast and Inland Coastal Plain regions. In Tennessee Valley and Mountain region, local and rare to uncommon in all seasons, but increasing. Found in suburbs, parks, and farm groves.

White-winged Dove *Zenaida asiatica*. Possible breeder. Uncommon in spring and fall, rare in winter, and occasional in summer in Gulf Coast region. In other regions, occasional in summer, fall, and winter. Found on farms and in woodlots and grasslands. Low Conservation Concern.

Mourning Dove *Zenaida macroura*. Breeder. Common in all seasons and regions. Found on farms, and in towns, woodlots, agricultural fields, and grasslands. Lowest Conservation Concern. **(Fig. 130, p. 165)**

Passenger Pigeon *Ectopistes migratorius*. **Extinct**. Once overwintered in mature, mast producing woodlands.

Common Ground-Dove *Columbina passerina*. Breeder. Uncommon in all seasons in Gulf Coast and Inland Coastal Plain regions. Rare in all seasons in Tennessee Valley and Mountain regions. Found in sandy open areas, sparsely vegetated grasslands, and on farms and roadsides. MODERATE CONSERVATION CONCERN.

PARROTS
ORDER PSITTACIFORMES

LORISES, PARAKEETS, MACAWS, AND PARROTS - FAMILY PSITTACIDAE

Carolina Parakeet *Conuropsis carolinensis*. **Extinct**. Historical breeder. Thought to have been a breeding, permanent resident of the Coastal Plain.

CUCKOOS AND ALLIES
ORDER CUCULIFORMES

CUCKOOS, ROADRUNNERS, AND ANIS - FAMILY CUCULIDAE

Black-billed Cuckoo *Coccyzus erythropthalmus*. Occasional breeder. Uncommon in spring and rare in fall in Gulf Coast region. In other regions, rare in spring and fall, and occasional in summer. Found along forest edges and open woodlands.

Yellow-billed Cuckoo *Coccyzus americanus*. Breeder. Common in spring, summer, and fall in all regions. Found in woodlands and on farmlands with scattered trees and orchards. Low Conservation Concern.

Groove-billed Ani *Crotophaga sulcirostris*. Rare in fall and winter in Gulf Coast region. Found in early successional scrub, pastures, and orchards.

OWLS
ORDER STRIGIFORMES

BARN OWLS - FAMILY TYTONIDAE

Barn Owl *Tyto alba*. Breeder. Uncommon to rare in all seasons and regions. Found in open and partly open country and abandoned buildings. MODERATE CONSERVATION CONCERN.

TYPICAL OWLS - FAMILY STRIGIDAE

Eastern Screech-Owl *Otus asio*. Breeder. Common in all seasons and regions. Found in woodlands, especially near open areas, and orchards. MODERATE CONSERVATION CONCERN. **(Fig. 131, p. 165)**

Great Horned Owl *Bubo virginianus*. Breeder. Fairly common in all seasons and regions. Found in woodlands and parklands. MODERATE CONSERVATION CONCERN.

Snowy Owl *Nyctea scandiaca*. Accidental.

Burrowing Owl *Athene cunicularia*. Rare in winter, spring, and fall in Gulf Coast region. Found in open country and on beaches.

Barred Owl *Strix varia*. Breeder. Common in all seasons and in all regions. Found in moist woodlands and wooded swamps. Low Conservation Concern. **(Fig. 132, p. 165)**

Long-eared Owl *Asio otus*. Occasional in fall and winter in all regions. Found in woodlands, especially conifer groves.

Short-eared Owl *Asio flammeus*. Rare in winter, spring, and fall in Tennessee Valley and Inland Coastal Plain regions. Occasional in Gulf Coast region. Found in marshes, on dunes, and in grassy fields. **HIGH CONSERVATION CONCERN.**

Northern Saw-whet Owl *Aegolius acadicus*. Occasional in winter and fall in Inland Coastal Plain, Mountain, and Tennessee Valley regions. Found in dense evergreen thickets.

GOATSUCKERS, OILBIRDS, AND ALLIES
ORDER CAPRIMULGIFORMES

GOATSUCKERS - FAMILY CAPRIMULGIDAE

Lesser Nighthawk *Chordeiles acutipennis*. Accidental.

Common Nighthawk *Chordeiles minor*. Breeder. Uncommon to locally common in spring, summer, and fall, and rare in winter in all regions. Found in open and semi-open areas, grasslands, fields, cities, and towns. Low Conservation Concern.

Chuck-will's-widow *Caprimulgus carolinensis*. Breeder. Common in spring, summer, and fall, and occasional in winter in Gulf Coast region. In other regions, common in spring, summer, and fall. Found in deciduous and pine woodlands. MODERATE CONSERVATION CONCERN.

Whip-poor-will *Caprimulgus vociferus*. Breeder. Locally common in spring, summer, and fall in Tennessee Valley and Mountain regions. In Gulf Coast region, uncommon in winter, spring, and fall. In Inland Coastal Plain region, rare in spring and fall, and locally rare in summer. Found in open and mixed-forest woodlands. MODERATE CONSERVATION CONCERN.

SWIFTS AND HUMMINGBIRDS
ORDER APODIFORMES

SWIFTS - FAMILY APODIDAE

Chimney Swift *Chaetura pelagica*. Breeder. Common in spring, summer, and fall in all regions. Found in open areas, especially around human habitations. Low Conservation Concern.

HUMMINGBIRDS - FAMILY TROCHILIDAE

Green Violet-ear *Colibri thalassinus*. Accidental.

Buff-bellied Hummingbird *Amazilia yucatanensis*. Occasional in fall, winter, and spring in Gulf Coast region.

Blue-throated Hummingbird *Lampornis clemenciae*. Accidental. Hypothetical.

Magnificent Hummingbird *Eugenes fulgens*. Accidental.

Ruby-throated Hummingbird *Archilochus colubris*. Breeder. Common in spring, summer, and fall, and rare in winter in Gulf Coast regions. In other regions, common in spring, summer, and fall. Found in woodlands, gardens, along forest edges, and at feeders. Low Conservation Concern.

Black-chinned Hummingbird *Archilochus alexandri*. Rare in winter, spring, and fall in all regions. Found in open woodlands, parks, and gardens.

Anna's Hummingbird *Calypte anna*. Accidental.

Calliope Hummingbird *Stellula calliope*. Occasional in late fall, winter, and early spring in Gulf Coast, Inland Coastal Plain, and Mountain regions.

Broad-tailed Hummingbird *Selasphorus platycercus*. Occasional in late fall, winter, and early spring, mainly in Gulf Coast region.

Rufous Hummingbird *Selasphorus rufus*. Rare to uncommon in winter, spring, and fall in Gulf Coast region. In other regions, rare in winter, spring, and fall. Found in suburban gardens and at feeders.

Allen's Hummingbird *Selasphorus sasin*. Occasional in fall and winter in all regions. Found in suburban gardens and at feeders.

ROLLERS, MOTMOTS, KINGFISHERS, AND ALLIES
ORDER CORACIIFORMES

KINGFISHERS - FAMILY ALCEDINIDAE

Belted Kingfisher *Ceryle alcyon*. Breeder. Common in all seasons and regions. Found along wooded rivers, streams, lakes, ponds, and in marshes. MODERATE CONSER-VATION CONCERN.

PUFFBIRDS, JACAMARS, TOUCANS, WOODPECKERS, AND ALLIES
ORDER PICIFORMES

WOODPECKERS AND ALLIES - FAMILY PICIDAE

Red-headed Woodpecker *Melanerpes erythrocephalus*. Breeder. Fairly common in spring, summer, and fall, and uncommon in winter in all regions. Found in open woods, especially of oak and pine. MODERATE CONSERVATION CONCERN. **(Fig. 133, p. 165)**

Red-bellied Woodpecker *Melanerpes carolinus*. Breeder. Common in all seasons and regions. Found in woodlands. Low Conservation Concern.

Yellow-bellied Sapsucker *Sphyrapicus varius*. Fairly common in winter, spring, and fall in all regions. Found in mixed hardwood and conifer forests and urban areas. Low Conservation Concern.

Downy Woodpecker *Picoides pubescens*. Breeder. Common in all seasons and regions. Found in woodlands, orchards, suburban areas, parks, and farm woodlots. MODER-ATE CONSERVATION CONCERN.

Hairy Woodpecker *Picoides villosus*. Breeder. Uncommon in all seasons and regions. Found in pine, hardwood, and mixed woodlands. MODERATE CONSERVATION CONCERN.

Red-cockaded Woodpecker *Picoides borealis*. Breeder. Rare and local in all seasons in Mountain, Inland Coastal Plain, and Gulf Coast regions. Found in old growth pine forests. **Listed as *endangered* by the U.S. Fish and Wildlife Service. HIGHEST CONSERVATION CONCERN.**

Northern Flicker *Colaptes auratus*. Breeder. Fairly common in all seasons and regions.

Found in open woodlands and fields and on lawns and open meadows with large trees. **Designated the official state bird by the Alabama Legislature.** Low Conservation Concern. (**Fig. 134, p. 165**)

Pileated Woodpecker *Dryocopus pileatus*. Breeder. Fairly common in all seasons and regions. Found in mature woodlands with coniferous and hardwood trees. Low Conservation Concern.

Ivory-billed Woodpecker *Campephilus principalis*. **Extirpated.** Historic breeder. Was found in virgin cypress and bottomland hardwoods. **Listed as *endangered* by the U.S. Fish and Wildlife Service.**

PASSERINE BIRDS

ORDER PASSERIFORMES

TYRANT FLYCATCHERS - FAMILY TYRANNIDAE

Olive-sided Flycatcher *Contopus cooperi*. Rare in spring and fall in all regions. Found in forest habitats, primarily with emerging dead limbs.

Eastern Wood-Pewee *Contopus virens*. Breeder. Common to fairly common in spring, summer, and fall in all regions. Found in open woodlands, parks, and along forest edges. Low Conservation Concern.

Yellow-bellied Flycatcher *Empidonax flaviventris*. Rare in spring and fall in all regions. Found in forest interiors and along edges, and in low shrubby growth.

Acadian Flycatcher *Empidonax virescens*. Breeder. Common in spring, summer, and fall in all regions. Found in moist deciduous woods, dense woodlands, and wooded swamps. Low Conservation Concern.

Alder Flycatcher *Empidonax alnorum*. Occasional to rare in spring and fall in Tennessee Valley and Mountain regions. Occasional in fall in Gulf Coast regions. Found in shrubby thickets, primarily of alder and willow.

Willow Flycatcher *Empidonax traillii*. Possible breeder. Occasional to rare in spring and fall in all regions, and occasional in summer in Mountain region. Found in shrubby thickets, primarily of alder and willow.

Least Flycatcher *Empidonax minimus*. Uncommon in fall and occasional to rare in spring in all regions. Found in open woodlands, orchards, and parks.

Hammond's Flycatcher *Empidonax hammondii*. Accidental.

Fig. 110. Common Loon, *Gavia immer,* *p. 137.* *Photo–AOS Educational Slide Collection*

Fig. 111. Pied-bill Grebe, *Podilymbus podiceps,* **p. 137.** *Photo–Greg Harber*

Fig. 112. American White Pelican, *Pelecanus erythrorhynchos,* **p. 139.** *Photo–Walt Burch*

Fig. 113. Brown Pelican, *Pelecanus occidentalis,* **p. 139.** *Photo–Malcolm Pierson*

Fig. 114. Double-crested Cormorant, *Phalacrocorax auritus,* **p. 139.** *Photo–Malcolm Pierson*

Fig. 116. Tricolored Heron, *Egretta tricolor,* **p. 140.** *Photo–Malcolm Pierson*

Fig. 115. Great Blue Heron, *Ardea herodias,* **p. 140.** *Photo–Malcolm Pierson*

Fig. 118. White Ibis, *Eudocimus albus,* **p. 141.** *Photo–Malcolm Pierson*

Fig. 117. Cattle Egret perched on cow, *Bubulcus ibis,* **p. 140.** *Photo–Greg Harber*

Fig. 119. Turkey Vulture, *Cathartes aura,* **p. 142.** Photo–Malcolm Pierson

Fig. 120. Blue-winged Teal, *Anas discors,* **p. 143.** Photo–Malcolm Pierson

Fig. 121. Northern Pintail, *Anas acuta,* **p. 144.** Photo–Malcolm Pierson

Fig. 122. Osprey, *Pandion haliaetus,* **p. 146.** Photo–Dan Brothers

Fig. 123. Bald Eagle, *Haliaeetus leucocephalus,* **p. 146.** Photo–USFWS

Fig. 124. Clapper Rail *Rallus longirostris,* **p. 148.** Photo–AOS Educational Slide Collection

Fig. 125. Sora, *Porzana carolina,* **p. 149.** Photo–Malcolm Pierson

Fig. 126. Purple Gallinule, *Porphyrio martinica,* **p.149.** Photo–Malcolm Pierson

Fig. 127. Sandhill Crane, *Grus canadensis,* **p. 149.** Photo–Malcolm Pierson

Fig. 128. Ring-billed Gull, *Larus delawarensis,* **p. 155.** Photo–Greg Harber

Fig. 129. Black Skimmer
Rynchops niger, **p. 157.**
Photo–AOS Educational Slide Collection

Fig. 130. Mourning Dove, *Zenaida macroura*, **p. 157.** *Photo–James C. Leupold/USFWS*

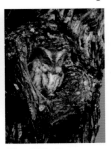

Fig. 131. Eastern Screech-Owl, *Otus asio*, **p. 158.** *Photo–Greg Harber*

Fig. 132. Barred Owl, *Strix varia*, **p. 159.** *Photo–Malcolm Pierson*

Fig. 133. Red-headed Woodpecker, *Melanerpes erythrocephalus*, **p. 161.** *Photo–ADCNR, Bob McCollum*

Fig. 134. Northern Flicker, *Colaptes auratus*, **p. 161.** *Photo–Walt Burch*

Fig. 135. Purple Martins, *Progne subis*, **p. 169.** *Photo–ADCNR, Bob McCollum*

Fig. 136. Barn Swallow, *Hirundo rustica*, **p. 170.** *Photo–AOS Educational Slide Collection*

Fig. 137. Eastern Bluebird, *Sialia sialis*, **p. 172.** *Photo–AOS Educational Slide Collection*

Fig. 138. American Robin, *Turdus migratorius*, **p. 172.** *Photo–ADCNR, Bob McCollum*

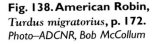

Fig. 139. Cedar Waxwing, *Bombycilla cedrorum,* **p. 173.**
Photo–ADCNR, Bob McCollum

Fig. 140. Yellow Warbler, *Dendroica petechia,* **p. 174.**
Photo–AOS Educational Slide Collection

Fig. 141. Ovenbird, *Seiurus aurocapillus,* **p. 177.**
Photo–AOS Educational Slide Collection

Fig. 142. Field Sparrow, *Spizella pusilla,* **p. 179.**
Photo–Walt Burch

Fig. 143. Northern Cardinal, *Cardinalis cardinalis,* **p. 181.**
Photo–Walt Burch

Fig. 144. Indigo Bunting, *Passerina cyanea,* **p. 181.**
Photo–Ralph Mirarchi

Fig. 145. Red-winged Blackbird, *Agelaius phoeniceus,* **p. 182.**
Photo–AOS Educational Slide Collection

Fig. 146. Boat-tailed Grackle, *Quiscalus major,* **p. 182.** *Photo–Malcolm Pierson*

Fig. 147. Baltimore Oriole, *Icterus galbula,* **p. 183.** *Photo–David Pond*

Fig. 148. American Goldfinch, *Carduelis tristis,* **p. 184.**
Photo–Ralph Mirarchi

Dusky Flycatcher *Empidonax oberholseri*. Accidental.

Eastern Phoebe *Sayornis phoebe*. Breeder. Fairly common in all seasons in Tennessee Valley and Mountain regions. In Inland Coastal Plain, common in winter, spring, and fall, and uncommon to rare in summer. In Gulf Coast region, common in winter, spring, and fall. Found in open deciduous woodlands near bridges, cliffs, caves, porches, and little-used or abandoned buildings. Lowest Conservation Concern.

Say's Phoebe *Sayornis saya*. Accidental.

Vermilion Flycatcher *Pyrocephalus rubinus*. Rare in winter, spring, and fall in Gulf Coast region. In Mountain and Inland Coastal Plain regions, occasional in winter, spring, and fall. Found in open country, especially in pastures, agricultural lands, and early successional scrub.

Ash-throated Flycatcher *Myiarchus cinerascens*. Rare in winter and fall, and occasional in spring, in Gulf Coast region. In other regions, occasional in fall and winter. Found in open woodlands.

Great Crested Flycatcher *Myiarchus crinitus*. Breeder. Common in spring, summer, and fall in all regions. Found in woodlands, open country with scattered trees, and parks. Lowest Conservation Concern.

Brown-crested Flycatcher *Myiarchus tyrannulus*. Accidental.

La Sagra's Flycatcher *Myiarchus sagrae*. Accidental.

Sulphur-bellied Flycatcher *Myiodynastes luteiventris*. Accidental.

Couch's Kingbird *Tyrannus couchii*. Accidental.

Western Kingbird *Tyrannus verticalis*. Uncommon to rare in fall, and rare in winter, spring, and summer in Gulf Coast region. In other regions, occasional in spring and fall. Found in open country with scattered trees, especially agricultural lands.

Eastern Kingbird *Tyrannus tyrannus*. Breeder. Common in spring, summer, and fall in all regions. Found in open rural areas with scattered trees and shrubs, along woodland edges, and in agricultural fields with hedgerows, especially near ponds or rivers. Low Conservation Concern.

Gray Kingbird *Tyrannus dominicensis*. Breeder. Rare in spring, summer, and fall in Gulf Coast region. Found in open habitats and on beaches and sand dunes with scattered trees and scrub vegetation. MODERATE CONSERVATION CONCERN.

Scissor-tailed Flycatcher *Tyrannus forficatus*. Breeder. Uncommon in fall, rare in winter and spring, and occasional in summer in Gulf Coast region. In other regions, rare in spring, summer, and fall. Found in open country, dry grasslands, and agricultural lands. Low Conservation Concern.

Fork-tailed Flycatcher *Tyrannus savana*. Accidental.

SHRIKES - FAMILY LANIIDAE

Loggerhead Shrike *Lanius ludovicianus*. Breeder. Fairly common in winter, spring, and fall, and uncommon in summer in all regions. Found in open country with scattered trees and shrubs and in hedgerows along agricultural fields. MODERATE CONSERVATION CONCERN.

VIREOS - FAMILY VIREONIDAE

White-eyed Vireo *Vireo griseus*. Breeder. Common in spring, summer, and fall, and uncommon in winter in Gulf Coast region. In Inland Coastal Plain region, common in spring, summer, and fall, and rare in winter. In Tennessee Valley and Mountain regions, common in spring, summer, and fall. Found in undergrowth, early successional fields, streamside thickets, and along woodland edges. Low Conservation Concern.

Bell's Vireo *Vireo bellii*. Rare in fall and occasional in spring in Gulf Coast region. In other regions, occasional in spring and fall. Found in dense thickets.

Yellow-throated Vireo *Vireo flavifrons*. Breeder. Common in spring, summer, and fall in Mountain, Tennessee, and Inland Coastal Plain regions. In Gulf Coast region, common in spring and fall, and fairly common in summer. Found in tall, open woodlands, especially near water. Low Conservation Concern.

Blue-headed Vireo *Vireo solitarius*. Breeder. Fairly common in winter, spring, and fall in Gulf Coast region. In Inland Coastal Plain region, uncommon in winter, spring, and fall. In Mountain region, uncommon in spring and fall, rare in winter, and rare to locally uncommon in summer. In Tennessee Valley region, uncommon in spring and fall, and rare in winter. Found in woodlands. Lowest Conservation Concern.

Warbling Vireo *Vireo gilvus*. Local breeder. In Tennessee Valley region, rare in spring, summer, and fall. In other regions, rare in spring and fall. Found in open, park-like woodlands, with tall trees, especially near water. Low Conservation Concern.

Philadelphia Vireo *Vireo philadelphicus*. Fairly common in fall, and rare in spring in all regions. Found in woodlands.

Red-eyed Vireo *Vireo olivaceus*. Breeder. Common in spring, summer, and fall in all regions. Found in deciduous woods, mixed forests, shade trees, and woodlots. Lowest Conservation Concern.

Black-whiskered Vireo *Vireo altiloquus*. Rare in spring and occasional in fall in Gulf Coast region. Found in coastal trees and thickets.

CROWS AND JAYS - FAMILY CORVIDAE

Blue Jay *Cyanocitta cristata*. Breeder. Common in all seasons and regions. Found in forests, open woodlands, wooded residential areas, and parks. Low Conservation Concern.

American Crow *Corvus brachyrhynchos*. Breeder. Common in all seasons in all inland regions. In Gulf Coast region, uncommon in all seasons. Found in woodlands, farmlands, and suburban areas. Lowest Conservation Concern.

Fish Crow *Corvus ossifragus*. Breeder. Common in all seasons in Gulf Coast region. In Inland Coastal Plain region, fairly common in all seasons. In Mountain region, uncommon in spring, summer, and fall. Found around beaches, bays, swamplands, riverine areas, urban and suburban areas, and farmlands. Low Conservation Concern.

Common Raven *Corvus corax*. **Extirpated**. Historical breeder. Was a rare, permanent resident of the mountains of northern Alabama.

LARKS - FAMILY ALAUDIDAE

Horned Lark *Eremophila alpestris*. Breeder. Fairly common in winter, spring, and fall, and uncommon in summer in Tennessee Valley and Mountain regions. In Inland Coastal Plain region, rare and local in winter and late fall, and occasional in spring and summer. Found in open country habitats with short grass and bare ground patches, cultivated fields, and stubble fields. Low Conservation Concern.

SWALLOWS–FAMILY HIRUNDINIDAE

Purple Martin *Progne subis*. Breeder. Common in spring, summer, and early fall in inland regions. In Gulf Coast region, common in spring, summer, and fall, occasional in midwinter, and uncommon in late winter. Found in open rural and suburban areas and open farmlands, especially near water. Lowest Conservation Concern. **(Fig. 135, p. 165)**

Tree Swallow *Tachycineta bicolor*. Breeder. Common in winter, spring, and fall in Gulf Coast region. In Inland Coastal Plain, common in fall, fairly common in spring, and rare in winter. In Tennessee Valley and Mountain regions, common in fall, fairly common in spring, and rare in winter and summer. Open areas, ponds, lakes; nests in cavities in dead, standing timber and boxes. Lowest Conservation Concern.

Northern Rough-winged Swallow *Stelgidopteryx serripennis*. Breeder. Fairly common in spring, summer, and fall, and rare in early winter in Gulf Coast region. In other regions, common in spring, summer, and fall. Found in open areas, fields, swamps, and on ponds and lakes; nests in burrows in road cuts and steep banks. Lowest Conservation Concern.

Bank Swallow *Riparia riparia*. Historical breeder. Common in spring and fall, rare in late summer in Gulf Coast region. In other regions, fairly common in spring and fall, occasional in summer. Found in open habitats, especially near water.

Cliff Swallow *Petrochelidon pyrrhonota*. Breeder. Common in spring, summer, and early fall in Tennessee Valley. In Gulf Coast region, fairly common in spring, summer, and fall. In Mountain and Inland Coastal Plain regions, uncommon in spring, fall, and summer. Found in open habitats near water; nests on dams and bridges. Low Conservation Concern.

Cave Swallow *Petrochelidon fulva*. Rare in spring in Gulf Coast region. Found in open habitats.

Barn Swallow *Hirundo rustica*. Breeder. Common in spring, summer, and fall in inland regions. In Gulf Coast region, common in spring, summer, and fall, and occasional in winter. Found in open habitats, under bridges and culverts, and in barns. Low Conservation Concern. **(Fig. 136, p. 165)**

CHICKADEES AND TITMICE - FAMILY PARIDAE

Carolina Chickadee *Poecile carolinensis*. Breeder. Common in all seasons and regions. Found in woodlands and wooded suburbs. Low Conservation Concern.

Tufted Titmouse *Baeolophus bicolor*. Breeder. Common in all seasons and regions. Found in woodlands and wooded suburbs. Lowest Conservation Concern.

NUTHATCHES - FAMILY SITTIDAE

Red-breasted Nuthatch *Sitta canadensis*. Uncommon and erratic in winter, spring, and fall in all regions. Found in coniferous and mixed pine-hardwood woodlands. Lowest Conservation Concern.

White-breasted Nuthatch *Sitta carolinensis*. Breeder. Fairly common in all seasons in Tennessee Valley and Mountain regions. In Inland Coastal Plain, rare in all seasons. Found in deciduous woodlands. Low Conservation Concern.

Brown-headed Nuthatch *Sitta pusilla*. Breeder. Common in all seasons and regions, but local in Tennessee Valley region. Found in open pine forests. MODERATE CONSERVATION CONCERN.

CREEPERS - FAMILY CERTHIIDAE

Brown Creeper *Certhia americana*. Uncommon in winter, spring, and fall in Tennessee Valley and Mountain regions. In Gulf Coast region, uncommon in fall and rare in winter and spring. In Inland Coastal Plain, rare in winter, spring, and fall. Found in woodlands. MODERATE CONSERVATION CONCERN.

WRENS - FAMILY TROGLODYTIDAE

Rock Wren *Salpinctes obsoletus*. Accidental.

Carolina Wren *Thryothorus ludovicianus*. Breeder. Common in all seasons and regions. Found in thickets in woodlands, farmlands, and suburbs. Lowest Conservation Concern.

Bewick's Wren *Thryomanes bewickii*. Historical breeder. Occasional in winter, spring, and fall in all regions. Found in farmlands, hedgerows, and thickets. No breeding season records since 1976. **HIGHEST CONSERVATION CONCERN.**

House Wren *Troglodytes aedon*. Breeder. Common in winter, spring, and fall in Gulf Coast region. In Inland Coastal Plain, fairly common in fall, uncommon in winter and spring. In Tennessee Valley and Mountain regions, fairly common in fall, uncommon in spring, and rare in winter and summer. Found in farmlands, thickets, and suburban yards with dense hedgerows. Lowest Conservation Concern.

Winter Wren *Troglodytes troglodytes*. Fairly common in winter, spring, and fall in Tennessee Valley and Mountain regions. In Inland Coastal Plain and Gulf Coast regions, uncommon in winter, early spring, and fall. Found among fallen trees, vine tangles, and in ravines. Low Conservation Concern.

Sedge Wren *Cistothorus platensis*. Common in winter, spring, and fall in Gulf Coast region. In Inland Coastal Plain, fairly common in winter, spring, and fall. In Tennessee Valley and Mountain regions, uncommon in spring and fall, and rare in winter. Found in sedge marshes, grassy thickets, brush piles, and open pine savannahs. Low Conservation Concern.

Marsh Wren *Cistothorus palustris*. Breeder. Common in all seasons in Gulf Coast region. In Inland Coastal Plain, uncommon in winter, spring, and fall. In Tennessee Valley and Mountain regions, uncommon in spring and fall, and rare in winter. Found in marshes with cattails, cordgrass, and rushes. MODERATE CONSERVATION CONCERN.

KINGLETS- FAMILY REGULIDAE

Golden-crowned Kinglet *Regulus satrapa*. Common in winter, spring, and fall in inland regions. In Gulf Coast region, fairly common in fall, and uncommon in winter and spring. Found in woodlands, especially with conifers. Lowest Conservation Concern.

Ruby-crowned Kinglet *Regulus calendula*. Common in winter, spring, and fall in all regions. Found in woodlands. Lowest Conservation Concern.

OLD WORLD WARBLERS AND GNATCATCHERS - FAMILY SYLVIIDAE

Blue-gray Gnatcatcher *Polioptila caerulea*. Breeder. Common in spring, summer, and fall, and fairly common in winter in Gulf Coast region. In other regions, common in spring, summer, and fall, and rare in winter. Found in open woodlands, forest edges, and tree-lined fence rows. Low Conservation Concern.

THRUSHES - FAMILY TURDIDAE

Northern Wheatear *Oenanthe oenanthe*. Accidental.

Eastern Bluebird *Sialia sialis*. Breeder. Common in all seasons and regions. Found in open rural areas, farmlands, fence rows, open suburban areas, and parks with scattered trees. Lowest Conservation Concern. **(Fig. 137, p. 165)**

Veery *Catharus fuscescens*. Possible breeder. Fairly common in spring and rare in fall in Gulf Coast region. In Mountain region, uncommon in spring and fall, and occasional in summer. In Tennessee Valley and Inland Coastal Plain regions, uncommon in spring and fall. Found in dense woodlands.

Gray-cheeked Thrush *Catharus minimus*. Fairly common in spring and rare in fall in Gulf Coast region. In inland regions, uncommon in spring and fall. Found in woodlands with dense undergrowth.

Swainson's Thrush *Catharus ustulatus*. Common in spring and fall in all regions. In Gulf Coast region, occasional in early winter. Found in woodlands with dense undergrowth.

Hermit Thrush *Catharus guttatus*. Fairly common in winter, spring, and fall in all regions. Found in woodlands with dense undergrowth. Lowest Conservation Concern.

Wood Thrush *Hylocichla mustelina*. Breeder. Common in spring, summer, and fall in all regions. In Gulf Coast region, occasional in early winter. Woodlands and wooded suburbs with understory. **HIGH CONSERVATION CONCERN.**

American Robin *Turdus migratorius*. Breeder. Common in all seasons in Tennessee Valley and Mountain regions. In Inland Coastal Plain region, common in winter, spring, and fall, and uncommon in summer. In Gulf Coast region, common in winter, spring, and fall, and rare in summer. Found in short grass areas with scattered trees in cities, towns, parks, suburbs, and rural areas in summer; primarily in woodlands with soft mast in winter. Lowest Conservation Concern. **(Fig. 138, p. 165)**

Varied Thrush *Ixoreus naevius*. Accidental.

MOCKINGBIRDS AND THRASHERS - FAMILY MIMIDAE

Gray Catbird *Dumetella carolinensis*. Breeder. Common in winter, spring, and fall in Gulf Coast region. In Inland Coastal Plain region, common in spring and fall, uncommon in winter and summer. In Tennessee Valley and Mountain regions, common in spring, and fall, fairly common in summer, and rare in winter. Found in hedgerows, thickets, fence rows, and dense brushy vegetation bordering ponds and lakes. Lowest Conservation Concern.

Northern Mockingbird *Mimus polyglottos*. Breeder. Common in all seasons and regions. Found in rural, suburban, and urban areas in openings with short grass, scattered shrubs, and trees. Low Conservation Concern.

Sage Thrasher *Oreoscoptes montanus*. Accidental.

Brown Thrasher *Toxostoma rufum*. Breeder. Common in all seasons and regions. Found in short ground cover vegetation near dense thickets, hedgerows, and shrubs. Low Conservation Concern.

STARLINGS - FAMILY STURNIDAE

European Starling *Sturnus vulgaris*. **Exotic**. Breeder. Common in all seasons and regions. Found in urban, suburban, and rural areas with open ground for foraging.

WAGTAILS AND PIPITS - FAMILY MOTACILLIDAE

American Pipit *Anthus rubescens*. Fairly common in winter, spring, and fall in all regions. Found in open country, especially on plowed fields and mudflats. Low Conservation Concern.

Sprague's Pipit *Anthus spragueii*. Occasional in winter, spring, and fall in all regions. Found in open, short-grass areas, such as pastures and airports.

WAXWINGS - FAMILY BOMBYCILLIDAE

Cedar Waxwing *Bombycilla cedrorum*. Breeder. Common in winter, spring, and fall, and rare in summer in Mountain and Tennessee Valley regions. In Gulf Coast and Inland Coastal Plain regions, common in winter, spring, and fall, and occasional in summer.

Found in areas with trees and shrubs that produce fruits, such as hackberry, red mulberry, eastern red-cedar, black cherry, and American holly. Lowest Conservation Concern. **(Fig. 139, p. 166)**

WOOD-WARBLERS - FAMILY PARULIDAE

Bachman's Warbler *Vermivora bachmanii*. **Extinct.** Historical breeder. Was found along swamp borders with blackberry thickets and cane.

Blue-winged Warbler *Vermivora pinus*. Breeder. Fairly common in fall, uncommon in spring and summer in Mountain and Tennessee Valley regions. In Gulf Coast region, fairly common in spring, uncommon in fall, and occasional in late summer. In Inland Coastal Plain, uncommon in spring and fall, and occasional in summer. Found in abandoned fields or cut-over areas, usually near water, that contain scattered saplings and dense ground cover; woodlands during migration. MODERATE CONSERVATION CONCERN.

Golden-winged Warbler *Vermivora chrysoptera*. Uncommon in fall and rare in spring in all regions. Found in woodlands.

Tennessee Warbler *Vermivora peregrina*. Common in spring and fall in all regions. Found in woodlands.

Orange-crowned Warbler *Vermivora celata*. Fairly common in winter, spring, and fall in Gulf Coast region. In Inland Coastal Plain, uncommon in winter, spring, and fall. In Tennessee Valley and Mountain regions, uncommon in spring and fall, and rare in winter. Found in woodlands.

Nashville Warbler *Vermivora ruficapilla*. Uncommon in fall and rare in spring in Tennessee Valley. In Mountain and Gulf Coast regions, rare in spring and fall. In Inland Coastal Plain, rare in fall. Found in woodlands.

Northern Parula *Parula americana*. Breeder. In Gulf Coast region, common in spring, summer, and fall, and occasional in winter. In inland regions, fairly common in spring, summer, and fall. Found in tall trees along streams, swamps, and lakes; woodlands during migration. MODERATE CONSERVATION CONCERN.

Yellow Warbler *Dendroica petechia*. Breeder. Common in spring and fall, and rare in summer in Tennessee Valley and Mountain regions. In Inland Coastal Plain region, common in spring and fall, and occasional in summer. In Gulf Coast region, common in spring and fall. Found in small trees and shrubs near water. Lowest Conservation Concern. **(Fig. 140, p. 166)**

Chestnut-sided Warbler *Dendroica pensylvanica*. Occasional breeder. Common in fall, fairly common in spring, and rare in summer in Mountain region. In Tennessee Valley and Gulf Coast regions, common in fall and fairly common in spring. In Inland Coastal Plain region, fairly common in fall and uncommon in spring. Found in woodlands.

Magnolia Warbler *Dendroica magnolia*. Common in fall, fairly common in spring, and occasional in summer in all regions. Found in woodlands.

Cape May Warbler *Dendroica tigrina*. Uncommon in spring, rare in fall, and occasional in winter in inland regions. In Gulf Coast region, fairly common in spring and rare in fall, and occasional in winter. Found in woodlands.

Black-throated Blue Warbler *Dendroica caerulescens*. Uncommon in spring and fall in Gulf Coast region. In inland regions, rare in spring and fall, especially in east. Found in woodlands, especially understory.

Yellow-rumped Warbler *Dendroica coronata*. Common in winter, spring, and fall in all regions. Found in woodlands. Lowest Conservation Concern.

Black-throated Gray Warbler *Dendroica nigrescens*. Occasional in spring and fall in Gulf Coast region.

Black-throated Green Warbler *Dendroica virens*. Breeder. Common in fall, fairly common in spring and summer, and occasional in winter in Mountain region. In Gulf Coast region, common in spring and fall, and occasional in winter. In Inland Coastal Plain and Tennessee Valley regions, common in fall, and fairly common in spring. In breeding season, found in coniferous and deciduous forests; in migration, found in woodlands. Lowest Conservation Concern.

Blackburnian Warbler *Dendroica fusca*. Fairly common in spring and fall, and occasional in summer in Mountain region. In Tennessee Valley region, fairly common in spring and fall. In Gulf Coast region, fairly common in fall, and uncommon in spring. In Inland Coastal Plain, uncommon in spring and fall. Found in woodlands.

Yellow-throated Warbler *Dendroica dominica*. Breeder. In Gulf Coast region, common in spring, summer, and fall, and rare in winter. In inland regions, fairly common in spring, summer, and fall, and occasional in winter. In breeding season, found in older pine forests and woodlands with sycamores, especially near water; in migration, found in woodlands. Low Conservation Concern.

Pine Warbler *Dendroica pinus*. Breeder. Common in all seasons and regions. Found in mature pine woodlands. Lowest Conservation Concern.

Kirtland's Warbler *Dendroica kirtlandii*. Accidental. Hypothetical.

Prairie Warbler *Dendroica discolor*. Breeder. Common in spring, summer, and fall; occasional in winter in inland regions. In Gulf Coast region, common in spring and fall, uncommon in summer, and occasional in winter. Found in brushy early successional growth, particularly regenerating clearcuts. MODERATE CONSERVATION CONCERN.

Palm Warbler *Dendroica palmarum*. Common in spring and fall, and fairly common in winter in Gulf Coast region. In Inland Coastal Plain region, common in spring, fairly common in fall, and uncommon to locally common in winter. In Tennessee Valley and Mountain regions, common in spring, fairly common in fall, and rare in winter. Found in open areas with scattered shrubs and trees. MODERATE CONSERVATION CONCERN.

Bay-breasted Warbler *Dendroica castanea*. Fairly common in spring and fall in all regions. Found in woodlands.

Blackpoll Warbler *Dendroica striata*. Common in spring in all regions, and occasional in fall, mostly in Gulf Coast region. Found in woodlands.

Cerulean Warbler *Dendroica cerulea*. Breeder. Uncommon in spring and fall, and rare and local in summer in Mountain region. In Tennessee Valley, uncommon in spring and fall, and occasional in summer. In Gulf Coast region, uncommon in spring, and rare in fall. In Inland Coastal Plain, rare in fall and occasional in spring. In breeding season, found in mature bottomland forests along streams; in migration, found in woodlands. **HIGHEST CONSERVATION CONCERN**.

Black-and-white Warbler *Mniotilta varia*. Breeder. Common in spring, summer, and fall, and occasional in winter in Tennessee Valley and Mountain regions. In Inland Coastal Plain, common in spring and fall, rare in summer, and occasional in winter. In Gulf Coast region, common in spring and fall, and rare in winter. In breeding season, found in hardwood and mixed hardwood-coniferous forests; in migration, found in woodlands. Low Conservation Concern.

American Redstart *Setophaga ruticilla*. Breeder. Common in spring and fall, and fairly common in summer in Inland Coastal Plain and Gulf Coast regions. Common in spring and fall in Tennessee Valley and Mountain regions, and rare to uncommon in summer. In breeding season, found in deciduous woods, especially riverine systems; in migration, found in woodlands. Low Conservation Concern.

Prothonotary Warbler *Protonotaria citrea*. Breeder. Common in spring, summer, and early fall in all regions. Found in swamp and bottomland forests. MODERATE CONSERVATION CONCERN.

Worm-eating Warbler *Helmitheros vermivorus*. Breeder. Uncommon in spring, summer, and fall in Tennessee Valley and Mountain regions. In Inland Coastal Plain region, uncommon in spring and fall, and rare in summer. In Gulf Coast region, fairly common in spring, uncommon in fall, and rare in late summer. In breeding season, found in shrubby, wooded hillsides and ravines; in migration, found in woodlands and thickets. **HIGH CONSERVATION CONCERN.**

Swainson's Warbler *Limnothlypis swainsonii*. Breeder. Fairly common in spring and summer, and uncommon to rare in fall in Gulf Coast, Inland Coastal Plain, and Mountain regions. In Tennessee Valley, rare in spring, summer, and fall. Found in dense thickets in swamps, along streams, and in woodland areas. HIGH CONSERVATION CONCERN.

Ovenbird *Seiurus aurocapillus*. Breeder. Fairly common in spring and fall, and locally uncommon to rare in summer in Tennessee Valley and Mountain regions. In Gulf Coast region, common in spring, fairly common in fall, and occasional in winter. In Inland Coastal Plain region, fairly common in spring, and uncommon in fall. In breeding season, found in deciduous forests; in migration, found in woodlands, especially with dense understory. Lowest Conservation Concern. **(Fig. 141, p. 166)**

Northern Waterthrush *Seiurus noveboracensis*. Common in spring and fall, and occasional in winter in Gulf Coast region. In inland regions, fairly common in spring and fall. Found along shorelines of swamps, lakes, ponds, and streams.

Louisiana Waterthrush *Seiurus motacilla*. Breeder. Common in spring, summer, and early fall in inland regions. In Gulf Coast region, common in spring, and rare in late summer and early fall. Found in older bottomland forests along streams. MODERATE CONSERVATION CONCERN.

Kentucky Warbler *Oporornis formosus*. Breeder. Common in spring, summer, and fall in all regions. Found in moist woodlands with dense herbaceous ground cover. **HIGH CONSERVATION CONCERN.**

Connecticut Warbler *Oporornis agilis*. Rare in spring and occasional in fall inland. In Gulf Coast region, occasional in spring and fall. Found in brushy, semi-open, moist woodland areas.

Mourning Warbler *Oporornis philadelphia*. Rare in spring and summer in inland regions. In Gulf Coast, rare in fall. Found in thickets, weedy fields, scrub, and woodland undergrowth.

Common Yellowthroat *Geothlypis trichas*. Breeder. Common in spring, summer, and fall, and fairly common in winter in Gulf Coast region. In Inland Coastal Plain region, common in spring, summer, and fall, and uncommon in winter. In Tennessee Valley and Mountain regions, common in spring, summer, and fall, and rare in winter. Found along woodland edges, and in hedgerows, thickets, marshes, and wet meadows. Low Conservation Concern.

Hooded Warbler *Wilsonia citrina*. Breeder. Common in spring, summer, and fall in all regions. In breeding season, found in shrubby forests; in migration, found in woodlands, especially in understory. Low Conservation Concern.

Wilson's Warbler *Wilsonia pusilla*. Uncommon in fall, rare in spring, and occasional in winter in all regions. Found in shrubby areas, especially near water.

Canada Warbler *Wilsonia canadensis*. Fairly common in fall and spring in Tennessee Valley and Mountain regions. In Inland Coastal Plain region, uncommon in spring and fall. In Gulf Coast region, uncommon in fall and rare in spring. Found in woodlands, especially understory.

Painted Redstart *Myioborus pictus*. Accidental.

Yellow-breasted Chat *Icteria virens*. Breeder. Common in spring, summer, and fall, and occasional in winter in all regions. Found in early successional growth areas. Lowest Conservation Concern.

TANAGERS - FAMILY THRAUPIDAE

Summer Tanager *Piranga rubra*. Breeder. Common in spring, summer, and fall, and occasional in winter in all regions. In breeding season, found in open, mixed hardwood-coniferous forests and along forest edges. Lowest Conservation Concern.

Scarlet Tanager *Piranga olivacea*. Breeder. Common in spring, summer, and fall in Tennessee Valley and Mountain regions. In Inland Coastal Plain and Gulf Coast regions, common in spring and fall. In breeding season, found in hardwood forests; in migration, found in woodlands. Low Conservation Concern.

Western Tanager *Piranga ludoviciana*. Rare in spring and fall, and occasional in winter in primarily Gulf Coast region. Found in older pine woodlands.

EMBERIZIDS - FAMILY EMBERIZIDAE

Green-tailed Towhee *Pipilo chlorurus*. Accidental.

Eastern Towhee *Pipilo erythrophthalmus*. Breeder. Common in all seasons and regions. Found in brushy woodlands and early successional growth. Low Conservation Concern.

Bachman's Sparrow *Aimophila aestivalis*. Breeder. Uncommon in spring, summer, and fall, and rare in winter in Inland Coastal Plain and Gulf Coast regions. In Mountain and Tennessee Valley regions, rare in spring, summer, and fall, and occasional in winter. Found in open pine forests and regenerating clearcuts. **HIGH CONSERVATION CONCERN.**

American Tree Sparrow *Spizella arborea*. Rare in winter and occasional in spring in primarily Mountain and Tennessee Valley regions. Found in brushy and weedy areas.

Chipping Sparrow *Spizella passerina*. Breeder. Common in all seasons in Tennessee Valley and Mountain regions. In Inland Coastal Plain region, common in winter, spring, and fall, and fairly common in summer. In Gulf Coast region, common in winter, spring, and fall, and rare in summer. Found in open areas with short grass and scattered trees, especially conifers. Lowest Conservation Concern.

Clay-colored Sparrow *Spizella pallida*. Rare in fall, and occasional in winter and spring in primarily outer coast of Gulf Coast region. Found in open woodlands with small trees and open shrubby areas.

Field Sparrow *Spizella pusilla*. Breeder. Common to fairly common in all seasons in inland regions. In Gulf Coast region, fairly common in winter, spring, and fall. Found in early successional growth areas, especially with dense ground cover. Low Conservation Concern. **(Fig. 142, p. 166)**

Vesper Sparrow *Pooecetes gramineus*. Fairly common in winter, spring, and fall in Gulf Coast and Inland Coastal Plain regions. In Tennessee Valley and Mountain regions, uncommon in spring and fall, and rare in winter. Found in short grass fields.

Lark Sparrow *Chondestes grammacus*. Breeder. Uncommon in fall, and rare in winter and spring in primarily outer coast of Gulf Coast Plain region. In Inland Coastal Plain region, rare in spring, summer, and fall. In Tennessee Valley, rare in spring, summer and fall, and occasional in winter. In Mountain region, occasional in spring and fall. Found in open, short-grass and bare-ground areas. Low Conservation Concern.

Lark Bunting *Calamospiza melanocorys*. Accidental.

Savannah Sparrow *Passerculus sandwichensis*. Common in winter, spring, and fall in all regions. Found in open grassy fields. Low Conservation Concern.

Grasshopper Sparrow *Ammodramus savannarum*. Breeder. Uncommon to fairly common in spring, summer, and fall, and rare in winter, in Inland Coastal Plain. In Tennessee Valley, fairly common in spring, summer, and fall, and occasional in winter. In Mountain region, uncommon in spring, summer, and fall, and rare in winter. In Gulf Coast region, uncommon in spring, and rare in fall and winter. Found in old fields, grasslands. MODERATE CONSERVATION CONCERN.

Henslow's Sparrow *Ammodramus henslowii*. Rare to locally uncommon in winter, spring, and fall in Inland Coastal Plain and Gulf Coast regions. Occasional in fall, winter, and spring in Tennessee Valley and Mountain regions. Found in open areas with grass and forb ground cover, especially in bogs. **HIGHEST CONSERVATION CONCERN.**

Le Conte's Sparrow *Ammodramus leconteii*. Uncommon and local in winter and fall, and rare in spring in Gulf Coast region. In inland regions, rare in winter, spring, and fall. Found in moist, grassy fields. MODERATE CONSERVATION CONCERN.

Nelson's Sharp-tailed Sparrow *Ammodramus nelsoni*. Fairly common in winter, spring, and fall in Gulf Coast region. In inland regions, occasional in spring and fall. Found in coastal salt marshes. **HIGH CONSERVATION CONCERN.**

Seaside Sparrow *Ammodramus maritimus*. Breeder. Fairly common and local in all seasons in Gulf Coast region. Found in coastal salt marshes. **HIGH CONSERVATION CONCERN.**

Fox Sparrow *Passerella iliaca*. Uncommon in winter, spring, and fall in inland regions. In Gulf Coast region, rare in winter and fall. Found in woodlands and thickets. Low Conservation Concern.

Song Sparrow *Melospiza melodia*. Breeder. Common in winter, spring, and fall, and uncommon to rare in summer in Tennessee Valley and Mountain regions. In Inland Coastal Plain and Gulf Coast regions, common in winter, spring, and fall. Found in open brushy and weedy areas. Lowest Conservation Concern.

Lincoln's Sparrow *Melospiza lincolnii*. Uncommon in fall, rare in winter and spring in Tennessee Valley. In other regions, rare in winter, spring, and fall. Found in brushy, open areas. Low Conservation Concern.

Swamp Sparrow *Melospiza georgiana*. Common to fairly common in winter, spring, and fall in all regions. Found in freshwater marshes and shrubby and weedy areas, especially near water. Low Conservation Concern.

White-throated Sparrow *Zonotrichia albicollis*. Common in winter, spring, and fall, and rare in summer in all regions. Found in thickets and shrubby areas. Low Conservation Concern.

Harris's Sparrow *Zonotrichia querula*. Occasional in winter, spring, and fall in all regions. Found in brushy, weedy areas, hedgerows, and brush piles.

White-crowned Sparrow *Zonotrichia leucophrys*. Uncommon in winter, spring, and fall in Inland Coastal Plain and Tennessee Valley regions. In Gulf Coast region, fairly common in fall, and rare in winter and spring. In Mountain region, rare in winter, spring, and fall. Found in thickets, hedgerows, and along woodland borders. Low Conservation Concern.

Dark-eyed Junco *Junco hyemalis*. Common in winter, spring, and fall, and occasional in summer in inland regions. In Gulf Coast region, uncommon in winter and rare in spring and fall. Found in open woodlands and brushy and grassy areas. Low Conservation Concern.

Lapland Longspur *Calcarius lapponicus*. Locally fairly common in winter and spring, and uncommon in late fall in Tennessee Valley region. In other regions, rare in winter, spring, and fall. Found on beaches and in open areas with short grass and bare ground, especially plowed fields and fields with stubble. Lowest Conservation Concern.

Smith's Longspur *Calcarius pictus*. Accidental.

Snow Bunting *Plectrophenax nivalis*. Accidental. Hypothetical.

CARDINALS, SALTATORS, AND ALLIES - FAMILY CARDINALIDAE

Northern Cardinal *Cardinalis cardinalis*. Breeder. Common in all seasons and regions. Found in shrubby areas, hedgerows, thickets, and suburban gardens. Lowest Conservation Concern. **(Fig. 143, p. 166)**

Rose-breasted Grosbeak *Pheucticus ludovicianus*. Common in spring and fall, and occasional in winter in mostly Gulf Coast region. Found in woodlands, especially in the canopy.

Black-headed Grosbeak *Pheucticus melanocephalus*. Occasional to rare in winter, spring, and fall in all regions. Found in woodlands.

Blue Grosbeak *Passerina caerulea*. Breeder. Common in spring, summer, and fall in all regions. Found in open thickets and hedgerows, especially along field borders.

Indigo Bunting *Passerina cyanea*. Breeder. Common in spring, summer, and fall, and rare in winter in Gulf Coast region. Common in spring, summer, and fall, and occasional in winter in inland regions. Found in brushy and weedy area, in early successional stages and woodland openings, and along woodland and field borders. Low Conservation Concern. **(Fig. 144, p. 166)**

Painted Bunting *Passerina ciris*. Breeder. Fairly common in spring, uncommon in summer and fall, and occasional in winter in Gulf Coast region. In Mountain and Inland Coastal Plain regions, rare in spring, and occasional to rare in summer and fall. Found in brushy areas, especially near water.

Dickcissel *Spiza americana*. Breeder. Uncommon to locally fairly common in spring and summer, and fairly common in fall in Inland Coastal Plain. In Tennessee Valley, fairly common in spring, summer, and fall, and occasional in winter. In Gulf Coast region, fairly common in spring, uncommon in fall, and rare in winter and summer. In Mountain region, uncommon in spring, rare in summer and fall, and occasional in winter. Found in weedy, brushy, and cultivated fields. MODERATE CONSERVATION CONCERN.

BLACKBIRDS - FAMILY ICTERIDAE

Bobolink *Dolichonyx oryzivorus*. Common in spring, and uncommon to rare in fall in all regions. Found in marshes and fields, especially those cultivated with oats, alfalfa, and clover.

Red-winged Blackbird *Agelaius phoeniceus*. Breeder. Common in all seasons and regions. Found in marshes, brushy, weedy and grassy areas, and especially in wet, cultivated areas. Low Conservation Concern. **(Fig. 145, p. 166)**

Eastern Meadowlark *Sturnella magna*. Breeder. Common in all seasons and regions. Found in grassy, weedy fields, especially high grass. Low Conservation Concern.

Western Meadowlark *Sturnella neglecta*. Accidental.

Yellow-headed Blackbird *Xanthocephalus xanthocephalus*. Rare in fall, and occasional in winter and spring in Gulf Coast region. In inland regions, occasional in fall and spring. Found in marshes and wet fields.

Rusty Blackbird *Euphagus carolinus*. Fairly common in winter and spring, and rare to uncommon in late fall in Tennessee Valley region. In Mountain and Inland Coastal Plain regions, uncommon in winter, spring, and fall. In Gulf Coast region, rare in winter, spring, and fall. Found along edges of ponds, flooded fields, sloughs, streams, and swamps. MODERATE CONSERVATION CONCERN.

Brewer's Blackbird *Euphagus cyanocephalus*. Fairly common in winter, early spring, and late fall in Inland Coastal Plain. In Tennessee Valley and Gulf Coast regions, uncommon in winter, spring, and fall. In Mountain region, rare in winter, spring, and fall. Found in feedlots and pastures with livestock. Low Conservation Concern.

Common Grackle *Quiscalus quiscula*. Breeder. Common in all seasons and regions. Found in open woodlands, especially those with pines and grassy areas; also fields with short grasses or in cultivated fields. Low Conservation Concern.

Boat-tailed Grackle *Quiscalus major*. Breeder. Common in all seasons in Gulf Coast region. Found in coastal marshes and open, grassy areas near marshes. Low Conservation Concern. **(Fig. 146, p. 166)**

Great-tailed Grackle *Quiscalus mexicanus*. Accidental.

Shiny Cowbird *Molothrus bonariensis*. Rare in spring and occasional in summer and fall in Gulf Coast region. Found in early successional scrub.

Bronzed Cowbird *Molothrus aeneus*. Accidental.

Brown-headed Cowbird *Molothrus ater*. Breeder. Common in all seasons and regions. Found in short-grass areas, especially with livestock. Lowest Conservation Concern.

Orchard Oriole *Icterus spurius*. Breeder. Common in spring, summer, and fall in all regions, and occasional in winter in Mountain and Gulf Coast regions. In breeding season, found in open areas, with scattered trees, especially near water. In migration, found in woodlands. Low Conservation Concern.

Bullock's Oriole *Icterus bullockii*. Rare in winter and fall, and occasional in spring in primarily Gulf Coast region. Found in woodlands.

Baltimore Oriole *Icterus galbula*. Breeder. Common in spring and fall, and rare in winter and summer in Gulf Coast region. In Tennessee Valley region, fairly common in spring and fall, and rare in summer. In Mountain and Inland Coastal Plain regions, fairly common in spring and fall, and rare in summer and winter. In breeding season, found in open areas, with scattered trees, especially near water. In migration, found in woodlands. Lowest Conservation Concern. **(Fig. 147, p. 166)**

FRINGILLINE AND CARDUELINE FINCHES AND ALLIES-FAMILY FRINGILLIDAE

Purple Finch *Carpodacus purpureus*. Uncommon and erratic in winter, spring, and fall in inland regions. In Gulf Coast region, rare and erratic in winter, spring, and fall. Found in woodlands, especially deciduous. Low Conservation Concern.

House Finch *Carpodacus mexicanus*. Breeder. Common in all seasons in inland regions. In Gulf Coast, fairly common in all seasons. Found in open woodlands, especially those associated with buildings, homes, and gardens. Lowest Conservation Concern.

Red Crossbill *Loxia curvirostra*. Local breeder. Rare and erratic in all seasons in primarily Mountain region. Found in coniferous woodlands. Low Conservation Concern.

Common Redpoll *Carduelis flammea*. Occasional in winter and spring in all regions. Found in early successional stages, especially willow and alder; sightings mostly at feeders.

Pine Siskin *Carduelis pinus*. Fairly common and erratic in winter, spring, and fall in Tennessee Valley and Mountain regions. In Inland Coastal Plain and Gulf Coast regions, uncommon in winter, spring, and fall. Found in open woodlands; often seen at feeders. Lowest Conservation Concern.

American Goldfinch *Carduelis tristis*. Breeder. Fairly common in all seasons in Tennessee Valley and Mountain regions. In Inland Coastal Plain, common in winter, spring, and fall, and uncommon in summer. In Gulf Coast region, common in winter, spring, and fall. Found in open woodlands, brushy areas, and willow thickets. Lowest Conservation Concern.. **(Fig. 148, p. 166)**

Evening Grosbeak *Coccothraustes vespertinus*. Uncommon and erratic in winter, spring, and fall in Mountain region. In other regions, rare and erratic in winter, spring, and fall. Found in woodlands; often seen at feeders. Lowest Conservation Concern.

OLD WORLD SPARROWS - FAMILY PASSERIDAE

House Sparrow *Passer domesticus*. **Exotic**. Breeder. Common in all seasons and regions. Found in urban and suburban areas and on farms, especially those with livestock.

MAMMALS

Raccoon
Procyon lotor

INTRODUCTION

Although geographic distributions of Alabama's 64 species of native mammals are reasonably well known, there generally is a paucity of knowledge relative to genetics, physiology, parasites, pathogens, dynamics of populations, diet, reproduction, and other basic aspects of their biology. Small size, nocturnal activity, and secretive natures of most mammals make them difficult to study. A variety of trapping and monitoring techniques has allowed acquisition of information on distribution and habitat of most species, but significant effort often results in few captures or observations. For example, mist nets to capture bats and rodents traps used for small mammals often yield no captures, even when placed into what appear to be favorable habitats for several consecutive nights.

Ignorance and fear have led to needless destruction of populations of certain mammals, especially large carnivores and bats. Fortunately, educational efforts by public schools, conservation organizations, television programs, availability of information on the Internet, and other efforts are increasing public awareness of the need to protect all of our native flora and fauna.

Many habitats that were occupied by mammals in Alabama have been cleared and cultivated, degraded by erosion, harvested for timber, converted to shopping centers and housing developments, and otherwise made less desirable or unsuitable for native species. Although significant efforts are being made to restore some areas to native wildlife habitat, this will take decades to accomplish, and more species may be lost in the interim.

Scientific classification, common names, and order in which species are presented in the checklist follow Vaughan *et al.* (2000) and Wilson and Reeder (1993). All taxa, including exotics known to breed in the state, and those extirpated in historic times, have been included on the checklist.

Troy L. Best

COMMITTEE

Dr. Troy L. Best, Department of Biological Sciences and Alabama Agricultural Experiment Station, Auburn University, AL, Chairperson/Compiler

Dr. Julian L. Dusi, Department of Zoology and Wildlife Sciences (Retired), Auburn University, AL

Mr. Barry D. Hart, Alabama Natural Heritage Program, The Nature Conservancy, Huntingdon College, Montgomery, AL

Mr. Travis Hill Henry, Regional Natural Heritage Program, Tennessee Valley Authority, Norris, TN

Mr. M. Keith Hudson, Alabama Department of Conservation and Natural Resources, Division of Wildlife and Freshwater Fisheries, Florence, AL

Mr. J. Ralph Jordan, Tennessee Valley Authority, Norris, TN

Mr. W. Mark Kiser, Bat Conservation International, Austin, TX

Ms. Jo Ashfield Lewis, Alabama Department of Conservation and Natural Resources, State Lands Division, Natural Heritage Section, Montgomery, AL

Dr. Michael S. Mitchell, U. S. Geological Survey, Alabama Cooperative Fish and Wildlife Research Unit, School of Forestry and Wildlife Sciences, Auburn University, AL

Dr. Michael C. Wooten, Department of Biological Sciences, Auburn University, AL

MAMMALS
CLASS MAMMALIA

NEW WORLD OPOSSUMS
ORDER DIDELPHIMORPHIA

OPOSSUMS - FAMILY DIDELPHIDAE

Virginia Opossum *Didelphis virginiana*. Found statewide and common in all habitats, including urban areas. Typically, one litter born in early winter and another in spring. Gestation 12-13 days resulting in four to 20 young. Tiny young climb directly into marsupium and attach to one of 13 mammae; neonates failing to attach quickly perish. Diet includes fruits, other vegetative matter, invertebrates, eggs, and small vertebrates. Lowest Conservation Concern. **(Fig. 149, p. 201)**

INSECTIVORES
ORDER INSECTIVORA

SHREWS - FAMILY SORICIDAE

Northern Short-tailed Shrew *Blarina brevicauda*. Poorly known. Occurs only in northeastern Alabama. Occupies broad variety of habitats, including woodlands, grasslands, brushy fencerows, and marshy areas. Breeding begins in late winter and continues through summer, although there may be a lull in early and mid-summer. Gestation 21-22 days, with six to seven young per litter. Diet includes larval and adult insects, snails, slugs, spiders, centipedes, millipedes, earthworms, fungi, and plant material. MODERATE CONSERVATION CONCERN.

Southern Short-tailed Shrew *Blarina carolinensis*. Poorly known. Found statewide except for northeastern region. Little is known about species in Alabama, but may be common in a variety of habitats. MODERATE CONSERVATION CONCERN.

Least Shrew *Cryptotis parva*. Poorly known. Found statewide in grasslands and other upland areas, weedy fencerows, fields, roadsides, and meadows. Parturition occurs from early spring to mid-autumn. Several litters each averaging four to six young, produced annually. Young from early litters may breed later in same season. Plant and animal materials important in diet, which includes adult and larval insects, earthworms, spiders, centipedes, and snails. MODERATE CONSERVATION CONCERN.

Pygmy Shrew *Sorex hoyi*. Poorly known. Known only from northeastern Alabama. Occupies a diversity of habitats, but probably prefers mesic sites. Pregnant and lactating females recorded July-August, but little else known about reproductive biology. Probably one litter born annually. Diet primarily invertebrates. **HIGH CONSERVATION CONCERN.**

Southeastern Shrew *Sorex longirostris*. Poorly known. Found statewide, except southern tier of counties. Occupies a variety of habitats from bogs and marshes to upland grassy areas and forests, and even bare hillsides and dry upland hardwoods. May favor moist areas bordering swamps, marshes, lakes, and streams. More than one litter averaging four young may be produced annually. Important foods are spiders, larval insects, centipedes, slugs, snails, earthworms, and plant material. MODERATE CONSERVATION CONCERN.

MOLES - FAMILY TALPIDAE

Eastern Mole *Scalopus aquaticus*. Poorly known. Found statewide and common in a variety of habitats in both forested and unforested areas. Occupies moist, loose, sandy or loamy soils, and spends most of life underground. Gestation about five weeks, one litter produced annually, and, on average, four young born. Diet includes earthworms, larval and adult insects, other invertebrates, and plant material. Low Conservation Concern.

BATS
ORDER CHIROPTERA

VESPERTILIONID BATS - FAMILY VESPERTILIONIDAE

Little Brown Myotis *Myotis lucifugus*. Found statewide; although common throughout its distribution, is rare in Alabama with no breeding colonies known. Elsewhere in distribution, groups of several thousand females form maternity colonies in buildings. Mating occurs before hibernation, but copulating pairs may be found in hibernacula throughout winter. In spring, a single young is born. Lifespans of greater than 30 years documented in wild. Diet includes a variety of insects, including flies, moths, and small beetles. **HIGH CONSERVATION CONCERN.**

Southeastern Myotis *Myotis austroriparius*. Occurs in southern half and western half of Alabama, but may be most common in southern tier of counties. Active year-round, it occupies caves, mines, and buildings, but may go into torpor for a few days when daily temperatures approach freezing. Only one maternity colony known in Alabama. Twins are born in spring and become volant in five to six weeks. **HIGH CONSERVATION CONCERN.**

Gray Myotis *Myotis grisescens*. Found statewide, except for southwestern quarter. Occupies deep caves near permanent water in winter and summer. Breeds in autumn before hibernation, but mating probably occurs in winter. One young born in June becomes volant in 20-25 days. Forages primarily over water, along streams, and over lakes and ponds. Consumes a variety of small insects, including moths and mayflies. Lifespan may exceed 15 years. **Listed as *endangered* by the U.S. Fish and Wildlife Service. HIGHEST CONSERVATION CONCERN.**

Northern Long-eared Myotis *Myotis septentrionalis*. Poorly known. Found statewide, except southwestern region. Forested ridges appear favored over riparian woodlands. Hibernacula include caves and mines, but may use crevices in walls or ceilings. Summer roosts include tree holes, birdhouses, or behind loose bark or shutters of buildings. One young born in late spring or early summer weaned about a month after birth. **HIGH CONSERVATION CONCERN.**

Small-footed Myotis *Myotis leibii*. Probably occurs in northeastern Alabama because is known from adjacent areas of Tennessee and Georgia. Distribution maps often depict it occurring in Alabama, but no specimens known from state. MODERATE CONSERVATION CONCERN.

Indiana Myotis *Myotis sodalis*. Rare. Occurs in northern and eastern half of Alabama, but populations continue to decline distribution wide. Hibernates in caves, mostly in tight clusters. In summer, females form small maternity colonies in tree hollows and behind loose bark. A single offspring born in June or early July is weaned in 25-35 days. Diet includes small, soft-bodied insects, such as moths, flies, and beetles. **Listed as *endangered* by the U.S. Fish and Wildlife Service. HIGHEST CONSERVATION CONCERN.**

Silver-haired Bat *Lasionycteris noctivagans*. Poorly known. Probably found statewide, except for southern tier of counties. Little known of distribution and habits in Alabama. Probably present as a winter resident, or in spring and autumn migration, but apparently not in summer. In winter, hibernates in a variety of shelters, including buildings, caves, mines, crevices, and hollow trees. Not known to breed in Alabama. MODERATE CONSERVATION CONCERN.

Eastern Pipistrelle *Pipistrellus subflavus*. Found statewide and common. Occupies hollow trees, tree foliage, caves, mines, rock crevices, and buildings. Hibernates in winter, often with beads of water forming on fur from humid surroundings. In late May through early July, an average of two young are born. Diet includes a variety of insects, including leafhoppers, beetles, and flies. Lowest Conservation Concern.

Big Brown Bat *Eptesicus fuscus*. Found statewide and common. Roosts typically in human-made structures, but also in caves, mines, hollow trees, and crevices, or behind loose bark. Commonly inhabits bat houses, attics, and louvered attic vents. Copulates in autumn and winter, ovulation occurs in spring, and two young are born in late spring. Diet consists primarily of beetles, but flies, moths, bugs, and cicadellids also consumed. Lowest Conservation Concern. **(Fig. 150, p. 201)**

Eastern Red Bat *Lasiurus borealis*. Found statewide and common. Roosts in a variety of trees, but frequently uses clumps of Spanish moss. Often emerges early, while sun is in the western sky. Breeding may take place during southward migration in autumn, and copulation in flight has been observed. An average of four young are born in spring. Lowest Conservation concern.

Seminole Bat *Lasiurus seminolus*. Found statewide. Common in mixed coniferous and deciduous woodlands; often associated with Spanish moss. Parturition occurs late-May and early June, with two to four young born. Mostly forages at treetop level in forests, although also flies over open water, forest clearings, and along forest edges. Diet consists of flies, beetles, dragonflies, and hymenopterans. Lowest Conservation concern. **(Fig. 151, p. 201)**

Hoary Bat *Lasiurus cinereus*. Poorly known. Found statewide, but are few records of this large (avg. 25 g [1 oz.]) species in Alabama. Roosts in trees or shrubs, usually three to five meters (9-15 feet) above ground. Females bear two young in late spring. Migratory and may not breed in state, but some females may raise young here. MODERATE CONSERVATION CONCERN. **(Fig. 152, p. 201)**

Northern Yellow Bat *Lasiurus intermedius*. Rare and poorly known. Only a few records from the southern tier of counties. This relatively large (14-31 g [0.5-1.1 oz.]) bat inhabits coniferous and deciduous woodlands near permanent water. Often roosts in clumps of Spanish moss, but also in trees. Breeds in autumn and winter; two to four young born in spring. Diet consists of flies, bugs, dragonflies, beetles, and hymenopterans. **HIGH CONSERVATION CONCERN.**

Evening Bat *Nycticeius humeralis*. Found statewide, but may be most common in southern half. Primary habitat is deciduous forest where it roosts in hollow trees, under loose bark, and in human-made structures, such as outbuildings, churches, belfries, and attics. One to three young (usually two) born in early June. Diet consists of a variety of insects, including moths, beetles, flies, bugs, and flying ants. Lowest Conservation Concern.

Rafinesque's Big-eared Bat *Corynorhinus rafinesquii*. Poorly known. Found statewide, but among least-known bats in region. In summer, roost sites may be behind loose bark, in caves, crevices, and hollow trees, and in unoccupied buildings, abandoned mines and wells, and other human-made structures. In winter, may hibernate briefly in open and well-lighted hibernacula. Mating occurs in autumn and winter; one young born in late spring. Diet primarily moths. **HIGHEST CONSERVATION CONCERN.**

FREE-TAILED BATS - FAMILY MOLOSSIDAE

Brazilian Free-tailed Bat *Tadarida brasiliensis*. Poorly known. Possibly found statewide, but most remaining populations are in southern half. Occurs only in human-made structures. Essentially nonmigratory and does not hibernate, but summer and winter roosts may be in different localities. Breeds in March, gestation is 11-12 weeks, and one young born in June. Diet primarily moths. **HIGH CONSERVATION CONCERN.**

ARMADILLOS, SLOTHS, AND ANTEATERS
ORDER XENARTHRA
ARMADILLOS - FAMILY DASYPODIDAE

Nine-banded Armadillo *Dasypus novemcinctus*. Found statewide and common in woodlands, forest edges, savannas, and brushy areas. Breeding occurs in summer, implantation is delayed about 14 weeks, and four quadruplets are born in late winter or early spring after a gestation of 120 days. Diet consists primarily of insects, their larvae, and invertebrates, but fruits, mushrooms, eggs, and small vertebrates also consumed. Lowest Conservation concern. **(Fig. 153, p. 201)**

RABBITS, HARES, AND PICAS
ORDER LAGOMORPHA
RABBITS AND HARES - FAMILY LEPORIDAE

Marsh Rabbit *Sylvilagus palustris*. Poorly known. Restricted to southernmost counties. Primarily occurs in and around marshes and swamps. Sexually active year-round, gestation period 30-37 days, several litters averaging three to five young born annually. Feeds on variety of lowland plants, including cattails, rushes, and cane, and also consumes twigs and leaves of trees, shrubs, and woody vines. **HIGH CONSERVATION CONCERN.**

Swamp Rabbit *Sylvilagus aquaticus*. Poorly known. Distributed statewide, except for southern tier of counties along Florida Panhandle. Found in floodplain forests, wooded bottomlands, briar and honeysuckle patches, and canebrakes. Produces up to eight litters averaging three to six young annually. Diet includes a variety of plant material, such as grasses, sedges, shrubs, twigs, and bark. Low Conservation Concern.

Eastern Cottontail *Sylvilagus floridanus*. Common and found statewide. Primarily occurs in deciduous forests and forest edges, but also in grasslands, along fencerows, and in urban areas. Produces up to seven litters averaging three to five young annually; gestation about 30 days. Forbs and grasses comprise most of diet in summer, but consumption of twigs and tree bark increases in winter. Lowest Conservation Concern. **(Fig. 154, p. 201)**

Appalachian Cottontail *Sylvilagus obscurus*. Poorly known. Records only from northern third of Alabama. Inhabits dense woodlands and mountainous areas. Gestation 28 days; average litter size is five with two to three young produced annually. Diet mostly grass and clover; other foods include herbaceous plants and shrubs, twigs, buds, seeds, and fruit. **HIGH CONSERVATION CONCERN.**

RODENTS
ORDER RODENTIA

SQUIRRELS - FAMILY SCIURIDAE

Eastern Chipmunk *Tamias striatus*. Common. Found statewide, except for extreme southwestern and southeastern regions. Occupies wooded areas with dense canopy and sparsely covered forest floor, open brushy habitats, ravines, deciduous growth along streams, and urban areas. Gestation 31-32 days; two litters averaging four to five young produced each year. Seeds, nuts, insects, other invertebrates, and fungi are important foods. Lowest Conservation Concern.

Woodchuck *Marmota monax*. Poorly known. Distribution includes northern two-thirds of state. Occupies forest edges and open fields and pastures near brushy fencerows or other cover Breeding occurs upon emergence from hibernation in spring. Gestation 31-33 days; one litter averaging four to five young produced annually. Diet includes various weedy plants, but clover and alfalfa favored. Fruits and agricultural crops also consumed. Lowest Conservation Concern. **(Fig. 155, p. 201)**

Gray Squirrel *Sciurus carolinensis*. Common. Found statewide in hardwood forests, mixed forests, and urban areas. An important game species, active throughout year. Two litters of two to four young born annually, one in late winter and another in summer; gestation about 44 days. Diet includes seeds, fruits, flowers, leaves, bark, and some insects, eggs, and young birds. Lowest Conservation Concern. **(Fig. 156, p. 201)**

Fox Squirrel *Sciurus niger*. Found statewide, this large tree squirrel favors mature deciduous and pine-oak woodlands, but also occurs at forest edges and in riparian woodlands. Two reproductive peaks occur in late winter and mid-late summer. Gestation about 45 days, with an average of three young born. Diet is acorns, pine seeds, other nuts, and a wide variety of plant and animal material, including fruits, corn, and other grains. Low Conservation Concern. **(Fig. 157, p. 201)**

Southern Flying Squirrel *Glaucomys volans*. Found statewide. Most common in mature, broad-leaved forests, but also found in coniferous-deciduous woodlands, and urban areas. Nocturnal existence belies its common occurrence. Breeds in mid-summer to early winter. Gestation about 40 days, with an average litter size of two to three. Foods are nuts of deciduous trees, such as oaks and hickories, but also consumes seeds, fruits, buds, bark, fungi, insects, eggs, and small vertebrates. Lowest Conservation Concern. **(Fig. 158, p. 201)**

POCKET GOPHERS - FAMILY GEOMYIDAE

Southeastern Pocket Gopher *Geomys pinetis*. Poorly known. Seemingly less common now than previously; once occupied southern half of Alabama. Usually occurs in dry, sandy soils, but may inhabit well-drained, gravelly, upland sites. Peaks of reproductive activity occur February-March and June-August. Females produce two litters of about two young annually. **HIGH CONSERVATION CONCERN.**

BEAVERS - FAMILY CASTORIDAE

Beaver *Castor canadensis*. Once extirpated, or nearly so, now common. Found statewide in all habitats with open water. Considered a pest in some areas, because of flooding caused by construction of dams. In April-June, three to five young born after a gestation of about 107 days. Sexual maturity reached at two years. Diet includes leaves, branches, and bark of most kinds of woody plants that grow near water. Lowest Conservation Concern. (**Fig. 159, p. 202**)

RATS AND MICE - FAMILY MURIDAE

Marsh Rice Rat *Oryzomys palustris*. Common and found statewide in wet meadows and dense vegetation near marshes, swamps, streams, ponds, and ditches. Probably breeds throughout year. Gestation 21-28 days, average litter size four to five, and sexual maturity attained at six to eight weeks. Diet includes seeds and green plants, but insects, snails, and other animal materials are consumed. Lowest Conservation concern.

Eastern Harvest Mouse *Reithrodontomys humulis*. Poorly known. Once common in old fields containing dense stands of weeds and grasses, but may be declining in Alabama. Breeds throughout year, gestation 21-22 days, and litter of two to three. Seeds comprise most of diet, but insects and green vegetation also eaten. MODERATE CONSERVATION CONCERN.

Oldfield Mouse *Peromyscus polionotus*. Poorly known. Primarily distributed in sandy-soiled habitats in eastern and southern Alabama, but also occurs in west-central and northwestern parts of state. Occurs in fallow fields with herbaceous vegetation, and along roadsides in agricultural areas. Breeds throughout year. Gestation about 22 days with an average of four young born. Diet mostly consists of seeds of grasses and herbs, but green plants and insects also consumed. MODERATE CONSERVATION CONCERN. (**Fig. 160, p. 202**)

Alabama Beach Mouse *P. polionotus ammobates*. Known only from coastal dune areas of Baldwin County, Alabama. Distribution continues to shrink due to construction of beach-front buildings and associated destruction of habitat. Monogamous, with strong pair bonds; reproduction peaks in late autumn and early winter. Gestation about 28 days; litter size varies from two to eight. Diet includes sea oats, bluestems, and a variety of insects. **Listed as *endangered* by the U.S. Fish and Wildlife Service. HIGHEST CONSERVATION CONCERN.**

Perdido Key Beach Mouse *P. polionotus trissylepsis*. Known only from Perdido Key, Baldwin County, Alabama. Storms and habitat destruction have reduced distribution from entire length of Perdido Key to a few remnant and reintroduced populations.

Although there are distinct morphological and genetic differences, ecology and reproduction similar to the Alabama beach mouse. **Listed as *endangered* by the U.S. Fish
and Wildlife Service. HIGHEST CONSERVATION CONCERN.**

Cotton Mouse *Peromyscus gossypinus*. Common. Found statewide in dense underbrush,
bottomland hardwood forests, and a variety of other habitats, including old fields, upland
forests, hammocks, and swamps. Except for summer, breeds year-round. Gestation about
23 days; litter size averages four. This opportunistic omnivore consumes insects, spiders,
slugs, and snails, but also eats seeds and fungi. Lowest Conservation concern.

White-footed Mouse *Peromyscus leucopus*. Poorly known. Occurs in northern two-thirds
of state. Common in woodlands with fallen logs, brush piles, and rocks, and in shrubs
along fencerows and streams. Breeds year-round, with reduced activity in summer.
Several litters of three to four produced annually; gestation 22-23 days. Females may be
pregnant and lactating simultaneously. Diet includes seeds, nuts, fruits, other plant materials, and small invertebrates. Lowest Conservation concern.

Golden Mouse *Ochrotomys nuttalli*. Common in a variety of habitats, including woodlands, floodplains, borders of fields, and thickets bordering swamps and dense woods.
Highly social; up to eight have been found in same nest. Breeding occurs all year.
Gestation 25-30 days; litter size usually two to three. Seeds and invertebrates form
majority of diet. Lowest Conservation concern.

Hispid Cotton Rat *Sigmodon hispidus*. Found statewide, especially in grassy areas of fields
and along roadways. Populations fluctuate greatly among years, but usually abundant in
densely vegetated habitats. Active day and night. Prolific breeder; gestation about 27
days; one to 15 young per litter; and young mature in about eight weeks. Primarily herbivorous, but will consume invertebrates, small vertebrates, and bird eggs. Lowest
Conservation Concern. **(Fig. 161, p. 202)**

Eastern Woodrat *Neotoma floridana*. Poorly known. No recent surveys; populations may
be declining. Occupies woodland and brushy habitats south of Tennessee River. Usually
found associated with rocky outcrops, but also in areas with dense vegetation. Mating
occurs throughout year with an average of two to three young born after a gestation of
about 35 days. MODERATE CONSERVATION CONCERN.

Allegheny Woodrat *Neotoma magister*. Probably restricted to region north of Tennessee
River. Possibly confined to areas with rocky outcrops, crevices, caves, and boulder fields,
but also may occupy woodlands and brushy areas. Breeds throughout year; litter size of
two to three; gestation about 35 days. Diet consists of plant materials. **HIGH CON-
SERVATION CONCERN.**

Prairie Vole *Microtus ochrogaster*. Poorly known. Occupies areas with dense grasses, such
as pastures, roadsides, and edges of fields in north-central Alabama. Breeds throughout

year with peaks in spring and autumn. After a gestation of about 21 days, three to five young are born. Green vegetation commonly eaten in summer, whereas roots, seeds, bark, and stems commonly eaten in winter. MODERATE CONSERVATION CONCERN.

Pine Vole *Microtus pinetorum*. Found statewide, except for southwestern section. Occupies a wide range of habitats, including leaf litter, grassy fields with brush and brambles, and beneath mats of dense vegetation. Breeds throughout year; gestation about three weeks; average litter size three; young fully mature at 10-12 weeks. Diet includes grasses, stems, roots, seeds, nuts, and bark, which are stored in burrows. Low Conservation Concern.

Muskrat *Ondatra zibethicus*. Found nearly statewide, except counties bordering Florida Panhandle. Habitats include saline, brackish, and freshwater streams; marshes; ponds; lakes; ditches; and rivers. Produces up to five to six litters of six to seven young annually. Gestation about 30 days. Feeds mostly on roots and basal parts of aquatic vegetation, but also crayfish, fishes, mollusks, turtles, and other animal matter. Lowest Conservation Concern. (**Fig. 162, p. 202**)

Black Rat *Rattus rattus*. **Exotic.** Breeder. Also called "roof rat" because of its climbing capabilities. A commensal ("sharing the table") rodent brought to the United States by early European colonists. Produces up to 12 litters of eight young annually. Gestation period about 24 days. Requires food, water, and harborage provided by humans. Often displaced by Norway rat, but when co-inhabiting same areas, usually spatially separated vertically. Often targeted for eradication because of potential economic damage and health concerns.

Norway Rat *Rattus norvegicus*. **Exotic.** Breeder. Also known as "sewer or wharf rat." A commensal rodent brought to the United States by early European colonists, albeit considerably later (ca. 1775) than the black rat and house mouse. Produces up to 12 litters of eight or nine young annually. Gestation period about 24 days. Requires food, water, and harborage provided by humans. Often targeted for eradication because of potential economic damage and health concerns.

House Mouse *Mus musculus*. **Exotic.** Breeder. A commensal rodent brought to the United States by early European colonists. Produces up to 14 litters of five or six young annually. Gestation period about 20 days. Not nearly as dependent on food, water, and harborage provided by humans as black and Norway rats; often found in habitats associated with native rodents fairly distant from human habitation. Often targeted for eradication because of potential economic damage and health concerns.

JUMPING MICE AND JERBOAS - FAMILY DIPODIDAE

Meadow Jumping Mouse *Zapus hudsonius*. Poorly known. Populations may be declining, but no recent surveys. Found primarily in Piedmont region of northeastern

Alabama. Occupies variety of habitats with dense vegetation, including overgrown fields and thick vegetation near ponds, marshes, and streams. Up to three litters of about five young may be produced April-August. Seeds, grasses, fruits of some woody shrubs, insects, and fungi are consumed. **HIGH CONSERVATION CONCERN**.

NUTRIAS - FAMILY MYOCASTORIDAE

Nutria *Myocaster coypus*. **Exotic.** Breeder. A South American native introduced into the United States for fur farming and weed control. Occupies fresh and brackish wetlands in southern Alabama. Known to cause damage to crops, drainage systems, and natural plant communities.

CARNIVORES
ORDER CARNIVORA

WOLVES, DOGS, FOXES, AND JACKALS - FAMILY CANIDAE

Coyote *Canis latrans*. Found statewide, including urban areas. Common in all habitats. Usually breeds February-March. Gestation about 60 days; litter size about six. Diet extremely varied and includes rodents, rabbits, birds, eggs, many kinds of fruits, domestic poultry, livestock, and watermelons. Lowest Conservation Concern.

Red Wolf *Canis rufus*. **Extirpated.** Once inhabited a variety of habitats statewide. Roamed in small groups and fed on small to mid-sized wild mammals. Also, often fed on small domestic animals such as sheep, goats, pigs, and sometimes calves. Reported on verge of extinction in Alabama in 1921. Last stronghold was rough, hilly region from Walker County northwestward to Colbert County. **Listed as *endangered* by the U.S. Fish and Wildlife Service.**

Red Fox *Vulpes vulpes*. Common statewide in forested uplands interspersed with pastures and farmland. Breeding occurs January-February; gestation about 50 days; litter size four to five. Mice and rabbits are important components of diet, but birds, eggs, plant material, and insects also consumed. Lowest Conservation Concern. **(Fig. 163, p. 202)**

Gray Fox *Urocyon cinereoargenteus*. Common in forested habitats statewide. Breeding peaks in February-March; gestation 50-60 days; litter size three to five. Diet includes many plant and animal species, including rodents, birds, eggs, and carrion. Lowest Conservation Concern.

BEARS - FAMILY URSIDAE

Black Bear *Ursus americanus*. Rare. Once found statewide, but now extirpated from all except an area just north of Mobile, where they still breed. Transients from Georgia and Florida also occasionally enter the state. Occupies woodland and swampland habitats. Mating occurs May-July with two to three young born in January-February after a seven-month gestation. A variety of plant and animal materials, including some agricultural crops, consumed depending upon availability. **HIGHEST CONSERVATION CONCERN.**

EARED SEALS, FUR SEALS, AND SEA LIONS - FAMILY OTARIIDAE

California Sea Lion *Zalophus californianus*. Accidental. Known from a single observation at Sand Point Light, Mobile Bay, prior to 1984.

RACCOONS, RINGTAILS, AND COATIS - FAMILY PROCYONIDAE

Raccoon *Procyon lotor*. Common in all habitats statewide, including urban areas. Often associated with water, especially bottomland swamps, marshes, and flooded woodlands. This opportunistic omnivore consumes an unusually wide range of plant and animal foods. Breeding occurs December-June with a peak February-March; gestation about 65 days; litter size two to five. Lowest Conservation Concern. **(Fig. 164, p. 202)**

Ringtail *Bassariscus astutus*. Accidental. Known only from two animals collected in Chambers and Montgomery Counties that may have been released from captivity. No evidence of a breeding population in Alabama or adjacent states. Occupies a variety of habitats throughout distribution, which extends from California across Louisiana and from southwestern Oregon to southern Mexico. Principal foods are arthropods, small mammals, and fruits, but diet varies with availability and location. Breeds February-May, but most occurs March-April. Following about a 50-day gestation, one to four young are born.

WEASELS, BADGERS, AND OTTERS - FAMILY MUSTELIDAE

Long-tailed Weasel *Mustela frenata*. Poorly known. Probably found statewide, but little known about current status. Lives in woodlands, forest edges, fencerows, agricultural, and urban areas. Small mammals form important part of diet, along with other vertebrates and invertebrates. Mating occurs July-August, there is delayed implantation, and five to eight young are born mid-spring. **HIGH CONSERVATION CONCERN.**

Mink *Mustela vison*. Poorly known. This semiaquatic species occurs statewide, usually near permanent water. Status of populations unknown. Breeding occurs February-April; gestation about 30 days; and average litter size of four. Diet consists primarily of rodents, but also includes a variety of other vertebrates and invertebrates. Low Conservation Concern.

River Otter *Lontra canadensis*. Poorly known. Probably present statewide in association with rivers, creeks, and lakes, especially open water bordered with wooded habitat. Current status of populations unknown. In late winter or early spring, copulation usually occurs in water, there is delayed implantation, and a litter of one to six young is born in 290-380 days. Low Conservation Concern.

SKUNKS - FAMILY MEPHITIDAE

Striped Skunk *Mephitis mephitis*. Found statewide, especially in open areas, forest edges, and urban habitats. Although usually common, abundance varies significantly within Alabama; some regions having high populations and others having few, or no, individuals present. Most breeding occurs February-April. Low Conservation Concern. **(Fig. 165, p. 202)**

Eastern Spotted Skunk *Spilogale putorius*. Found in a variety of habitats such as pastures, woodlands, forest edges, and farmlands. Although statewide in distribution, little known about this species in Alabama. Breeding occurs March-April, and there may be a second litter in late summer. **HIGH CONSERVATION CONCERN**.

CATS - FAMILY FELIDAE

Puma *Puma concolor*. **Extirpated.** Probably was statewide in distribution in all habitats, especially remote upland woodlands, rough terrain, and bottomland swamps. Although sightings are still commonly reported in Alabama, these are likely misidentifications of domestic dogs and cats, coyotes, and bobcats. Some puma sightings have been traced back to escapees from captivity. The only known self-sustaining wild population closest geographically to Alabama is the Florida panther (*P. c. coryi*), which is **listed as *endangered* by the U.S. Fish and Wildlife Service.**

Bobcat *Lynx rufus*. Common statewide in a wide array of habitats including dense understory, bottomland hardwood forests, swamps, and farmlands. Breeding peaks December-April, but young may be born anytime during the year. Diet includes many kinds of vertebrates and invertebrates. Lowest Conservation Concern.

Jaguarundi *Herpailurus yagouaroundi*. Accidental. Rare sightings reported from southwestern and central Alabama, but there is no evidence of a breeding population in Alabama or adjacent states. **Listed as *endangered* by the U.S. Fish and Wildlife Service.**

SIRENIANS
ORDER SIRENIA

MANATEES - FAMILY TRICHECHIDAE

Manatee *Trichechus manatus*. Rare in Alabama waters; known from regular annual sightings in late spring, summer, and early fall in inland waterways around Mobile Bay. Individuals may be migrants from populations that occur along Gulf Coast of Florida. **Listed as *endangered* by the U.S. Fish and Wildlife Service. HIGHEST CONSERVATION CONCERN.**

EVEN-TOED HOOFED MAMMALS
ORDER ARTIODACTYLA

DEER, ELK, CARIBOU, AND MOOSE - FAMILY CERVIDAE

Elk *Cervus elaphus*. **Extirpated.** May have been found statewide, except for southern third. A mix of open and densely wooded habitats probably were occupied by the eastern subspecies (*C. e. canadensis*), which is now extinct. Re-introductions to states within former eastern distribution have been successfully made with some of the western subspecies.

White-tailed Deer *Odocoileus virginianus*. This common and important game species is a browser and grazer found statewide, including urban habitats. Throughout most of its distribution, breeding occurs October-January, but in Alabama, breeding usually takes place January-February with young born in late summer. Lowest Conservation Concern. **(Fig. 166, p. 202)**

Fallow Deer *Dama dama*. **Exotic.** Breeder. Native to Europe. Has been introduced widely around the world, including the area around Camden, Alabama. Still a very small population near Miller's Ferry.

SWINE - FAMILY SUIDAE

Feral Swine *Sus scrofa*. **Exotic.** Breeder. Probably introduced by European settlers originally, although subsequent releases of European "wild boars" and illegal trap and transplant operations by hunting enthusiasts have encouraged their hybridization and spread. Considered a direct and aggressive competitor with native wildlife and destroyer of natural plant communities of the state. Every opportunity for eradication should be undertaken.

ANTELOPES, BISON, CATTLE, GOATS, SHEEP - FAMILY BOVIDAE

Bison *Bison bison*. **Extirpated.** Plains subspecies (*B. b. bison*) once occupied mixed habitats associated with open grasslands and adjacent woodlands. Distribution was throughout most of state, except southernmost counties.

Fig. 151. Seminole Bat, *Lasiurus seminolus,* **p.191.**
Photo–J. Scott Altenbach

Fig. 150. Big Brown Bat, *Eptesicus fuscus,* **p.190.** *Photo–J. Scott Altenbach*

Fig. 152. Hoary Bat, *Lasiurus cenereus,* **p.191.**
Photo–J. Scott Altenbach

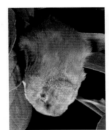

Fig. 149. Virginia Opossum, *Didelphis virginiana,* **p. 188.**
Photo–ADCNR, Mark Sasser

Fig. 153. Nine-banded Armadillo, *Dasypus novemcinctus,* **p. 192.**
Photo–Ericha Shelton

Fig. 154. Eastern Cottontail, *Sylvilagus floridanus,* **p. 192.**
Photo–Ericha Shelton

Fig. 155. Woodchuck, *Marmota monax,* **p. 193.** *Photo–Keith Guyse*

Fig. 158. Southern Flying Squirrel, *Glaucomys volans,* **p. 193.** *Photo–ADCNR, Sam Spencer*

Fig. 156. Gray Squirrel, *Sciurus carolinensis,* **p. 193.**
Photo–Ralph Mirarchi

Fig. 157. Fox Squirrel, *Sciurus niger,* **p. 193.**
Photo–ADCNR, Mark Sasser

Fig. 159. Beaver, *Castor canadensis*, **p.194.**
Photo–USFWS

Fig. 160. Oldfield Mouse,
Peromyscus polionotus, **p. 194.**
Photo–Nick Holler

Fig. 161. Hispid Cotton Rat,
Sigmodon hispidus, **p. 195.**
Photo–Nick Holler

Fig. 162. Muskrat, *Ondatra zibethicus*, **p. 196.**
Photo–USFWS

Fig. 163. Red Fox, *Vulpes vulpes*,
p. 197. *Photo–USFWS*

Fig. 164. Raccoon, *Procyon lotor*, **p. 198.**
Photo–USFWS

Fig. 165. Striped Skunk, *Mephitis*
mephitis, **p. 199.** *Photo–ADCNR, Keith*
Guyse

Fig. 166. White-tailed Deer, *Odocoileus*
virginianus, **p. 200.** *Photo–Ralph Mirarchi*

REFERENCES CITED

Alabama Ornithological Society (AOS). 1999. Field checklist of Alabama birds. Alabama Ornithological Society home page. <http://www.bham.net/aos/abrc/ chklist.pdf> . Accessed July 2002.

American Ornithologists' Union (AOU). 1998. Check-list of North American birds. 7th ed. American Ornithologists' Union, Washington, DC. 829 pp.

Banks, R. C., C. Cicero, J. L. Dunn, A. W. Kratter, P. C. Rasmussen, J. V. Remsen, Jr., J. D. Rising, and D. F. Stotz. 2002. Forty-third supplement to the American Ornithologists' Union *Checklist of North American Birds*. Auk 119:897-906.

Boschung, H. T., ed. 1976. Endangered and threatened plants and animals of Alabama: the results of a symposium sponsored by Game and Fish Division of the Alabama Department of Conservation and Natural Resources and Alabama Museum of Natural History, the University of Alabama. University of Alabama, Tuscaloosa, AL. 92 pp.

_____. 1992. Catalog of freshwater and marine fishes of Alabama. Bull. Ala. Museum Natur. Hist. 14. 266 pp.

Crother, B. I., ed. 2000. Scientific and standard English names of amphibians and reptiles of North America north of Mexico, with comments regarding confidence in our understanding. SSAR Herpetological Circular 29.

Griffith, G. E., J. M. Omernik, J. A. Comstock, G. Martin, A. Goddard, and V. J. Hulcher. 2001. Ecoregions of Alabama. U.S. Environmental Protection Agency, National Health and Environmental Effects Research Laboratory, Corvallis, OR.

Holliman, D. C., G. A. Baldassarre, J. L. Dusi, T. A. Imhof, J. E. Keeler, R. E. Mirarchi, D. T. Rogers, and C. W. Summerour. 1984. Birds. Pp. 25-40 in R. H. Mount, ed. Vertebrate wildlife of Alabama. Ala. Agric. Expt. Sta., Auburn University, Auburn, AL.

Imhof, T. A. 1976. Alabama birds. 2nd ed. The University of Alabama Press, Tuscaloosa, AL. 445 pp.

Jackson, G. D. 2001. Distribution and frequency of occurrence charts. Pp. 308-340 in J. F. Porter, ed. A Birder's Guide to Alabama. The University of Alabama Press, Tuscaloosa, AL.

Keeler, J. E. 1972. Rare and endangered vertebrates of Alabama. Ala. Dept. Conserv. Natur. Res., Div. Game and Fish. 92 pp.

Leopold, A. 1949. A Sand County alamanac and sketches here and there. Oxford University Press, New York, NY. 226 pp.

Lydeard, C., and R .L. Mayden. 1995. A diverse and endangered aquatic ecosystem of the southeast United States. Conservation Biology 9:800-805.

McConnell, S. W. 2001. Report of the Alabama Bird Record Committee 2000. Alabama Birdlife 47:55–56.

Mettee, M. F., P. E. O'Neil, and J. M. Pierson. 1996. Fishes of Alabama and the Mobile Basin. Oxmoor House, Birmingham, AL. 820 pp.

_____, W. P. Henderson, Jr., and G. W. Crawford. 1993. Rivers and streams of Alabama, including Mobile Basin tributaries in adjacent states. Special Map 241. Geological Survey of Alabama.

Mount, R. H., ed. 1984. Vertebrate wildlife of Alabama. Ala. Agric. Expt. Sta., Auburn University, Auburn, AL. 44 pp.

_____, ed. 1986. Vertebrate animals of Alabama in need of special attention. Ala. Agric. Expt. Sta., Auburn University, Auburn, AL. 124 pp.

Partners in Flight (PIF). 2002. Bird conservation region assessment scores (Version 1.1). Partners in Flight home page. <http://www.partnersinflight.org> . Accessed July 2002.

Smith-Vaniz, W. F. 1968. Freshwater fishes of Alabama. Ala. Agric. Expt. Sta., Auburn University, Auburn, AL. 211 pp.

The Nature Conservancy. 2002. States of the Union. <http://www.natureserve.org/library/state of unions. pdf>. Accessed July 2003.

Trefethen, J. B. 1975. An American crusade for wildlife. Winchester Press, New York, NY. 383 pp.

Turgeon, D. D., J. F. Quinn, Jr., A. E. Bogan, E. V. Coan, F. G. Hochberg, W.G. Lyons, M. Mikkelsen, C. F. E. Roper, G. Rosenberg, B. Roth, A. Scheltema, M. J. Sweeney, F. G. Thompson, M. Vecchione, and J. D. Williams. 1998. Common and scientific names of aquatic invertebrates from the United States and Canada: Mollusks. 2nd ed. Am. Fisheries Soc. Special Publ. 26, Bethesda, MD. 526 pp.

Vaughan, T. A., J. M. Ryan, and N. J. Czaplewski. 2000. Mammalogy. Saunders College Publishing, New York, NY. 565 pp.

Wilson, D. E., and D. M. Reeder, eds. 1993. Mammal species of the world: a taxonomic and geographic reference. 2nd ed. Smithsonian Institution Press, Washington, DC. 1206 pp.

Wilson, E. O. 1992. The diversity of life. W. W. Norton & Co., New York, NY. 424 pp.

GLOSSARY OF TERMS

Aestivate – dormancy similar to hibernation in being characterized by greatly slowed metabolic processes, but occurring in response to heat or drought during the summer.

Arboreal – living in, or frequenting, trees.

Anadromous – species that migrate from estuarine or marine areas into freshwater to spawn.

Backwater – pooled water separated from the main stream channel.

Barrier island – an island located in close proximity to the mainland, but between it and the open ocean or sea; often composed of shifting sands and forming a barrier to tidal surges from storms that would otherwise damage the mainland.

Basin – a major group of drainages interconnected by a master river or estuary.

Basking – to lie in warmth; action taken by cold-blooded animals to increase their internal temperature.

Bay – a body of water partially enclosed by land, but with a wide mouth, affording access to the sea.

Benthic – deep or bottom parts of an aquatic environment.

Blackwater – water that is stained dark from the leaching of organic compounds such as tannins and lignins.

Bog – wetland ecosystem characterized by acidic conditions, the accumulation of peat, and dominance of sphagnum moss.

Borrow pit – pits or holes left in the ground after soil and/or gravel has been removed (*borrowed*) for use elsewhere; often fill with water over time.

Bottomland – low-lying alluvial land near a river.

Brackish – mixture of saltwater and freshwater.

Bryophyte – member of the division in the plant kingdom of nonflowering plants comprising mosses, liverworts, and hornworts.

Canopy – a forest's roof; consists of a network of branches and leaves and forms a covering that blocks sunlight from lower plants.

Catadromous – freshwater fish that feed and grow in fresh water but migrate to salt water to spawn.

Clear-cut – a forestry practice that cuts all trees at one time from a block of forest.

Cobble – rectangular stone that has been rounded naturally on top by the Earth's elements, usually water. Also defined by size in the sequence of silt, sand, gravel, cobble, rubble, boulder, and bedrock.

Copulation – coitus; the union of male and female reproductive organs to facilitate reception of sperm by the female.

Cryptic – protective coloration of animals that makes them resemble or blend into their habitats or backgrounds.

Cultured – living organisms grown in a specially prepared nutrient medium, or in captive facilities.

Detritus – fresh to partly decomposed plant and animal matter.

Disjunct – a population (or populations) of an organism isolated geographically from the main distribution of its (their) species.

Diurnal – active during daylight hours; opposite of nocturnal.

Drainage – a group of interconnected stream systems the main channel of which enters an ocean, estuary, or the mainstream of a basin.

Ecomorphs – closely related populations that exhibit similiar morphological characteristics that make them suited for development under local ecological conditions they experience.

Eddies – water currents moving contrary to the direction of the main current, especially in a circular motion.

Endemic – found only in one region to which it is native.

Estivate – see *Aestivate*.

Estuary – a partially enclosed body of water that has a connection with the sea and is diluted by freshwater.

Extant – still living or present.

Fall Line – the boundary between unconsolidated Coastal Plain sediments and the harder rocks of the Appalachian Highlands.

Feedlot – small fenced areas where domestic livestock are concentrated and fed grains to fatten them before slaughter.

Floodplain – a strip of relatively flat and normally dry land alongside a stream, river, or lake that is covered by water during a flood.

Forb – an herb, or nonwoody plant, other than grass, sedge, or rush.

Fragmentation – habitat disruption where natural habitat is broken into small, relatively isolated sections.

Friable – soil that is loose and large-grained in consistency, like sand.

Gestation – the period of development of the embryo in the uterus from conception to birth, in some cases protracted by delayed implantation.

Hammock – a tract of forested land that rises above adjacent marsh.

Headwaters –the source and upper reaches of a stream or reservoir.

Herbaceous – having the character of an herb; soft and succulent tissue that will die back after first frost.

Hibernaculum – (*pl.* hibernacula) a shelter occupied in the winter by a hibernating animal.

Hybrid – the offspring of mating between individuals of two separate but related species, the offspring often infertile.

Implantation – the process by which the blastula or blastocyst stage of the developing mammalian embryo imbeds in the lining of the uterus.

Intergrade – transitional stage or form.

Intermittent – alternately having or not having water.

Jetties – structures that project into a body of water to influence the current or tide or to protect a harbor or shoreline.

Karst topography – land form underlain with limestone; usually punctuated with caves and sinkholes.

Lanceolate – tapering from a rounded base toward an apex.

Lentic – pertaining to standing water, as in lakes and ponds.

Lotic – pertaining to flowing water, as in unimpounded rivers and streams.

Macrophytes – large forms of plant life.

Mammae – teats used to suckle mammalian young.

Marsh – formed when organic matter is deposited to the bottom of an open-water area and the substrate rises above groundwater level; sedges, cattails, and associated plants are typically associated with development.

Marsupium – the external pouch formed by folds of skin in the abdominal wall of many marsupials and some montremes, and in which are provided mammae and shelter for the young.

Mesic – an intermediate condition of environmental moisture, where there is neither an excess nor a lack of water.

Midstory – forest layer beneath the canopy; formed by the leaves and branches of shorter trees.

Monogamous – having a single mate for life, or at least for one breeding season.

Morphology – the form and structure (anatomy) of an organism or any of its parts.

Nocturnal – active during the night; opposite of diurnal.

Omnivore – feeding typically on both animal and vegetable foods.

Ovulation – release of eggs or ova from the ovary into the oviduct or fallopian tubes.

Oxbow – water bodies (lakes) formed when water currents gradually carve new channels that bypass and isolate the original path of the river; typical of meandering, low-gradient streams and rivers; become progressively shallower, develop aquatic vegetation, and lose many of its original riverbed's characteristics.

Panfish – any of numerous small food fishes often sought by sport fishers.

Parasitic – an organism living in, or on, another organism, and usually causing harm.

Parturition – the birth of offspring in most mammals; the process by which the fetus separates from the mother's uterine wall and leaves the mother's body.

Pelagic – species that lives in, or over, open water.

Piscivore – one who feeds on fish.

Relict – an organism or species of an earlier time surviving in an environment that has undergone considerable change.

Riffle – a stream habitat characterized by shallow depth, broken substrate, and swift flow.

Rubble – a mass or stratum of fragments or rock lying under the alluvium, and derived from the neighboring rock.

Run – a stream habitat that is transitional between fast, shallow riffles and slow, deeper pools.

Scrub vegetation – woody vegetation often associated with sandy, infertile soils; often stunted by a lack of moisture, and/or nutrients, and/or wind, and/or fire.

Seep – a spot where water trickles out of the ground to form a pool.

Seepage areas – areas formed by the slow movement of water through small cracks and pores of a material into or out of a body of surface or subsurface water.

Sessile – not free to move about; permanently attached to a substrate.

Shoal – a shallow place in a body of water.

Slough – a stagnant swamp, marsh, bog, or pond; primarily part of a bayou, inlet, or backwater.

Spawn – to produce or deposit eggs of aquatic animals such as bivalve mollusks, fishes, and amphibians.

Species complex – a grouping of closely related species.

Substrate – (*pl.* substrata) bottom material in lakes, streams, and rivers.

Successional – replacement of populations in a habitat through a regular progression to a stable state.

Swamp – wooded wetlands in which water is near or above ground level.

System – a smaller division of a drainage.

Tailwaters – a section of swift-flowing river immediately downstream of a lock or dam.

Talus – a slope formed by rocky debris at the base of a cliff or mountain.

Terete – cylindrical and tapering.

Torpor – a deep sleep.

Troglobitic – cave-dwelling.

Understory – forest layer between midstory and ground cover.

Unionids – a taxonomic order of freshwater mussels.

Unsculptured – lack of ridges, bumps, and other structures on the shell surface of a mollusk; relatively smooth.

Volant – pertaining to the ability to fly.

Xeric – a soil or habitat characterized by minimal moisture and in which plant production is limited by water.

REFERENCES USED TO SUPPORT THE GLOSSARY

Many definitions used in the glossary were derived entirely, or partially, from the following sources. Some definitions were formed by combining definitions from various sources. Others were developed by the chief editor.

American® Dictionary of the English Language. © 2000. Fourth Edition. Houghton Mifflin Company.

DeBlase, A. F., and R. E. Martin. 1981. A manual of mammalogy with keys to families of the world. Wm. C. Brown Co., Dubuque, IA. 436 pp.

Koford, R. R., J. B. Dunning, Jr., C. A. Ribic, and D. M. Finch. 1994. A glossary for avian conservation biology. Wilson Bulletin. 106: 121-137. Jamestown, ND: Northern Prairie Wildlife Research Center Homepage. <http://www.npwrc.usgs.gov/resource/literatr/avian.avian.htm> (Version 16JUL97).

U.S. Geological Survey. <http://www.Water.usgs.gov.>

Whitaker, J. O., Jr. and W. J. Hamilton, Jr. 1998. Mammals of the Eastern United States. Cornell University Press, Ithaca and London. 577 pp.

Mettee, M. F., P. E. O'Neil, and J. M. Pierson. 1996. Fishes of Alabama and the Mobile Basin. Oxmoor House, Birmingham, AL. 820 pp.

ABOUT THE EDITOR:

Ralph E. Mirarchi has degrees in biology from Muhlenberg College (1971, B.S.) and in wildlife biology and management from Virginia Polytechnic Institute and State University (1975, M.S.; 1978, Ph.D.). He currently is the William R. and Fay Ireland Distinguished Professor of Wildlife Science in the School of Forestry and Wildlife Sciences at Auburn University, Alabama, where he has taught numerous courses in wildlife science, advised undergraduate wildlife majors, and conducted research on doves and pigeons for the Alabama Agricultural Experiment Station for more than 25 years. He previously served as editor in chief of *The Journal of Wildlife Management* (1992-1993) and as a co-editor, compiler, and author of *Ecology and Management of the Mourning Dove* (1993), an award-winning Wildlife Management Institute sponsored text published by Stackpole Books. He also currently serves on the board of Alabama's Forever Wild Land Trust, which purchases wild lands for the people of Alabama to enjoy in perpetuity.